Richard Rogers
Partnership

Works and Projects

Edited by Richard Burdett

THE MONACELLI PRESS

To Winston Burdett

First published in the United States of America in 1996
by The Monacelli Press, Inc.,
10 East 92nd Street, New York, New York 10128.

Copyright © 1995 Electa
English text © 1996
The Monacelli Press, Inc.

Library of Congress Cataloging-in-Publication Data
Rogers, Richard George.
    [Richard Rogers. English]
    Richard Rogers : partnership : works and projects / edited by Richard
    Burdett.
        p.   cm.
    Includes bibliographical references.
    ISBN 1-885254-32-6 (paper)
    1. Rogers, Richard George.   2. Richard Rogers Partnership.
I. Burdett, Richard. II. Title.
NA997.R64A4   1996
720'.92—dc20   95-50547

Printed and bound in Italy

Acknowledgments
I would like to thank Francesco dal
Co and his colleagues at Electa for
their patience and understanding;
Harriet Watson, who played an
instrumental role in sourcing the
illustrations and directing me with
skill through the labyrinths of the
Richard Rogers Partnership; John
Young, Mike Davies, Laurie Abbott,
and Philip Gumudjian for their
insights and entertainment; and
Richard Rogers, who made the task
of writing a stimulating, warm, and
enjoyable experience. Finally, I
would like to thank Mika Hadidian
for her comments on the text and
support throughout the project.
Richard Burdett, May 1995

Contents

Richard Rogers Partnership

The Culture of Cities
Richard Rogers

Human life has always depended on the three variables of population, resources, and environment. But today, we're perhaps the first generation to face the simultaneous impact of expanding populations, depletion of resources, and erosion of the environment. All this is common knowledge, and yet, incredibly, industrial expansion carries on regardless.

Other societies have faced extinction—some, like the Easter Islanders of the Pacific, the Harappa civilization of the Indus Valley, and Teotihuacan in pre-Columbian America, due to ecological disasters of their own making. Historically, societies unable to solve their environmental crises have either migrated or become extinct. The vital difference today is that the scale of our crisis is no longer regional but global: it involves all of humanity and the entire planet.

The United Nations report "Our Common Future" laid down the concept of "sustainable development" as the backbone of a global economic policy. According to the report, our aim should be to meet our present needs without compromising future generations to direct our development positively in favor of the world's majority—the poor. At the core of this concept is a new notion of wealth, one that incorporates those environmental elements previously considered limitless and free: clean air, fresh water, an effective ozone layer, and a fertile land and sea. The means proposed to protect the environment were stringent regulations—you don't use CFCs—and a costing of the market's use of natural resources—you pay for the damage created by your use of resources.

Nowhere is this sort of implementation of "sustainability" more relevant than in the city. In fact, I believe environmental sustainability needs to become the guiding law of modern urban design—an innovation that would have an impact on the twenty-first-century city as radical as that of the Industrial Revolution on its nineteenth-century counterpart.

As it stands, cities and buildings are the most important destroyers of the ecosystem. In the United States, pollution rising from the cities has reduced crop production by 5 to 10 percent. In Japan, Tokyo alone dumps an estimated twenty million tons of waste every year. The city has already saturated its bay with waste and is now running out of sites on land. But although cities are breeding environmental disaster, there is nothing in the nature of city living that makes this inevitable. On the contrary, I believe that cities can be transformed into the most environmentally balanced form of modern settlement.

Cities concentrate physical, intellectual, and creative energy. It is this "social and cultural" dynamic—rather than an aesthetic balance created by the design of buildings—that, to my mind, is the essence of civic beauty. I am passionate about the choice and diversity of city life—from exhibitions to demonstrations, from bars to cathedrals, and from shops to opera. I love the combination of ages, races, cultures, and activities; the mix of the community with the unknown, anonymity/familiarity, and surprise—even the sense of dangerous excitement they can generate. I enjoy the animation that sidewalk cafés bring to the street, the informal liveliness of the public square, the mixture of shops, offices, and homes that makes a living neighborhood.

Strolling through Europe's great public spaces—the covered Galleria in Milan, the Ramblas in Barcelona, the parks of London—I feel part of the community of that city. One of the most exhilarating moments of my career was when the Parisian authorities agreed to give half the site they had set aside for the Centre Pompidou to a public piazza. When we were planning how the Centre Pompidou could invigorate its surrounding streets and communities, we had, in the back of our minds, the bustling public square at the heart of Siena—scene of the great Palio horse race, which thunders over its cobbles twice a year. Today, to my great delight, the Place Beaubourg and the Centre Pompidou teem with life, and this has led to a wholesale renewal of the areas that surround it.

A vibrant urban life is, to my mind, the essential ingredient of a good city. And yet today, this quality is increasingly missing. The public life of a city is enacted in its streets, squares, alleys, and parks, and it is these spaces that make up the public domain. This domain is an institution in its own right. It belongs to the community, and like any institution, it can enhance or frustrate our existence.

But just ask anybody what they think of city life today. He or she will more likely talk about congestion, pollution, and fear of crime than community, animation, or beauty. In all probability, a negative association will be made between city and quality of living. The essential problem is that cities have been viewed in instrumental or consumerist terms. Those responsible for them have tended to see it as their role to design cities to meet private material needs, rather than to foster public life. The result is that cities have been polarized into communities of rich and poor, and segregated into ghettos of single-minded activity—the business park, the housing estate, the residential suburb—or worse still, into giant single-function buildings, like shopping centers with their own private streets (which lead nowhere) built in.

But if we lament the recent transformations of our cities, we should acknowledge that cities can *only* reflect the values and character of the societies they contain. This relationship is well explored in the long tradition of attempts to make cities reflect society's ideals. Vitruvius, Leonardo da Vinci, Thomas Jefferson, Ebenezer Howard, Le Corbusier, Buckminster Fuller, and others have proposed *ideal* urban forms to propel society through its traumas. These architectural and social utopias exert a constant and profound influence on our great architects and patrons, and they filter through to developers and city builders. In a democratic age, you might expect contemporary architecture to express democratic ideals and egalitarian values. But recent transformations of cities reflect the workings of businesses committed to short-term profit, where the pursuit of wealth has become an end in itself, rather than a means to achieve broader goals. City planning worldwide is dominated by market forces and short-term financial imperatives—an approach most spectacularly illustrated by the chaotic and office-dominated development on the Isle of Dogs in London. Not only have such developments eliminated variety of function from our city centers, but in this single-minded search for profit, we have ignored the needs of the wider community.

But if, as I have claimed, cities are where life is often at its most precarious, they are also where we have the greatest tangible opportunity for improvement, intervention, and change. Humankind's capacity to learn and to transmit accumulated knowledge from generation to generation, to anticipate and solve problems, is its greatest asset. I find it amazing that only seventy seventy-year life-spans separate our own epoch, which has the ability to build a city in space, from the first mud cities along the Euphrates. It is the irrepressible power of mind that has accelerated the development of our species.

Knowledge, technology, and our capacity for forethought have transformed our world, often in the face of our pessimism. In 1798, the economist Malthus warned the world that the rate of population growth is infinitely greater than the power of the earth to feed future generations. If he was proved wrong, as he was in the case of Britain, it was because he had not foreseen the remarkable capacity of technology. In the hundred years following his ominous prediction, the population of Britain quadrupled, but technological advances brought a fourteenfold increase in agricultural production.

The problem is not with technology, but with its application. Today technology destabilizes and transforms the modern age: as Marx famously said, "All that is solid melts into air." Caught in this endless upheaval, technology *can* be used to positive ends—to advance social justice—one of modernity's greatest ideals. Perhaps we can say that when technology is used to secure the fundamentally modern principles of universal human rights—shelter, food, health care, education, and freedom—the modern age attains its full potential. It is here that the "spirit of modernity" finds its very expression.

The challenge we face today is to break with a system that treats technology and finance as a route to short-term profit, rather than a means to social and environmental ends. The urban planner who drives a motorway through the middle of a city, merely to advance the single-minded goal of mobility, employs technology for the wrong ends.

(Extracted from "Cities for a Small Planet," 1995 Reith Lectures.)

"Long Life, Loose Fit, Low Energy":
The Architecture of the Richard Rogers Partnership
Richard Burdett

Located in an old factory along the Thames River in London, the offices of the Richard Rogers Partnership are a living example of the practice's belief in the regenerative and social potential of architecture. The complex of buildings includes a refurbished warehouse, a new apartment block, a successful restaurant, and a public garden that provides the community with direct access to the river. The nineteenth-century brick building has been converted in a "low-tech" manner: oversized mechanical blinds creak noisily to screen the sun's rays; windows are opened and closed in response to changes in external temperature—a far cry from the anemic, controlled environments of soulless "high-tech" architecture. As professional opportunities have come and gone, the office has grown and contracted within the existing framework of buildings. It is an aesthetic, environmental, and social synthesis of the "loose-fit, long-life, low-energy" approach that has characterized Rogers' radical architecture for more than thirty years.

The practice is, in many ways, a hybrid: part community, part workshop, part front office of one of the best-known "signature firms" in the profession. Despite its informal atmosphere, the Rogers office plays an increasingly influential role in contemporary architecture and urban design, with an expanding range of projects around the world, from eco-cities and airports to teaching units, offices, and housing. Yet its prodigious international reputation has been built on the strength of relatively few completed buildings, including at least two of the undisputed canonical buildings of the late twentieth century: the Centre Pompidou and the Lloyd's Building.

The practice's multicultural population fluctuates between fifty and one hundred architects. Organized as a partnership of individuals rather than a commercial company—all employees share in the company's profits and contribute regularly to selected charities—the practice's constitution underlines the commitment to high social, ethical, and professional goals. Today the practice still revolves around the founding members—Richard Rogers, John Young, Marco Goldschmied, and Mike Davies—each bringing his own specific area of expertise, enthusiasms, and interests to bear on the design and implementation of buildings and projects. In one configuration or another—Team 4 (with Norman and Wendy Foster), Richard + Su Rogers, Piano + Rogers, Richard Rogers + Partners—they have worked together for nearly thirty years, joining as a group with Renzo Piano in the early days of the Centre Pompidou project in 1971. Younger members of the office have recently taken on greater responsibilities, opening up new lines of inquiry that reflect the urban, environmental, and formal concerns of the generation of designers educated in the 1970s and 1980s.

While communication in the practice is open and accessible, the sense of duty and commitment verges on the evangelical. Clear lines of accountability (the word *hierarchy* is not loved in the Rogers office) ensure the direct involvement of the partners in every single project on the drawing boards. Members of the office are kept informed of progress on all projects, including the outcome of competitions and the likelihood of new commissions. An array of architectural models—the yellow Zip-Up House, a Lego version of the Centre Pompidou in primary colors, and the latest competition entry—hang precariously from industrial metal shelves above the large numbers of visitors, clients, and consultants who crowd the office's reception area. Behind the generally low-key atmosphere lies a highly professional machine that operates with the largest corporations in the world, including Lloyd's of London and the government of China.

Environment and Culture

Rogers' position within the architectural debate cannot be defined in conventional stylistic terms. The variety, scale, and motivation of the work transcends its restrictive high-tech label. It is a paradigmatic attitude toward environmental culture that sets the practice apart from many contemporary architects. Reyner Banham, whose critical writings strongly influenced Rogers' generation, perceptively described the difference between environmental cultures in the form of a parable: "A savage tribe arrives at an evening campsite and finds it well supplied with fallen timber. Two basic methods of exploiting the environmental potential of that timber exist: either it may be used to construct a windbreak or rain-shed— the structural solution—or it may be used to build a fire—the power-operated solution. An ideal tribe of noble rationalists would consider the amount of wood available, make an estimate of the probable weather for the night—wet, windy, or cold—and dispose of its timber resources accordingly. A real tribe, being the inheritors of ancestral cultural predispositions, would do nothing of the sort, of course, and would either

make fire or build a shelter according to prescribed custom—and that is what Western civilised nations do, in most cases" (*The Architecture of the Well-Tempered Environment* [London, 1969], 19).

Freedom from prescribed custom, exploitation of environmental potential, and the use of appropriate structural and power-operated solutions are the fundamental ingredients of Rogers' "loose-fit, long-life, low-energy" architecture. Apparently unshackled from "ancestral cultural predispositions," the Rogers "tribe of noble rationalists" has developed a tabula rasa approach to design, drawing inspiration from outside the strict confines of the architectural discipline, contributing to a paradigmatic shift in the theory and practice of environmental culture.

It is for this reason that developments in science and technology, statistics on social trends in world cities, the energy and structural performance of materials from the aerospace or car industry are more likely to act as primary generators of architectural form than conventional volumetric or tectonic concerns. The practice acts as a synthesizer and enabler: it brings together people and ideas from diverse disciplines and backgrounds, it marshals new concepts into a building or urban form. It is this turnover of ideas and information that accounts for a certain restless dynamism in the built work. The "loose-fit" notion applies as much to the intellectual framework of the practice as it does to the physical design of its buildings.

In the 1960s Mike Davies was engaged in the design of artificial environments where man, as he put it, could live autonomously in a totally self-sufficient environment: a concept captured by the image of a man in a space suit in the middle of the desert plugged into a rock, communicating happily with the rest of the world. Just as Davies believes that current telecommunications technology allows the individual access to an extraordinary range of information—the "downloaded air-conditioned gypsy"—the practice believes that buildings have to be designed to respond to their environments, to be used for twenty-four hours a day, to be plugged into the system anywhere in the world.

Despite this process of constant renewal, there are recurrent themes that run through Rogers' oeuvre since the experimental structures of the 1960s, such as the mobile Zip-Up House and Autonomous House projects that could be transported to any site and simply plugged into the system. For Rogers and his

colleagues, the functional and social requirements of the brief have always been the primary generators of architectural form. The unabated quest for the ultimate "loose-fit" building is a reaction to the inflexibility, cost, and rigidity of traditional building forms and techniques. Each new project is an opportunity to challenge conventional solutions and explore new options that optimize flexibility in planning, organization and servicing. While most buildings are built to last between fifty and seventy-five years, the patterns of occupation and lifestyles change far more frequently. Mechanical and telecommunications systems, for example, will last at best between ten and twenty-five years, while working practices and methods of production change in two- to five-year cycles.

Reflecting the profound influence of Buckminster Fuller's pioneering concerns with energy, flexibility, and durability in design (his Dymaxion House, designed in 1927, six years before Rogers' birth, was an autonomous, lightweight geodesic dome with services suspended from the main structure), Rogers notes: "A building that is easy to modify has a longer useful life and uses its resources more efficiently. In social and ecological terms, a building designed for flexibility enlarges the sustainable life of a society. Designing greater flexibility into our modern buildings inevitably moves architecture away from fixed and perfect forms. Palladian architecture, for example, derives its beauty from harmonious composition. Nothing can be added to it, nothing can be taken away. But when a society needs buildings that are capable of responding to changing requirements, then, I believe, we must seek to provide flexibility and search for new forms that express the power of change . . . Inflexible buildings hinder the evolution of society by inhibiting new ideas" ("Cities for a Small Planet," 1995 Reith Lectures).

With its completely column-free interior spaces as large as two football fields, the Centre Pompidou, conceived in 1971, is the ultimate flexible plan (both Renzo Piano and Richard Rogers concede that it may have been too flexible for the function it was to perform). The Lloyd's Building, designed a few years later, is a further variation on the theme, but this time all services and vertical circulation are placed on the exterior, leaving a pure, unencumbered plan for one of the world's most volatile organizations (the fluctuating fortunes of the insurance market have recently put the Lloyd's Building to the test; it has responded well to radical reorganization and the introduction of new forms

VIENNA

of technology). Many of the practice's smaller industrial buildings designed at the time of Pompidou and Lloyd's (including the Inmos Microprocessor Laboratory, PA Technology, and Fleetguard) are more subtle reinterpretations of the pioneering work of the postwar American architects Craig Ellwood and, in particular, Ezra Ehrenkrantz, whose experimental SCSD school prototypes set the standard for infinitely adaptable clear space between floor and roof planes. In Rogers' work, the section and planning of the buildings allow unlimited horizontal expansion, a hypothesis that has been successfully tested at Inmos and Patscentre, which have grown and adapted in response to demand and changing methods of production. The placement of the structure outside the waterproof skin has an added advantage: the buildings can be extended without removing cladding or disrupting operations, thus enhancing its "long-life" potential.

Rogers' concern with the autonomy of structure and servicing accounts for the repeated use of tension structures, designed mainly by the greatly missed engineer and collaborator Peter Rice and his team at Ove Arup & Partners. Tension structures are considerably lighter than equivalent conventional internal structures. Visual mass and internal volume are minimized, reducing costs and construction time. The structure is designed as a kit of parts, with pin joints, masts, rods, ties, connections, and precisely calibrated steel components assembled off-site, in ideal factory conditions, and easily erected on site with a minimal amount of site-welding and labor-intensive activity. In their simplicity, these buildings are technological in the purest sense of being made by machine, yet the application of technology is neither particularly advanced nor sophisticated. It is for this reason that "appropriate" technology, rather than "high" technology, captures the essence of Rogers' approach to design, with each structural or servicing system designed in response to the precise requirements of the brief, the budget, and the functional program of the building.

Architecture and Ethics

Rogers' belief in the ethical responsibility of the architect is deeply rooted in the heroic social mission of the early modern movement. He is, after all, "old enough to be immersed in modernism but young enough to have inherited the mantle of modernism rather than to have invented it" (Robert Maxwell, *Casabella*, Apr. 1994, 16). For Rogers, furthering the modernist cause has become a personal campaign, a matter of moral integrity. He takes every opportunity to drive home the message that the quality of architecture and the public realm is a key issue in contemporary society. In the deeply conservative and anti-architectural climate of post-Thatcher Britain, Rogers' invitation to give the prestigious annual series of Reith Lectures for the BBC—he was the only architect ever invited in its fifty-year history—reflects his status as a public proselytizer for modern architecture and the modern city designed for society at large. In this respect, Rogers' activity and his architecture "undertake the purpose of avant-garde art which is to change consciousness and prepare for the future" (Maxwell, *Casabella*, Apr. 1994, 17). This confirms his fundamental mission: to put the quality of the built environment firmly on the political agenda.

Manfredo Tafuri identified the fundamental crisis of postwar architecture as the inability of the profession to deliver the "utopia of social democracy" to which the modern movement had been committed. Reyner Banham argued that the failure of modernism is also to be blamed on the inability of the profession to engage with the "business of actually putting buildings together." Rogers has tackled the predicament of contemporary architecture on both fronts. He has made the deliverance of the "utopia of social democracy" his mission, yet his architecture is about "the business of actually putting buildings together properly." In 1977 Banham singled out the Centre Pompidou as "the only public monument of international quality the 1970s has produced" and applauded the design for challenging "Le Corbusier's increasingly geriatric understanding of monumentality as mere mass and impenetrable substance" (*Architectural Review*, Mar. 1977, 277). In 1982 he identified the Lloyd's Building as an exemplar of "elaborate and painstaking detailing . . . a reminder of the architectural quality that ought to be part of the heritage of Modernism" (*Architectural Review*, Oct. 1982, 55). In its search for craftsmanship and technical know-how, the Rogers practice is a direct descendant of the pioneering work of Jean Prouvé, a prominent member of the Pompidou jury, and Pierre Chareau, whose work was the subject of detailed analysis by Rogers in the 1950s.

Design Process and Architectural Form

There is a certain reticence among the members of the practice to talk about their work in conventional architectural terms. This is not merely a sign of British anti-intellectualism but reflects

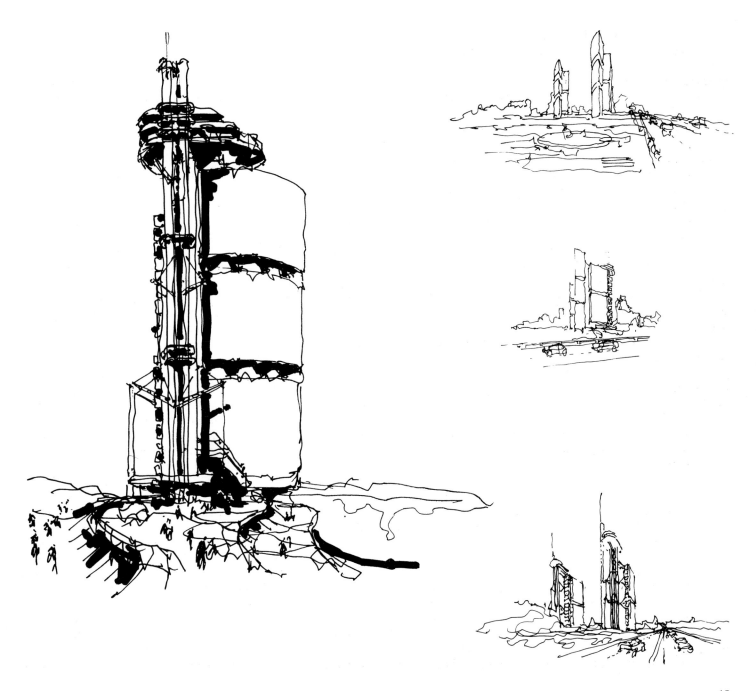

Twin Towers, Vienna, 1992,
preliminary sketches.

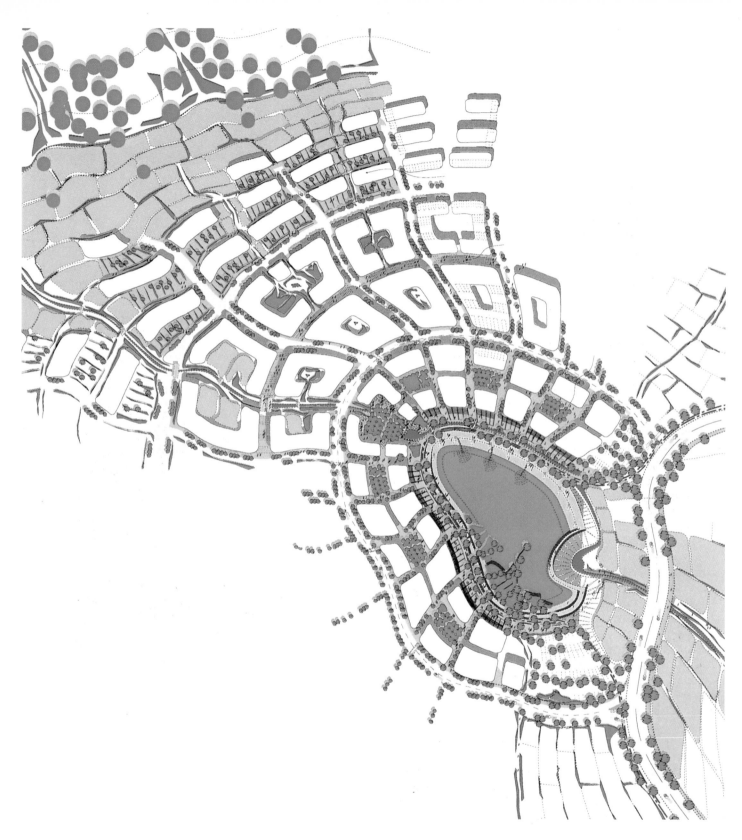

the collective view that architecture is the complex product of social, political, and environmental processes that cannot be reduced to mere formal or stylistic issues. Rogers has often been quoted as saying that he doesn't mind what style a building is, "as long as it's good." The concept of volumetric form is considered restrictive, an *a priori* that does not allow sufficient flexibility to satisfy the specific requirements of a given brief. To Rogers, the brief generates its own solution with its own language, reflecting a specific set of physical, intellectual, and aesthetic contexts.

The regular design sessions held in the office reflect the nature of this process of design. A handful of ongoing projects are reviewed by senior partners and their design teams with a small group of close collaborators, including environmental and structural engineers, planners, and cost consultants. Rather than being asked to solve the technical problems of the design, they are an integral part of the design team, helping the architects to dissect the brief and explore alternative solutions. It is in this context that Peter Rice played an instrumental role, encouraging the designers to search for the authenticity of materials and to exploit their natural structural properties. For the Rogers office, design is a linear evaluative process in which assumptions can be falsified or verified, discarded or developed in relation to the requirements of the brief and the strategic priorities of the project.

It is in this spirit that the "findings" of each project inform the next generation of designs. Developments in passive environmental control of the Turbine Tower project (with its lozenge-shaped volume that harnesses wind power to generate electricity and to assist natural ventilation) and the Inland Revenue scheme (with its curved roof serving a precise environmental function) have influenced the spatial organization and formal profile of Terminal 5 at London's Heathrow Airport and a new generation of energy-efficient designs for Lloyd's Register and Daimler Benz. Nearly twenty years of lived experience of the Centre Pompidou and the Place Beaubourg, the most popular postwar cultural center in France, with more than thirty thousand visitors a day, have been assimilated and reinterpreted in the designs for London's South Bank Centre and the Potsdamerplatz project in Berlin. Fast-track construction, prefabrication, and off-site assembly techniques used at Inmos, PA Technology, and Lloyd's have been applied to industrialized housing projects for Korea and the Channel 4 Building in London.

Despite the declared integrity and autonomy of the design process, a Rogers building is always recognizable. It has clearly identifiable, highly articulated formal characteristics. There is a hierarchy of vertical and horizontal elements. The materials and detailing provide grain and scale. The structure and services are often, but not always, exposed. The entrance is given priority and emphasis. The public areas are transparent and legible. Circulation is clear. Internal functions are expressed on the exterior. There is an obvious distinction between public and private, between served and servant areas, between primary and support spaces. These are the elements of a formal and aesthetic language that transcends the exigencies of site, environment, context, and brief. Different groups of buildings that respond to similar conditions clearly reflect the presence of a deft compositional hand. The Law Courts in Bordeaux and the European Court of Human Rights in Strasbourg, in one instance, or the Channel 4 Television Headquarters, the Docklands Pump House, and the Reuters Data Centre, in another, exhibit a distinct yet identifiable architectural lineage that suggests a more relaxed attitude toward the conventions of architectural form and language (even though all formal decisions are explained in purely environmental and functional terms, as discussed below). These recent buildings, with their circular glazed volumes and articulated solid forms, show the influence of the organic expressionism of Erich Mendelsohn and Hans Scharoun and reflect a renewed interest in the compositional language of early modernism.

Robert Maxwell explains this apparent contradiction between form and function by arguing that "it is not that the high-tech architect eschews beauty. But beauty to be uncovered has to be identified with necessity, the result of applying reason along with necessity" (*Casabella*, Apr. 1994, 21). This view is reiterated by the abstract painter Patrick Heron who, in praising the visual force of the exposed circulation towers of the Lloyd's Building, notes: "If Rogers had not, as an artist, already *loved the appearance* of the shining, geometric forms . . . he would have adopted a different set of 'practical' solutions. Architecture all the time juggles function and pure aesthetic choice" (*Architectural Review*, Oct. 1976, 57).

Peter Rice's account of the evolution of the Centre Pompidou sheds further light on the relationship between form, structure, and function: "I had been wondering for some time what it was that gave the large engineering structures of the 19th cen-

tury their great appeal. It was not just their daring and confidence . . . One element I had latched onto was the evidence of the attachment and care their designers and makers had lavished on them. Like Gothic cathedrals they exude craft and individual choice . . . Cast steel could have this quality too" (*An Engineer Imagines* [London, 1993], 29). Rice identifies the fundamental compositional role of the cast steel frame and giant cantilevered gerberettes that give the Centre Pompidou its distinctive grain and scale, transcending its purely structural function: "Each piece was separate, an articulated assembly where the members only touched at discrete points. As in music, where the space between the notes defines the quality, here it was the space between the pieces which defined the scale" (*An Engineer Imagines*, 34).

A similarly neoformal analysis of pin-jointed, expressed structures in Rogers' industrial and commercial buildings is offered by Reyner Banham. The rediscovery of the art of pin jointing, traditionally employed in engineering structures and bridges from the mid-nineteenth century, is described as "a remarkable break against what has become an almost unarguable structural orthodoxy of rigid jointing ever since the aesthetic ascendancy of Miesian framing was underwritten by the rise of Plastic Theory structural mathematics in the 1950s, . . . an almost reassuring return to those elegant and self-sufficient structural diagrams on which classical statistics was based" (*Architectural Review*, Dec. 1982).

A New Environmental Culture

The long-standing concern with environmental performance reflects the personal interests of the founding partners and the increasing awareness of the severe social and economic impact of the global energy crisis. Since half of the world's energy is consumed by buildings, the design of intelligent, sustainable buildings that can reduce energy consumption without significantly reducing comfort levels has become a major priority for the architectural profession. Roughly three-quarters of everyday energy use in buildings is consumed by artificial lighting, heating, and cooling with CFC emissions from air-conditioning systems contributing to the depletion of the ozone layer. While the external climate is continually changing, hour by hour, day by day, season by season, most "modern" buildings are designed to be insensitive to these changes. They remain static and dumb

South Bank Centre Crystal Palace,
London, 1994, preliminary sketch;
Inland Revenue Headquarters,
Nottingham, 1992, model.

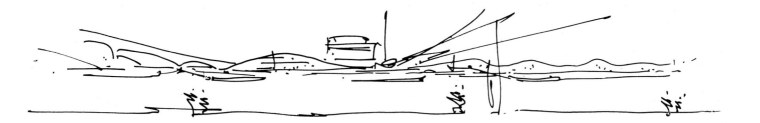

BIT Park master plan, Majorca,
1994, model.

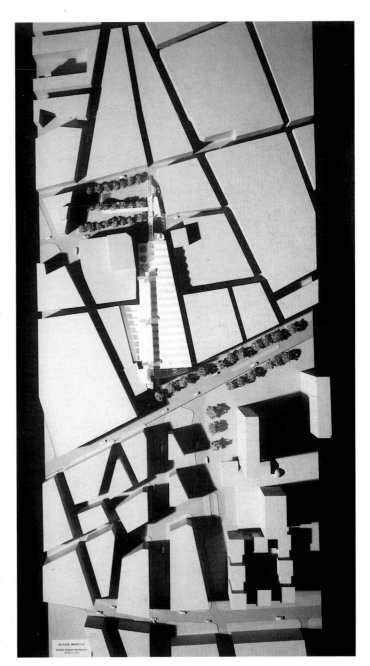

rather than interacting dynamically with the environment to exploit free energy and create comfortable living and working spaces.

The Rogers' office, together with other leading design and engineering practices, has pioneered the development of intelligent buildings that can contribute substantially (up to 75 percent) to reducing the running and maintenance cost during the life cycle of a building. Significantly, this new generation of buildings is not totally dependent on sophisticated equipment and high technology. They rely equally on conventional forms of passive environmental design (natural control of heat gain and loss through orientation, building form, thermal mass, etc.) and on new materials and systems (photovoltaic cells, responsive cladding skins, translucent insulating panels, stack effect, etc.) borrowed from other industries, including developments in fluid mechanics and energy performance for cars and airplanes. Computer techniques employed to test wind resistance and fuel consumption in cars are now used to simulate air movement and temperature distribution within buildings. There is an increased awareness that the design of a building can facilitate the use of renewable sources of energy (wind, sun, earth, and water), reducing the consumption of nonrenewable energy sources such as oil, coal, and gas.

To clarify the notion of passive environmental design (and to scotch the myth that the practice is dedicated to expensive, high-tech solutions), the designers often refer to nature or primitive examples of shelter, such as the igloo or the mud hut, that have successfully performed as ecologically balanced structures for thousands of years. Termites' nests, the two-meter-high spiral earth towers found in the African desert, are cited as prototypes of the perfect "intelligent" structure designed to conserve energy and reduce overheating. Termites inhabit a climate with temperatures that are low at night but extremely high during the day. The plan of the nest is a long thin oval. Its long axis is oriented east-west so that it gets maximum exposure to the early morning sun, warming up as quickly as possible. Its short axis faces north-south. As the sun rises, the amount of external wall exposed to the sun is reduced to a minimum, limiting the potential for overheating. In its own way, the termite's nest is a balanced sustainable development: a shelter that uses materials, form, and orientation to create a "high-quality" environment for the user by exploiting what is freely available (sunlight, heat,

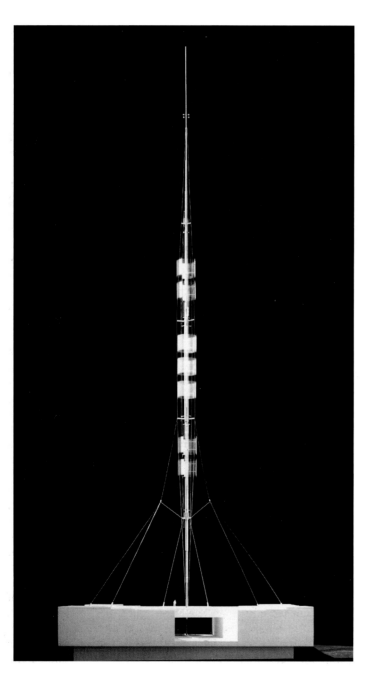

air) without using excessive amounts of energy or compromising the next generation's chances of survival.

Many of the practice's current design solutions seek an equally balanced solution to the environmental problem. Hence the emergence of long, thin buildings that offer the best orientation for natural daylighting (Lloyd's Register and the Berlin and Shanghai master plans); the presence of the distinctive curved glazed facade/roof that facilitates air movement and minimizes heat gain and loss (Terminal 5, Inland Revenue, and the South Bank Centre); the appearance of a new typology of patchwork facade composed of highly insulated translucent panels that optimize daylight penetration (reducing the need for artificial light) and keep buildings warm in the winter and cool in the summer. Passive environmental concerns account for the grand urban gestures at Shanghai and Berlin (landscaped avenues provide a civic amenity *and* improve ventilation and daylight in the buildings) or the organic configuration of the regional plans for Val d'Oise and Majorca (with their hierarchy of transport, water, and ecological systems).

The practice is pursuing an increasingly active research program into the environmental performance of buildings (receiving grants from the British government and the EEC), and Richard Rogers has taken on a major public role in promoting sustainability as a way of life. Rogers compares responsive reactive systems to automatic pilots in airplanes: they monitor all control functions and environmental parameters many times a second, continuously adapting and modifying the aircraft control systems to achieve optimal flight and passenger comfort. "Responsive systems, acting much like muscles flexing in a body, reduce mass to a minimum by shifting loads and forces with the aid of an electronic nervous system which will sense environmental changes and register individual needs" (*Architecture: A Modern View* [London, 1990]).

As a reminder of the poetic potential of this technological vision, Michael Davies describes the experience of living in a responsive building of the future: "Look up at a spectrum-washed envelope, whose surface is a map of its instantaneous performance, stealing energy from the air with an iridescent shrug, rippling its photogrids as a cloud runs across the sun, a wall which, as the night chill falls, fluffs up its feathers and, turning white on its north face and blue on the south, closes its eyes but not without remembering to pump a little glow down to the night porter, clear a view patch for the lovers on the south side of level 22 and so turn 12 percent silver just before dawn."

Toward the Sustainable City

Since the early 1980s the Rogers practice has become increasingly involved in the large-scale urban and regional master plans. This reflects the firm's growing professional reputation and constitutes a natural extension of the practice's long-standing commitment to the social and public dimension of architecture. In particular, the practice has developed a series of proposals for the restructuring of public space in London that amounts to a political and architectural blueprint for a new humanist city. Apart from the master plans for Florence, Berlin, and Shanghai, the firm has been commissioned to redevelop industrial areas in Liverpool and Dunkirque, the Alcatraz quarter in Marseille, and a new ecological regional plan for a science and industry park on the island of Majorca. The new generation of plans reveals the increasing influence of passive environmental design as a generator of architectural form, with dense clusters distributed in geometric or organic patterns across the natural or existing urban landscape.

Rogers' critique of the modern city shares the same intellectual ground as many postwar "revisionist" town planners and urban theorists. The alienating effect of zoning, the physical and environmental damage caused by the car, the demise of public transport, the unstoppable growth of suburban sprawl, the effect of out-of-town shopping centers on inner-city decline, and the increasingly negative impact of cities on the global environment are seen as the major ingredients of the crisis of the contemporary city.

Rogers' profound belief in the link between spatial form and social behavior is confirmed by his espousal of Jane Jacobs' crystal-clear analysis of the ills of modernist planning and the benefits of the traditional urban block published in her seminal book *The Death and Life of Great American Cities*. His rejection of the city of isolated monuments and his call for the city of streets and squares reflects the early influence of Team X's critique of CIAM and Le Corbusier's urban visions as well as the eloquent urban writings of Aldo Rossi, Robert Venturi, and the Krier brothers. The use of the Nolli plan of Rome and Colin Rowe's figure-ground drawing techniques in many of Rogers' presentations—as well as the employment of the "space syntax" computer-based techniques of spatial analysis pioneered by Bill Hillier—emphasizes Rogers' interest in the continuity and integration of the urban fabric. The search for a "seamless continuity" between old and new, between the public, semipublic, and private realms underlines many of the practice's urban schemes.

Yet Rogers' urban perspective recognizes that the city is a global phenomenon dependent for its survival on a complex web of spatial, social, ecological, and economic factors: a vision that rejects the fashionable and localized historicist reinterpretation of the traditional city. While the analysis of the problem is common, the formal resolution is dramatically diverse. Geometry, or in some cases supra-geometry, becomes the main structuring device of the urban plan, such as the grand circle in Shanghai, the curved terrace in Coin Street, or the radiating fan in Berlin's Potsdamerplatz.

The practice's comprehensive vision for the city of the future, which underlies many of the current urban projects, is characteristically bold and forward-looking: the compact, polycentric, sustainable city. The compact city, as opposed to the dispersed city of endless suburbs, fosters social contact and allows uses to overlap, keeping the city alive twenty-four hours a day. The more concentrated an urban system, the more efficient its public transport and services. Less energy is consumed on expensive commuting. Movement is by foot, cycle, or localized public transport networks, such as trams or nonpolluting buses. The polycentric city, enshrined in the Shanghai master plan, is based on a satellite neighborhood concept formed around local transport hubs for rail, buses, cars, cycles, and pedestrian networks. Each hub functions as the individual focus for discrete communities of an ideal size, providing all the necessary social and communal facilities to support and sustain social coexistence. The sustainable city offers the overall framework for the intelligent husbanding of resources, minimizing energy consumption and recognizing the key role that the economy of cities plays in the global ecological equilibrium. In Rogers' words, "Sustainability means healthier, livelier, more open-minded cities. And above all, it means life for future generations" ("Cities for a Small Planet").

Yet there is a tension between the formality of the plan of Rogers' urban vision and the informality of the sculptural, organic forms of the buildings—a potentially intended tension that reflects Rogers' wider belief in the interplay between framework and function. The structural grid of the Centre Pompidou, for example, is designed to accommodate a wide range of different activities while the regular, even rigid street pattern for Shanghai or Berlin can accommodate a highly differentiated mix of architectures, uses, and events: as Rogers points out, "the Pompidou was as much the exploration of the idea of a flexible institution as it was an exploration of flexible and fragmented form" (*Architecture: A Modern View*). To Rogers, the urban plan is an open and interactive framework, an elaboration of the seminal ideas of Buckminster Fuller's Dymaxion House or Cedric Price's "cybernetic toy" that first introduced the notion of architecture as an open-ended infrastructure for human activity.

The "Noble Tribe of Rationalists"

Fragmentation, flexibility, and fluidity render the architectural and spatial character of Rogers' buildings elusive. The insistence on process and function exacerbates the ability to grasp the essential architectural quality of their designs. But this is precisely the point of the practice's architecture. The quality ultimately resides in the ability to remain "loose fit," to escape the rigors and restrictions of form, to move on, keeping pace with the spirit of the age. The fine line between flexibility and uncertainty fades beyond recognition. It goes out of focus temporarily only to re-emerge—a few projects later—sharp, bold, and radical.

It is this structural uncertainty that makes the corpus of the work intriguing and relevant. At times the whole is more interesting than the parts: the arguments more satisfying than the results; the diagrams more pleasing than the built realities. The buildings are, in effect, *built manifestos* of contemporary culture. This is why they have such visual force and evocative power. In the space of thirty years, Rogers' "tribe of noble rationalists" has not only created some of the most influential buildings of their age: by turning the rational into the new convention, the Rogers practice has contributed to a radical shift in environmental culture that reflects the social and aesthetic concerns of the late twentieth century.

At the end of the Pompidou journey, Richard Rogers' close friend Peter Rice asked himself, "Was is worth it? No doubt at all. One day shortly after the opening I saw an old lady . . . just sitting quietly, stroking the side of the gerberette. She was not afraid, not intimidated" (*An Engineer Imagines*, 46).

A Worked Belief in the Modern
Peter Cook

Richard Rogers occupies an intriguing position in the cultural history of England and, in particular, where this applies to the forward thrust of architecture. The most significant aspect of his background is his cosmopolitanism, which obviously nourishes his wit and sharpens his antennae. So if we look at his remarkable office—which deals with factories, offices, housing, institutional monuments, and late-twentieth-century hybrids—we find it almost unique in holding to an identifiable aesthetic that runs across the limits of the building "type." A Rogers building always appears *as such*, yet the total range is memorable. His designs display an immediately recognizable set of gambits that are nonetheless evolving, and that make few compromises, a type of architecture that is sometimes "larger than life" and certainly does not hide behind pedantry and British caution. It clearly enjoys itself.

Perhaps such single-mindedness would have been possible in the nineteenth century, and at that time the buildings might have subscribed to the ideals of neoclassicism or romanticism. But as we move on into the twentieth century, the pressures of function upon the various building types tend to force them into compartmented references: a fate that is skillfully and sophisticatedly avoided by Rogers. There is so much thrust and dynamic afoot that many parts of buildings sing forth their presence.

Even Edwin Lutyens or James Stirling felt the need to shift pace noticeably when confronting different scales of operation. They had their "public" mannerisms and their "domestic" mannerisms. Rogers' work always holds to the power of being "supra-contextual." It stems from the enthusiasm for production and invention. It comes from that part of the English psychology that has not forgotten the audacities and imaginings of the young boy constructing a model airplane, or a few years later, lying under the engine of a small car, or later still, watching the technicians strip out the world's longest neoprene gasket.

The Rogers office is a very engaging place. It is full of original characters, many of them "schoolboys at heart." (Many of them, to my embarrassment, were my students!) It is as if Richard, their maestro, is able to play all their instruments (as many musical conductors can). What he possesses is the vision to see the wider picture and to strive continually for the relevance of these collective creative processes. Rogers believes strongly in the "multi-layering of cities . . . the shortness of life of buildings in relation to institutions . . . the essentialness of 'green' building . . . to integrate and design with the transportation systems." In a lecture at the Nara Triennale in 1992, Rogers said: "I am a great believer in symbiosis and the idea of continuity, but I do believe that we are getting ourselves confused again, as we did twenty or thirty years ago, when we seemingly forgot the importance of history and context. Unfortunately we see examples of history being borrowed piecemeal and being applied to the facades of buildings like wallpaper. I strongly object to the use of history in this way because it belittles our past . . . We must look optimistically into the future, I can see the formal classical approach to building becoming totally out of date as new technology supplants the old, where light and shadow will be handled in a totally different way. Buildings will become more lightweight and responsive to the changing climate. We are in the middle of an electronics revolution, computers and related technology are allowing us to explore hitherto unknown fields where climatic changes may alter the shade of the external skin of a building—more like the chameleon than the temple."

In the minds of most people, these statements were first made manifest in the Centre Pompidou. A special alchemy existed between Richard Rogers, Renzo Piano, and the great engineer Peter Rice. They had around them a complex team of young English, Japanese, and Austrian architects. The immensity of the task and the audacity of the proposition, as well as the necessity to complete the building for political reasons, led to an object that remains a feat of optimism, to be read by history alongside the great ocean liners, the Eiffel Tower, and the jumbo jet as phenomena that defied predicted defeat.

It is ironic in the light of such a trajectory that for a considerable period afterward Rogers did not know what would happen to the office and even considered becoming a full-time academic with memories of his one great building. Indeed, it must have been difficult to sustain the same momentum for the series of well-honed sheds that then occupied his team for a few years. Yet it is in these sheds—Patscentre, Inmos, and the rest—that the true maturity and strength of the office grew. Each shed was a test-bed for increasingly fine tuning without recourse to mere style, much more like an engine test-bed. Skins are stressed up here, the joints tweaked there, the struc-

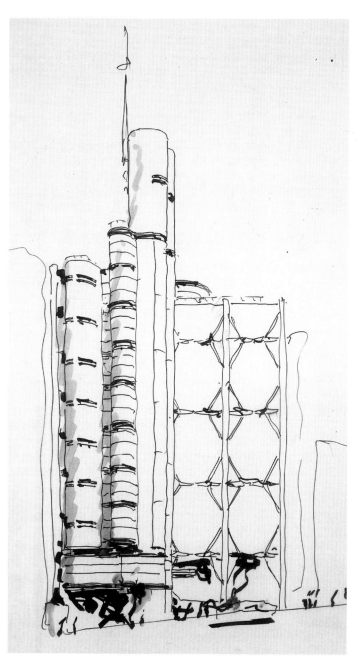

ture allowed to become a little more expressionist here, cooled down there. That these sheds actually developed the state-of-the-art (and the Rogers story is essentially one of the state-of-the-art) so far forward is one of those essential ironies of architecture. We can compare the relation of Christopher Wren's humbler churches in London with St. Paul's Cathedral, perhaps. The edging forward of idea piled upon idea and their cumulative power create a powerful force that is even able to withstand a national climate of the "belittled past" (in Rogers' own words) and is even able to move forward at a time when most of the generation below his seems happy to keep a low innovatory profile. Usually such a situation would lead to "coasting" or self-satisfaction—not for Rogers. His charm and insight whip up the enthusiasm of his lieutenants and they are again off into the unknown.

Lloyd's was, nonetheless, very necessary for the spirit of the office. Mere steady progress can become tedious. On close inspection, the margin of technological development that lies between these two buildings—Centre Pompidou (1971) and Lloyd's (1978)—is greater than the difference of years between them. Lloyd's has its own self-confidence: it is the product of mature specification and commodity of the parts rather than a single moment of passion. There is a further irony, for it does display some allegiances to the English arcade tradition in the design of the roof and to the work of Louis Kahn in plan, with its served and servant spaces, while at the same time being absolutely of its time. There is a confidence with which the compilation of extremely sophisticated elements is managed, there is a breadth with which the escalator bank, the lift shafts, the robotlike towers, and so on can exist as icons themselves—almost as in an urban design piece. So we can read Lloyd's as the springboard for a whole series of confident urban projects on a number of very different fronts.

Compounded towers and giant armatures play between vertical shafts, inclined shafts, stacks, towers, and trays. These are visible in buildings and proposals for Japan or China or France as well as London. If the Coin Street project with its bridge across the Thames River had to do with the continuity of London—and therefore offered technologized housing perhaps in the spirit of Victorian London, striving and optimistic—it was defeated by the obverse forces in today's society. Undaunted, the Rogers team offered an even more exotic bridge for their

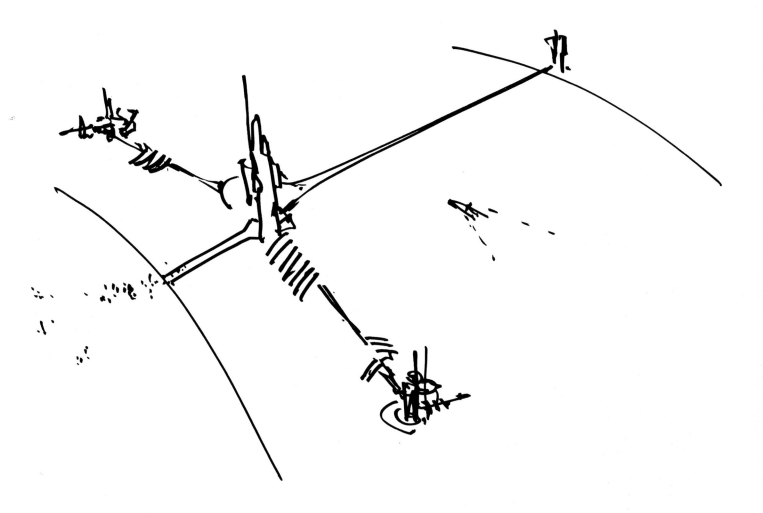

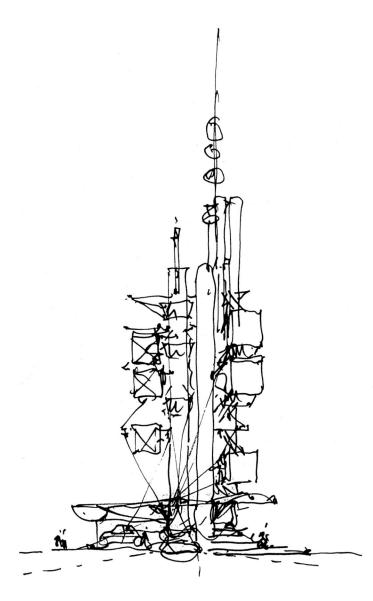

*Tomigaya Exhibition Building,
Tokyo, 1992–93, preliminary sketch.*

exhibit "London As It Could Be," a comprehensive vision for London exhibited at the Royal Academy in 1986. By this time the parts are even more confident and robotlike, and the focus moves toward the future. Linear parks and three-dimensionalization of transport are interwoven quite relaxedly. Such assuredness can come only from a machinery that knows that it can put up a superb tower, wrap a superb shed, and still play with the performance of play within space. All the time it suggests what the twentieth century should have been but was held back from by architects who were more concerned with retracing steps.

Richard himself is so quick on the uptake that he can sense the way in which a particular team is gaining or losing momentum. He is essentially a friendly person and uses psychology to keep the enthusiasm going long after it should have flagged. Perhaps it is his Italian blood that enables him to take a more rounded and less puritan approach to both people and processes, more than if he had been a typical "worried" Englishman. This same syndrome almost certainly accounts for the ease and clarity with which he is able to convey the power of the ideas to a lay audience.

From the days when he created a house for his parents in Wimbledon (1964), one that was not only technically cute but also very clear in its intentions, Richard Rogers has stuck to his guns. There are no secret buildings that were done purely to raise fees but abdicating the position taken, nor are there diversions or flirtations with revivalism. There is a refreshing avoidance of a certain British "homespun" detailing or overenthusiasm for archaic surfaces. True, there are better and worse buildings and the inevitable moments of self-imitation. But the general progression has been forward, right from the time of the Wimbledon house.

Richard and Ruthie Rogers live in a reconstructed interior in Chelsea which might be regarded as a sharp and metallic progression from Chareau's Maison de Verre. The late twentieth century inhabits the Georgian shell with a self-confident series of parts: manufactured, edgy, and ordered. It is a reminder that much of his work shares a spirit with that of today's Japan: a worked belief in the modern, rather than a modern style. This distinguishes his work from many of the younger "modernists" who are concerned with the *parti* rather than the *spirit* of modernism.

Rogers' work involves the exposure and enjoyment of the artifact that is simply and genuinely produced by the abilities of the time. It involves the exposure of these artifacts compounded together in such ways that they might, but also might not, create patterns of architecture that we immediately recognize. So there need be no embarrassment about simple rectangular pieces of metal, no problem about workmanlike stairs that are reminiscent of fire escapes, no problem with a surfeit of metal louvers, however many and however long, that may be necessary to make a wall.

The recent project for a housing tower in Korea looks as if it could be erected with the ease of a Lego model without any loss of spirit. The Tomigaya Turbine Tower in Tokyo looks as if it could take off and fly at any minute. This and other projects signal a new, even relaxed, phase in the Rogers work: the tautness of the junctions and skins and the environmental ambition are known prerequisites, but the building form itself is wholehearted, even flamboyant.

As it has moved into urbanism, the Rogers office has begun to show a delight in the simple and somewhat heroic power of the pivot, the armature, the spoke, the idea of centrality and rotation. These are strong circular elements: towers as pivots and then the creation of strong linear systems between. Tantalizingly, too, there are "floaters" that occur outside this system. It is as if the machine dynamic, which has always been in the work, has been given the mandate to express itself at the largest scale.

A geometrical directness has always been there, of course. Not for this office are the games and tricks of bifurcation, deformation, bending, twisting, overlaying, or slithering-off. Nor the accompanying languages of ambiguity, reference, metaphor, or quotation. The object should stand for itself and have the presence of mind to be what it is. For the Berlin central area of the Potsdamerplatz, there is therefore a clearheaded proposal, based on such a pivot, with thick avenues of trees alternating with strongly figured building (that would undoubtedly have a strong mechanical and environmental presence in contrast to the trees). It is directly in the tradition of this essentially full-bodied city. At the Royal Docks in London is again a direct series of boldly stated buildings announced by the series of pivot points, each of which has a different architectural scale, as thrusting and authoritative as the original nineteenth-century docks themselves.

All of this can be seen as an adjunct or a run-in toward the major urban project for China: the Lu Jia Zui district in Shanghai. The central park for this city-within-a-city is reminiscent of the center of Tokyo as a device. Avenues and sub-pivots sustain the rotational system. Inevitably, with the Thames-side experience in London, the development of bridges, docks, piers, and landing stages continues the "urbanism" into the water. The Kings' Dock project for Liverpool might serve as a glimpse into the detail of these city-scale pieces. Sheds have now developed into skinned-over pieces of city. The edges are more flamboyant than in the earlier industrial sheds, the ends and corners articulated by towers and piles-up pivots. Arms and legs might spring up at a moment's notice. There is, effectively, a whole *parti* available at every scale. So Rogers is able to offer a complete architectural response.

This is quite extraordinary in the light of the caution and introversion of most other contemporary British work. The team may well have benefited from exposure to a variety of different contexts, different scales, and the involvement of several different structural engineers: Peter Rice, Anthony Hunt, and various others of the innovative figures for whom London is justly famous. The close, even symbiotic, relation of, say, Anthony Hunt with Mike Davies is a key to the issue. There are certainly other territories—the links to boat design, computer development, race cars, stressed materials, sandwich plastics, "smart" glass—inevitably layered into the trajectory of the office. The straightforwardness of the juxtaposition of the parts is then a necessary adjunct: an element seen to be doing its task, a structural member enjoyed as it hangs out there, maybe in space; a skin delighting in the statement of a new definition: neither solid panel nor tent, neither translucent nor opaque, maybe heater as well as protector, maybe aperture as well as barrier. The clear geometry and the (usually) inevitable placement of routes, exits, or lines of force again serve as the necessary condition for these building machines to turn upon.

At this point, it would seem that the Rogers practice is one of the few that have followed directly upon the Miesian tradition, without having any of Mies van der Rohe's "dryness," a tradition that has not a little classical planning about it without in any way displaying classicism of form or detail. Like ships, though, most of the buildings are very concerned with performance, so like ships they have an ordered and assertive structuring. They keep afloat and keep plowing through.

Most imitators of this work seem to compromise the scale and power of the original. Rogers is not fearful about the size of an element or the components of a junction. In much British work there is an unnecessary proliferation of elements: each junction is treated as unique, each piece of metal is overenjoyed. So the imitators end up with a "high-tech" building of fussy cleverness. Rogers' buildings tend to plow through the vicissitudes of local conditions like a tank. A bolt is really a bolt and a corner is no cause for alarm. This genuine celebration of the large and the mechanically produced is immediately recognizable.

An intriguing strand crept into the work around the time of the ill-fated National Gallery extension in London's Trafalgar Square. It was in the form of the perspective drawings that accompanied the more rhetorically mechanistic presence of the model of the scheme. These drawings were in a bold manner of mass black as well as very assertive line. Bold tower forms and a powerful silhouette were repeated on a number of schemes, reminiscent of the fabulous drawings of Chernikhov of the 1920s, full of unbridled enthusiasm for the industrial or industrialized object, full of power and presence. Yet this imagery is clearly seen in a nighttime view of the Lloyd's Building. As the practice developed, however, the vertical "tubing" began to be a part of the vocabulary. The circular (or sometimes circular-ended) shafts became more and more assertive. Again, the elementalism of the high modernist moment is recalled, but carrying with it now the foreknowledge that, when built, the enclosure will no longer be made from brick or block that is smoothed over in order to make it seem "modern"; instead, it will actually be seen through as a piece of total enclosure technology.

The European Court of Human Rights in Strasbourg is probably the most developed product of this realized elementalism. It has all the assertiveness of the other work, but also a recognition of hierarchy and emphasis on the courtrooms and the entrance hall. The dominance of the shed and the loose-fit tower are thus being challenged in this latest work. It remains to be seen whether the enormous scale of the Shanghai master plan and Terminal 5 at London's Heathrow will cause the "shed" to reassert itself, or whether the compositional thrust of the work will be that of a total and hierarchical language. In parallel, we can ask a question about the detail of the buildings: will they (or need they) continue much further in the direction of delight in the skinning and jointing of the skins? Delightful (but intellectually irritating), the best parts of the Lloyd's Building are the staircase towers. They are essentially appendages to the main bulk, special, perhaps over designed, but terrific. There is a moment when the need for range of particularity or of emphasis reasserts itself like a ghost from architecture's past—or perhaps a need for expression. Except in his smallest buildings, Mies was unable to respond. Other architects of the twentieth century have over-responded. It is a challenge to which the power and enthusiasm of this marvelous machine can respond: extending and extending the density of their inventions and articulating the clarity of their thrust.

Domestic Environments

Creek Vean House, Feock, Cornwall, United Kingdom, 1966–68

This family house—the first major work by Team 4—is a single aspect masonry structure set into a steeply sloping site overlooking a creek in Cornwall. All main rooms are oriented toward spectacular views of the sea and surrounding wooded landscape. The building is divided into two elements, one housing the public spaces (living, kitchen, and dining areas in a single double-height volume) and the other containing the private bedrooms and guest apartment (in a linear structure). In this sense, the design is genuinely organic, shaped to maximize the relationship with its surroundings, reflecting the then recent acquaintance that Richard Rogers (and his fellow student Norman Foster) had made with the houses of Frank Lloyd Wright and Rudolph Schindler in the United States.

The fan-shaped plan is arranged around two main axes. The external east-west axis establishes a direct dialogue between the building and the landscape. It creates a visual link to the opposite side of the creek with a direct route from the car park and entrance bridge, along the outdoor staircase that cuts through the building, down to the lawn and boat house below, at the creek. The internal north-south axis is a circulation spine that provides access to all the main rooms, establishing a clear hierarchy between the different elements of the house. This toplit space is covered by a continuous strip rooflight—floodlit from the outside at night—acting as a gallery space that can be enjoyed from different points within the house. Sliding doors create a more varied internal environment, opening up views of the landscape and the

paintings from the deepest parts of the house. The roof and walls are covered with hanging creepers and the steps of the external staircase are planted with grass, emphasizing the integration of the house within its natural setting.

While the construction and materials are clearly traditional—the internal and external walls are fair-faced, honey-colored concrete blocks—the planning and spatial concerns of the building (flexibili-

ty, hierarchy, and relationship to context) can be seen to run through many of the designs of the Rogers practice over the following twenty-five years. The design team recognized the fundamental inefficiencies of employing labor-intensive and time-consuming traditional building techniques (the house took two years to complete). Su Rogers, one of the original members of the design team, stated at the time, "The pain and

the anguish of it all has forced us to realize that future homes must be built much more quickly and more simply"—an anguish that generated the development of a radical approach to construction techniques that has shaped all of Rogers' subsequent buildings and those of an entire generation of architects trained in Britain in the 1960s.

General views; site plan.

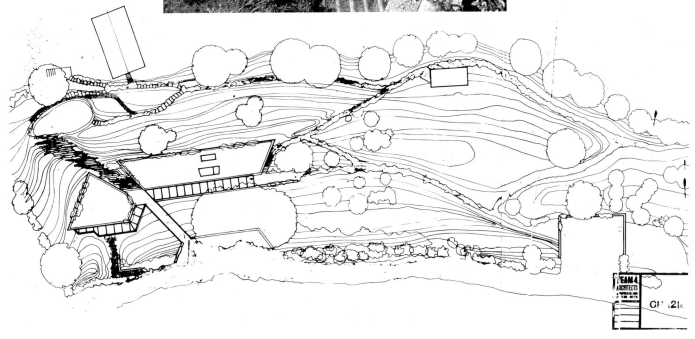

Section; view of garden.

Section; plans; interiors.

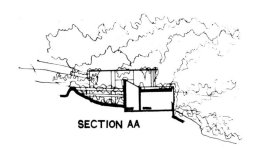

SECTION AA

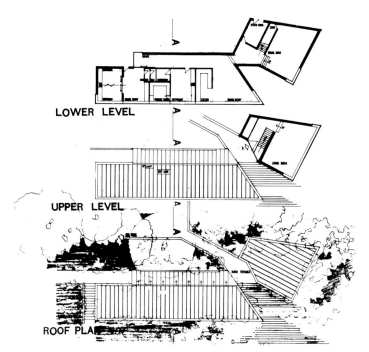

LOWER LEVEL

UPPER LEVEL

ROOF PLAN

WEST ELEVATION

EAST ELEVATION

Rogers House, Wimbledon, United Kingdom, 1968–69

The house for Richard Rogers' parents is an evocative reminder of the expressive potential of minimal architecture. Two simple single-story pavilions are carefully arranged along a deep garden plot creating a world of supreme tranquillity and order within the bourgeois suburb of Wimbledon, which is characterized by large, overdecorated Victorian mansions. The main pavilion, inhabited by Rogers' mother, Dada, who is a potter, occupies the central section of the plot sandwiched between the soft garden (with a cluster of elegant silver birch trees) and the hard paved courtyard facing the studio. A planted embankment acts as a buffer to the main street, engendering a sense of discovery as one moves deeper into the plot.

Both pavilions have floor-to-ceiling glazing along the main facades, establishing a layered axis of transparency that penetrates the garden, the main house, the courtyard, and the studio. The other sides of the box are solid with the exception of a service door to the garden passage. The interior spaces, with dual aspect, achieve a rare level of intimacy with nature. Wherever you turn you are unsure where the building ends and nature begins. Designed to be both open and private, the house succeeds in creating a sense of lightness and spaciousness with simple materials and a highly controlled economy of means.

The plan clearly separates the public and private functions of the house. A long kitchen counter (that doubles as storage) defines and integrates the kitchen with the open-plan living and dining areas. In this way, the collective activities of the house—cooking, eating, and talking—are not segregated into distinct spaces but celebrated at the very heart of the house. The open-plan zone is separated (when required) from the bedroom and bathroom areas by full-height green sliding screens. The master bedroom facing the garden leads to the main bathroom, which is illuminated by a flat glass skylight. A timber-and-glass furniture screen, designed by Richard Rogers' cousin, the eminent architect and critic Ernesto Nathan Rogers, sits in the master bedroom: a quiet testimony to the architectural pedigree of the building.

The building is supported by eight yellow steel portals, with expressed fascia and end columns, creating a clear internal span of fourteen meters. The main structure is enclosed within the external envelope to minimize maintenance, while the walls, composed of the yellow composite aluminum panels developed for the Zip-Up House, create a well-insulated internal environment with integrated heating in the ceiling. In its use of everyday, mass-produced materials and in its overall simplicity of form, this twenty-seven-year-old building is a refreshing reinterpretation of the Case Study Houses in California (with a particular affection for Ray and Charles Eames' house) reflecting Rogers' long-standing interest in clarity of plan and in the economy of structure and materials.

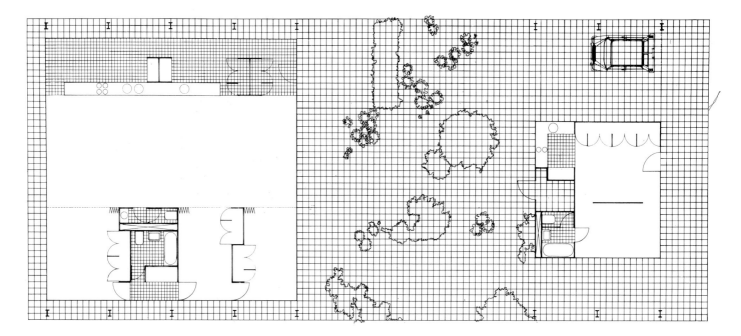

Plan; views of house.

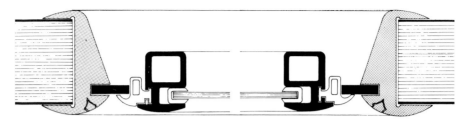

Construction detail; interiors.

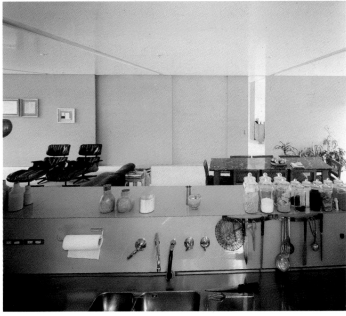

The appropriately termed Zip-Up House or Zip-Up Enclosure, named after the process of joining aluminum wall panels with a neoprene zipper, is a design manifesto for the modern house. Motivated by the need to find a more efficient way to build, it was a direct reaction to the laborious construction of the earlier Creek Vean House. This intentionally polemical design, which won second prize in the Ideal Home competition of 1969, is a three-dimensional statement for adaptability, flexibility, and autonomy.

The concept is simple: a bright yellow, waterproof, highly insulated box constructed from load-bearing panels. The floors, walls and roof are made of the same components, twenty-centimeter sandwiches of aluminum skins and structural foam plastic fastened together with neoprene zippers, commonly used to insert windows in buses. The panels have seven times the insulation value of traditional cavity brick walls, eliminating the need for expensive central heating in a moderate climate.

The self-contained structure creates a nine-meter clear span providing a highly flexible and infinitely adaptable domestic environment within. The absence of separate structural and cladding systems allows complete freedom in the disposition of internal partitions, which run on retractable castors and are locked in place by inflatable fixing gaskets. In this way, the interior can be rearranged—in twenty-four hours—to suit changes in family structure (a new baby, new family interests, and so on). The flexibility of the interior is mirrored by the adaptability of its exterior. Designed to sit on adjustable leveling jacks, the house does not require expensive foundations or a level site. It can be simply parked anywhere, on an irregular or even a sloping site, and "plugged in" to service mains.

Significantly, the house was designed in 1969 to be constructed from components already available on the market. Nearly thirty years later, the realization of such a building would still be perceived by many as radical and futuristic. Many of the ideas contained in this experimental project were given concrete form in two completed buildings: the Wimbledon House in London (1969) and the Universal Oil Products factory in Tadworth (1973) whose performance over time has proven the fundamental validity of the initial design concepts.

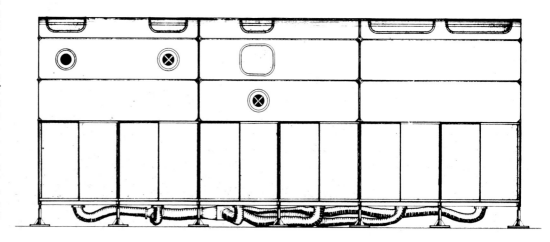

Elevation; axonometric; model.

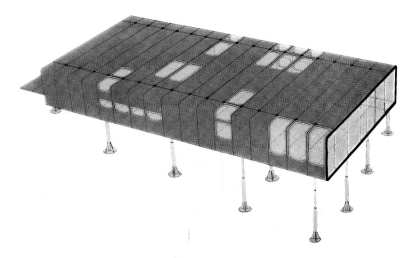

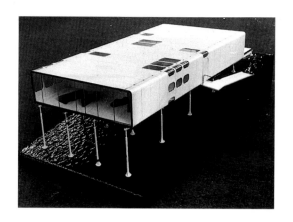

Model; axonometric sketch.

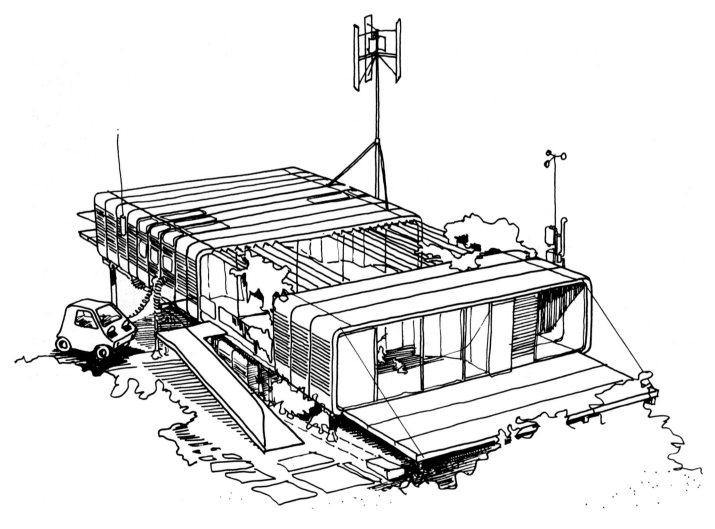

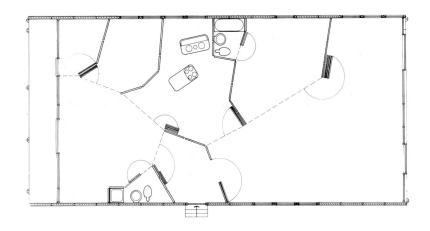

Plan; model.

Thames Reach Housing, London, 1984–87

The only completed housing project to date by the Rogers practice occupies a spectacular location along the Thames River in West London. Originally an oil storage depot and processing plant, the site contained a mixture of light industrial buildings and is surrounded by a residential neighborhood composed predominantly of two-story houses. The overall project, which contains apartments, offices, and workshops, is a microcosm of Rogers' belief in the mixed-use city: a place where people can live, work, and play within the same urban district, where old and new buildings are integrated to give new life to an otherwise derelict inner-city site. Rogers' own London office is located within the refurbished industrial building; John Young, one of the founding members of the practice, has designed his own apartment within the residential complex; and a successful restaurant creates a social focus for the development.

The project was designed to mediate the change in scale required by the broad vistas along the river frontage and the more delicate grain of the residential surroundings. Accordingly, the twenty-five residential units are pragmatically broken down into three distinct clusters of eight or nine apartments linked by lightweight steel bridges. Between the clusters, wide corridors allow views from the surrounding streets to the river. From the river, the buildings read as a single, articulated glass-and-steel structure with cantilevered balconies and fully glazed facades. From the rear, the three elements clad in brick and glass relate in scale and texture to the surrounding streets and terraced houses.

The distinction between "served" and "servant" spaces that characterizes so many of the practice's buildings is made manifest by the introduction of vertical circulation and service cores that link the apartments to the underground car parking. As a result, the living areas of the apartments are extremely spacious, maximizing daylight penetration and enjoyment of the views. All main living spaces and master bedrooms face the river, while other bedrooms and service areas face the street and neighboring housing blocks.

Designed while the Lloyd's Building was being completed, the formal expression of the buildings is highly articulated with strong vertical towers, horizontal layering, and cantilevered balconies. However, the restrained use of materials—brick, glass, and steel—is a reflection of the residential developers' view of a contemporary domestic vernacular that is more acceptable to traditional British tastes.

View along the Thames before construction.

Overall plan; general view.

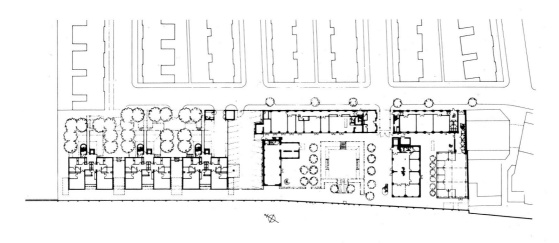

River elevation; views of balconies;
rear elevation.

View of towers; exterior details.

John Young Apartment, Thames Reach Housing, London, 1986–89

Designed for his own family by John Young, the practice's most experienced specialist in construction techniques and building production, the apartment is a tour de force of architectural detailing. While the Zip-Up House or the Autonomous House minimized the expression of their advanced technology, this design celebrates the integration of standardized industrial components with highly crafted one-off elements, revealing the lasting influence of Pierre Chareau and Jean Prouvé on the practice's work.

Placed on the two upper levels of Thames Reach Housing, the apartment has broad views, with dramatically changing light conditions at dawn and dusk, over the tidal waters of the Thames River. The sleeping platform (not an enclosed bedroom) is delicately suspended over the double-height living and dining area where a very shiplike wind beam braces the large expanse of glass against the strong winds. A lightweight cable-and-steel staircase in the living space sets up a *promenade architecturale* through the apartment that reaches its climax in the wonderfully self-indulgent master bathroom shrouded in a circular wall of glass blocks. A curved ramp wraps itself around the glass drum leading from a large terrace to the roof-level observatory with its upper deck viewing platform: a peaceful haven in the middle of the city.

Each space in this sequence allows the views to be enjoyed from different angles at different times of day. Below, the open kitchen faces a balcony with a teak timber deck emphasizing the maritime character of the design. A spacious workroom is flanked by a stack of mobile storage units that are accessed by turning the giant industrial-like wheels, while oversized circular plate-coil heaters create a visually striking vertical feature in the main living space.

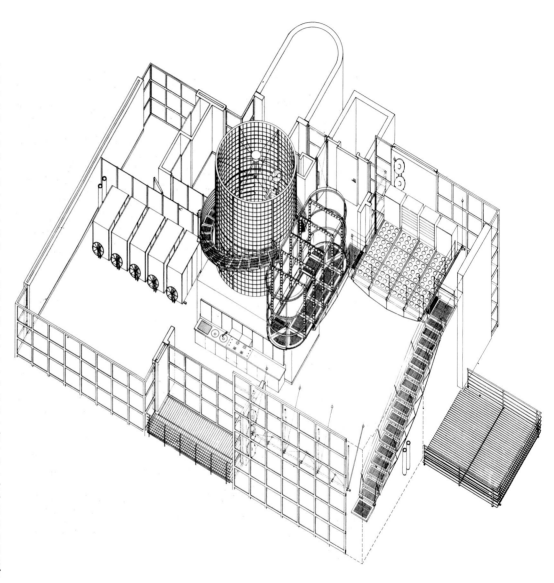

Axonometric; bathroom.

Interior; longitudinal section.

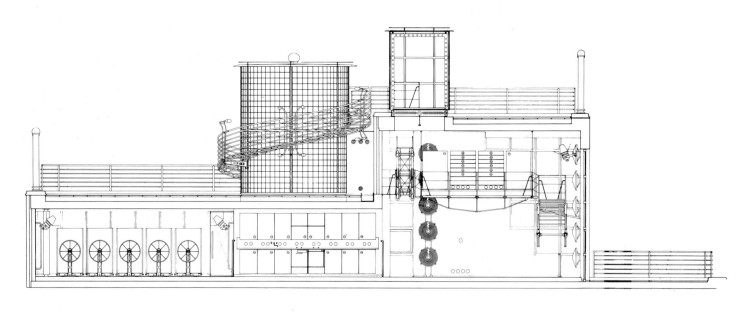

Interiors; cross section.

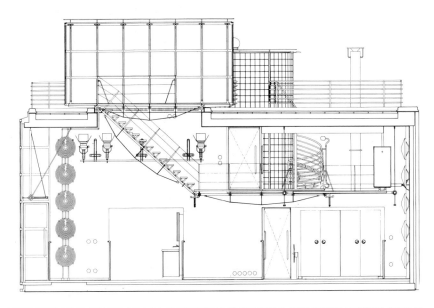

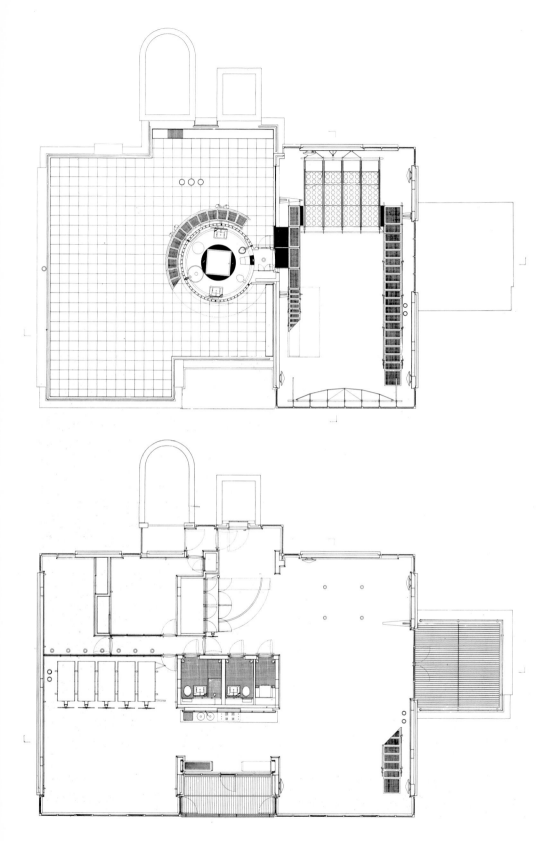

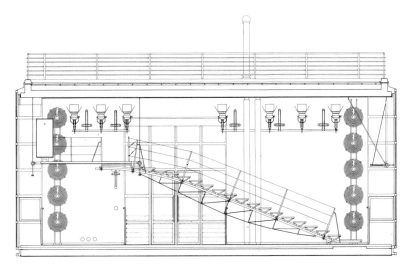

Michael Elias House, Los Angeles, California, 1990–91

The design for a family house in California is a clear tribute to the Case Study House movement of the 1950s and to the lasting influence on Rogers of the Eames House. Like an iceberg, the main volume of the building is concealed below ground, leaving a floating canopy suspended from a pair of steel masts to engage with the sloping terrain overlooking the Pacific Palisades in California.

Underneath the wafer-thin twenty-by-thirty-meter roof is a flexible arrangement of internal steel partitions that can be moved to suit the changing requirements of the household. While the external form is reminiscent of the simplicity of the early project for a movable Beach House (1975), with its retractable shutters and spiderlike internal plan, the house is well and truly anchored to the ground with concrete walls built into the underlying rock strata aiding its passive environmental performance. Heat is stored in cavities underground during the day and is recycled into the house through an "air floor" system to provide warmth on cool evenings.

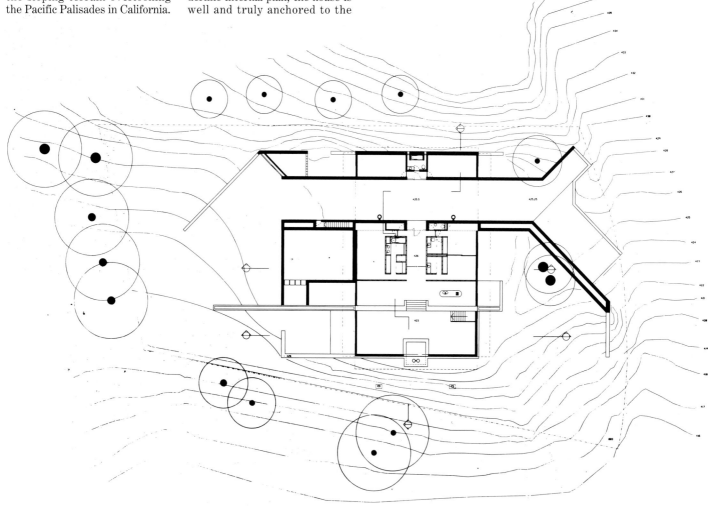

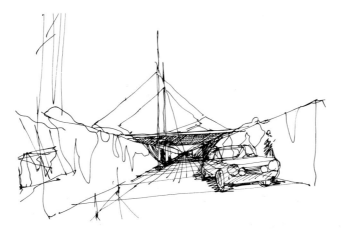

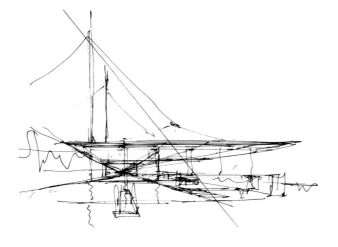

This experimental project for an industrialized housing system synthesizes the practice's approach to design. It represents a response to a global problem (how to build more decent houses at lower costs) rather than an idiosyncratic formal design solution. In its quest for ultimate flexibility and autonomy, it brings together many of the practice's earlier preoccupations (exemplified in the Zip-Up House and in the Inmos factory) with the growing concern for reduced costs, environmental performance, and energy-conscious design.

While the Zip-Up House was a simple yellow box, the industrialized housing system is a collection of "boxes," a kit of parts that can be combined to create residential towers or low-rise communities. The basic kit of parts includes a structural unit, a glazed unit, a staircase, a balcony, columns, and foundations. All units are assembled off-site in controlled factory conditions, then transported by truck and erected on different sites throughout the hilly terrain of Korea.

Thanks to computer-controlled cranes designed to stack containers in ships, the different housing units can be stacked vertically to create a completed building. Taking its cue from the manufacture of domestic appliances, such as refrigerator inserts, the project investigates the use of resin-injection and resin-transfer molding techniques with integrated electrical circuits that would considerably reduce the cost of basic building components and increase their long-term efficiency. The research project concluded that the industrialized housing system could deliver up to 100,000 fully furnished housing units at 20 percent of the conventional construction costs, providing a densely populated country like Korea with a solution to an increasingly global problem.

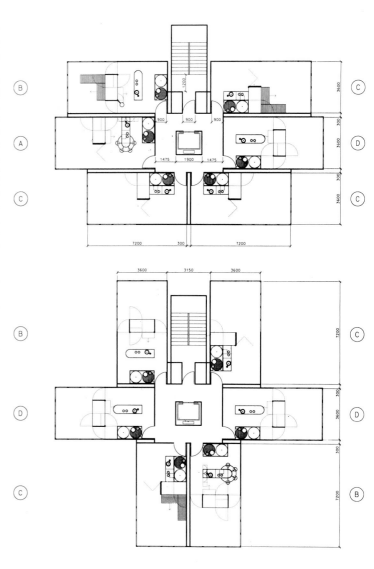

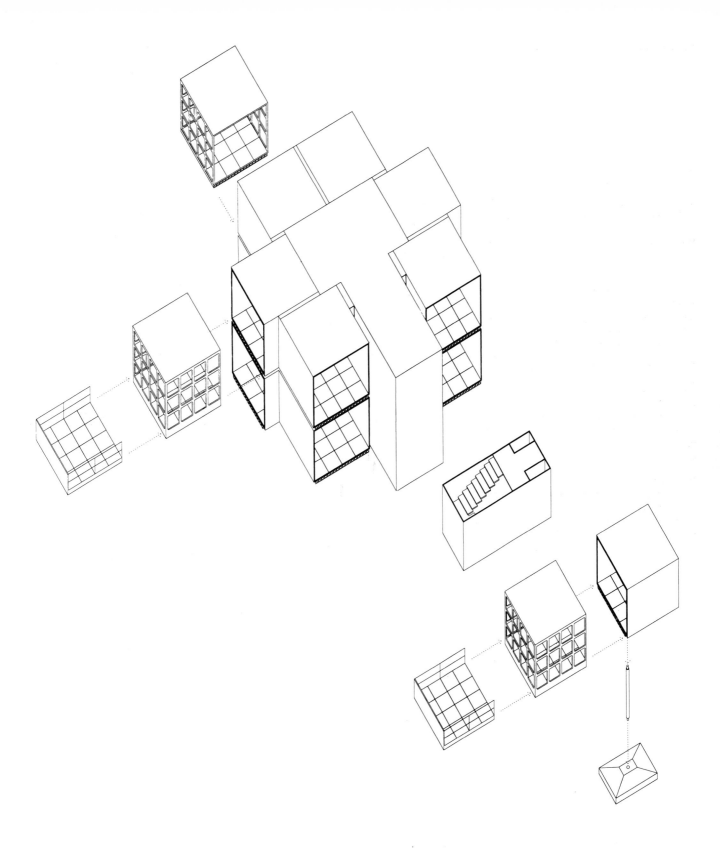

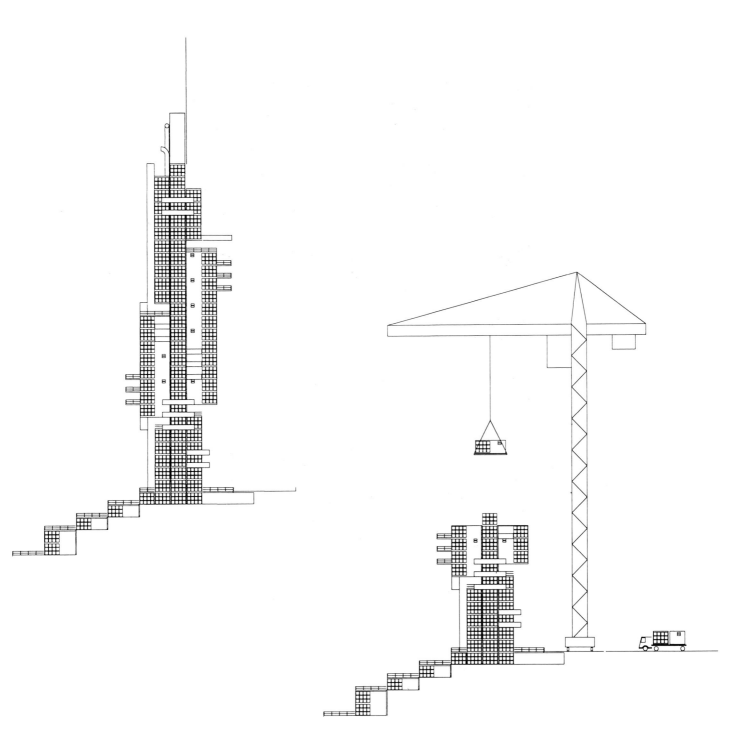

One of the practice's rare incursions into urban housing is situated on a key west-facing stretch of south bank of the Thames River in London (similar in character to the Thames Reach complex). The surrounding urban area is relatively fragmented, with a number of high-rise towers and clusters of neosuburban housing. On the southwestern corner of the site stands St. Mary's Church, marked by a prominent belfry.

The design responds to its special location with a sloping building that exploits views over the Thames. The building forms a thirty-degree gradient, stepping down from seventeen stories at its highest point (the northern corner of the site) to four stories as it reaches St. Mary's Church. The alignment of the building forms a triangular south-facing open space with gardens and playing fields defined by a covered pedestrian route running parallel to the main building. The riverside area is boldly landscaped with a radiating pattern of paths and planting that focuses on the river. At ground level the new building contributes a sense of order to the surrounding urban landscape. The design maximizes the potential of the river (one of Rogers' recurrent urban interests) with a generous waterside pedestrian walkway that is integrated into the surrounding street pattern and the new residential building.

The residential units are stacked between four distinct vertical circulation towers marked by twin service cores, providing a sense of rhythm and grain to what could otherwise have been a relentless facade. The vertical elements break down the scale of the housing units into identifiable visual clusters that echo, albeit at a different scale, the traditional pattern of Georgian houses. The apartments benefit from a riverside view with planted balconies, and glazed, inclined rooftop terraces add to the formal cohesion of the building form. Although designed in a bolder architectural language, its planning and formal organization are similar to the rigor and clarity of Team 4's housing projects of the early 1960s in Surrey and Cornwall, where low-rise units in linear clusters foster a sense of community and optimize views.

Site plan; model; elevations.

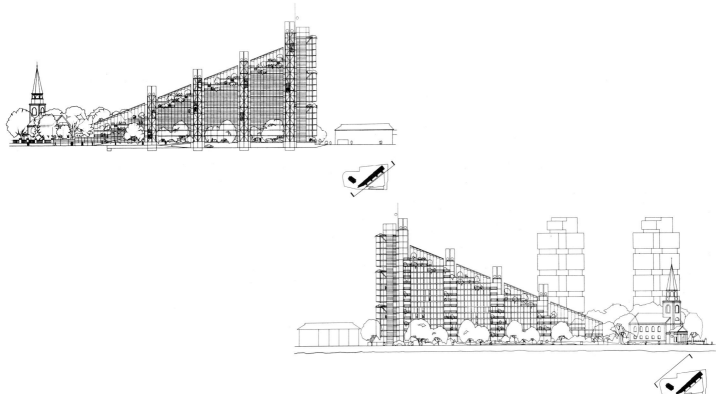

Model; sections.

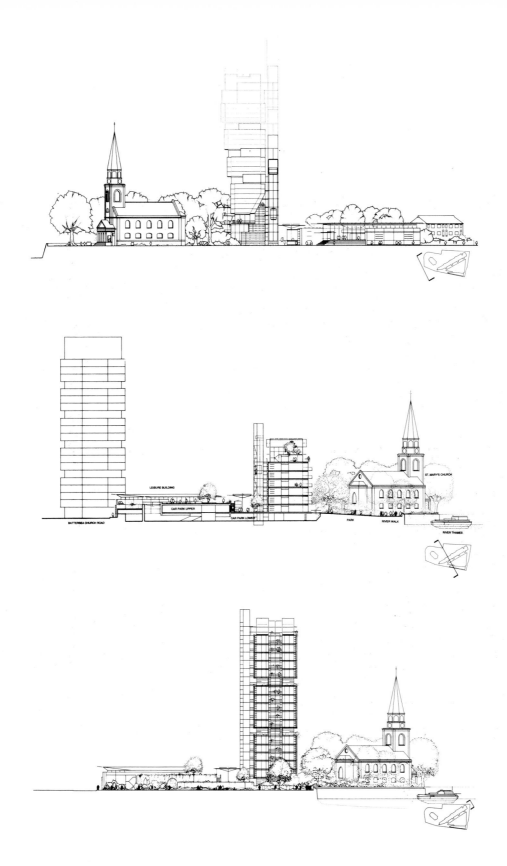

LEISURE BUILDING

CAR PARK UPPER

CAR PARK LOWER

BATTERSEA CHURCH ROAD

PARK

RIVER WALK

ST. MARY'S CHURCH

RIVER THAMES

The Workplace

Patscentre Research Laboratory, Melbourn, Hertfordshire, United Kingdom, 1976–83

Located in the countryside outside Cambridge, Patscentre is representative of the Rogers design approach to autonomous structures. The parent company, PA Technology, has a "holistic" view to problem solving similar to that of the Rogers practice; it offers its clients a range of skills and services, ranging from the design of toys and radar to graphics and presentation techniques.

As a building type, Patscentre is a hybrid. It is both a laboratory and an office building. Each staff member has two workstations: one in the laboratory to carry out experiments (bang-a-nail-anywhere workshop) and one in the office areas for administration and client contact. This potential conflict has been resolved by placing all laboratories in the middle, with offices on the perimeter and common rooms across the ends.

Conceived as an infinitely flexible structure, Patscentre is a building that has practiced what it preached. Following construction of the first phase in 1976, the building has been adapted and extended twice—in 1981 and 1983—in response to the company's growth and changing requirements. It is, in effect, a highly serviced "dumb box" with a difference. While the structure is conventional—a concrete slab on stilts with a steel-frame internal structure—the servicing strategy is novel. The services are suspended from the floor slab, in the void beneath the building—a subterranean precursor of the overhead expressed structures at Inmos and PA Technology in Princeton. The building appears to have been parked temporarily on the site and plugged into existing services, with the autonomy and self-

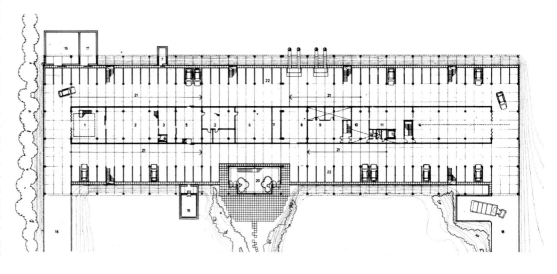

sustainability of a caravan or temporary shelter.

In order to integrate the structure with its surroundings, all car parking has been placed in the void beneath the building. An earlier intention to cover the building with planting partly survives in the built version in the form of a raised landscaped embankment that spills over into the lower-level void. The visual effect is to create a horizontal datum, an optical illusion where the building appears to hover over the grass, touching the ground only at the center. Here a double-height lobby acts as the main vertical circulation core with a pressed-steel-and-wire staircase,

inspired by the scaffolders' steps at the Centre Pompidou, marking the route to the offices and laboratories. Bunker zones, burrowed underneath the natural embankments, contain "quiet rooms" for special experiments, plant, and equipment. At night, the building describes a striking silhouette that emphasizes its structural independence from the surrounding context.

The building construction clearly defies methods of standard practice. The rather conventional concrete floor slab supports a yellow lightweight-steel roof frame. Prefabricated roofing panels, with the first layer of roofing material

bonded on one side and finished ceiling on the other, are bolted to the roof structure and an additional membrane added. The steel cladding system, with interchangeable glazed and vitreous enameled panels, is placed outside the frame so that the glass meets the sky. The absence of heavy Mies-like fascias increases the sense of lightness and impermanence of the building. As John Winter has noted, "The cool metallic building in a gentle landscape is one of the better legacies of the Modern Movement and Patscentre is a crisp example of the genre" (*Architects' Journal*, June 28, 1978).

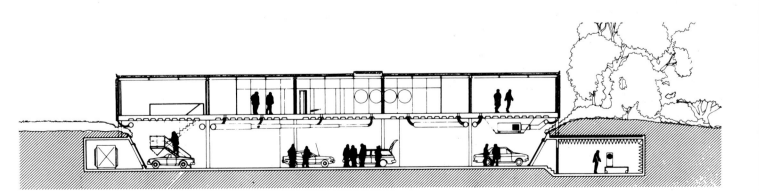

Section of first project; night view;
section.

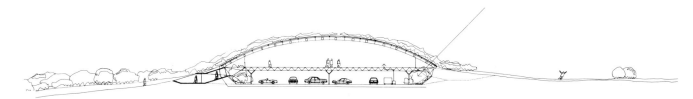

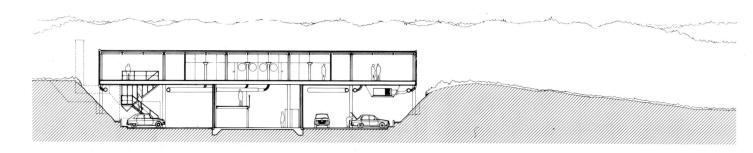

Axonometric showing structure;
interiors.

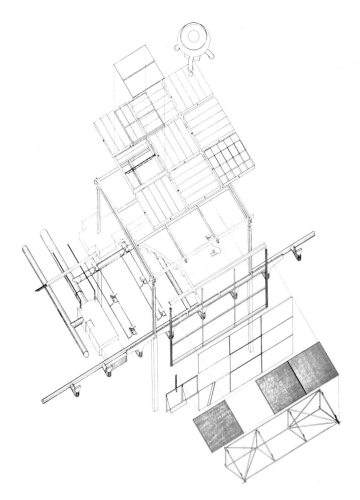

Fleetguard Manufacturing Plant, Quimper, Brittany, France, 1979–81

Fleetguard, an industrial building located in rural Brittany, in the far northwest of France, was the first building to follow the completion of the Centre Pompidou and the amicable separation of Richard Rogers and his partner, Renzo Piano. It is a manufacturing and distribution center for heavy-duty engine filters for Cummins, an American company well known for its patronage of distinguished architects in its hometown of Columbus, Indiana.

Cummins required a highly adaptable building that was capable of rapid expansion and response to changing needs and functions. Recommended by Kevin Roche, whose firm had designed many Cummins facilities in the United States, the Rogers office was selected because of their design of the ultimate flexible machine—the Pompidou—and, not least, for their ability to speak English and to practice in France.

The building occupies a prominent site on the most elevated point in the rolling countryside outside the town of Quimper. Known affectionately as *l'araignée* (the spider) and *le chapiteau* (the circus), the building makes its presence felt in a discreet yet definitive manner. A grid of red masts and weblike ties floats above the silvery structure that is dug into the ground to reduce its impact on the surrounding landscape. It is the structure, not the form, that acts as a sign for the building, quietly announcing its architectural content without resorting to rhetorical gestures or graphic excesses.

The extremely tight budget and schedule determined a straightforward approach to the design. It is a large, single-story, double-height box (8,750 square meters) with a steel-framed mezzanine element at the entrance end containing offices and plant rooms. The main circulation elements are conceived as distinct, plug-in components: the lightweight steel pedestrian bridge linking the car park to the entrance lobby barely touches the building (in the manner of a traditional drawbridge) while the main staircase is literally suspended from the building structure.

From the upper level there are clear, uninterrupted views of the cavernous production space below. The axial disposition of the staircase, framed by symmetrically arranged blue service ducts and generously lit by glazed partitions, emphasizes the hierarchical organization of the building. Explicit rhetorical use is made of color coding—as exemplified in the rear elevation of the Centre Pompidou—by identifying individual building components with different colors: red for structure, blue for services, and yellow for protective elements in the loading bay.

The choice of a suspended tension structure was motivated by the need to reduce the overall height of the building so as to minimize its environmental impact and reduce costs of construction by using less steel and cladding than a conventional solution. A grid of thin steel masts projects eight meters above the roofline, while the main volume—clad in precoated steel with a continuous band of high-level glazing—hugs the ground. The structure relies on the interrelationship of three load-carrying systems suspended from the tubular steel columns. Steel rods support the downward load of the roof on a six-meter

grid, while a secondary set of rods counteracts the upward loads caused by the extreme wind conditions on the site. A third set of crossing rods is placed along the axis of the main columns to limit deflection and control response to asymmetrical loadings of individual bays (in some areas eight-ton ovens are suspended from the roof).

*Entrance lobby; site plan; ground
floor plan.*

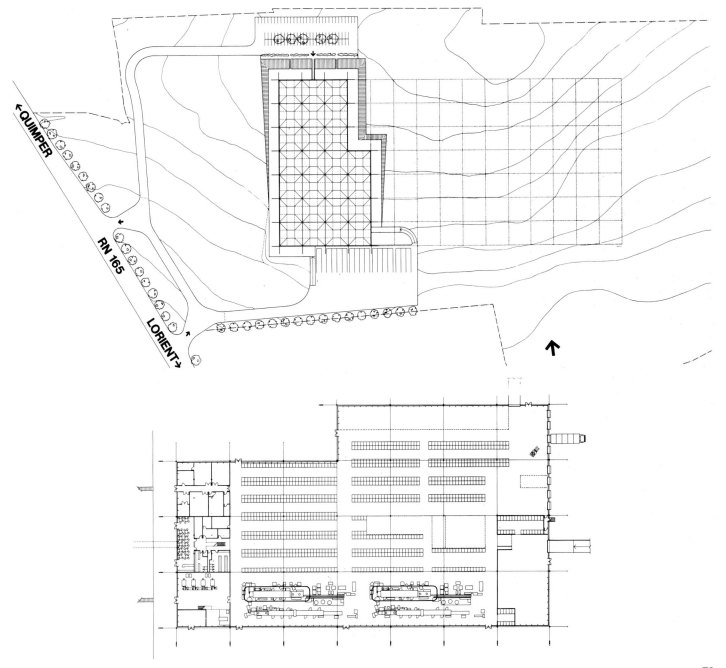

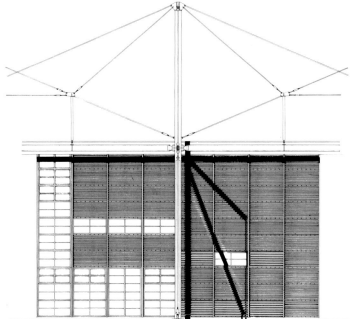

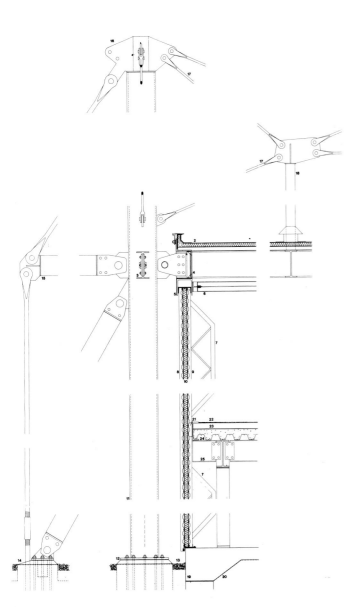

Section detail; pedestrian bridge.

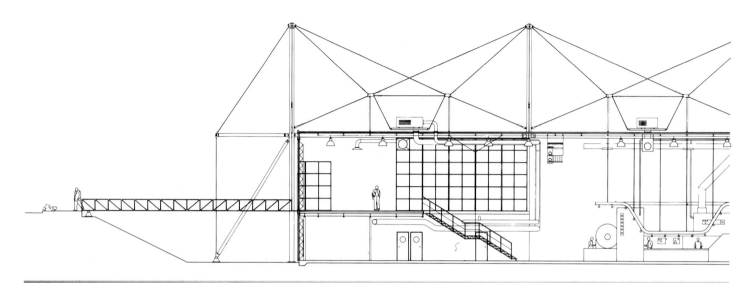

76

Section; exteriors.

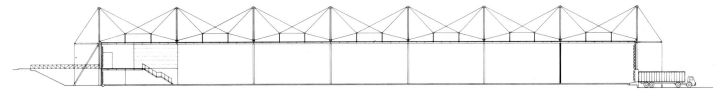

The Inmos factory, more than any of the firm's industrial buildings, renders explicit the relation between form and function. It is an undecorated shed that contains one of the most advanced yet delicate forms of modern industrial production: microchips for the computer industry. Microcomputer technology is the most rapidly developing sector of industry, and accordingly, flexibility of layout and servicing are of paramount importance. As if to prove its innate flexibility, the design of the building remained virtually intact despite a change in location from an inner-city site to its green field location in rural Wales.

The building achieves the required flexibility through simplicity of plan and section. It is an infinitely extendable rectangular box, an inside-out building with servicing and structure on the exterior. Inside, the spaces are column-free and adaptable. The building is divided in half by an internal toplit street that is marked by twin rows of brightly colored blue masts that give the building its distinctive external presence. The street, 7.2 meters wide and 106 meters long, acts as a social collector with reception, meeting areas, and information centers adding a degree of urban vivacity to the building's interior. On one side of the central axis is the production area—a highly controlled environment known as the "clean room"—while the offices, staff, and back-up areas are located in the facing wing.

The clean room—the holiest of holies—is where the manufacturing process of microchip wafers takes place. It requires phenomenally high-quality environmental control. Microchip technology reduces electrical circuits to a microscopic scale so as to speed up the passage of electrical impulses through the complex circuits. Typically, twelve

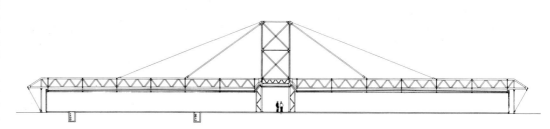

different layers of information are etched onto a quarter-inch tablet of pure silicon. The etching process is carried out to measurements of a thousandth of a millimeter. To achieve such an extreme degree of precision, the industrial process requires an exceptionally clean environment, ten times that of a hospital operating room. Air in the production facility must be absolutely clean to cut down on the failure rate of wafer production— sometimes as high as 90 percent.

The clean room is protected by a double barrier. The outer circulation zone, defined by a spine of lockers, forms a sort of air lock to the inner sanctum, where the most delicate equipment is located and only zero level contamination is tolerated. A service corridor in the outer *cordon sanitaire* gives access to the rear side of the workstations, so that all necessary servicing and maintenance of the equipment can be carried out from outside the clean room.

The two wings are identical in plan except for the omission of a thirteen-by-thirty-six-meter bay in the administrative wing that creates a south-facing courtyard between the restaurant and office areas. (Significantly, one of the courtyards has since been filled in, proving the capacity of the building to adapt to new situations.) On the exterior, the differentiation is accentuated by a marked variation in the cladding system. A continuous wall of pristine opaque panels encloses the inward-looking production areas, while a more random arrangement of opaque and glazed panels reflects the dynamic internal organization of the administrative and general laboratory areas.

Earlier design sketches reveal a less polite, more "gutsy" approach to the services—all intestinal services are fully exposed with a lower-level service trough running beneath the central street—but the completed building encloses the services and air-conditioning pods

within neat silver-gray containers that contrast elegantly to the blue structural framework. As in other Rogers buildings, there is a clear, albeit restrained, color-coding system: primary structure is blue, air intake is yellow, and waste is green.

The structure, which Banham described as "rational and unlikely," echoes the simplicity of its layout. Twin lattice beams spread out like wings from the central spine of H-frame pylons. Diagonal ties support the wings in midspan, at the points of maximum deflection, thereby eliminating the need for intermediate columns which would have had to pierce the clean-room box. The H-frames, composed of steel tubes that support the main service equipment and air-conditioning pods, are the only rigid components in the building. Everything else is pin-jointed. A large proportion of the components was prefabricated off-site, allowing accurate and quick assembly. The building was completed in fourteen months.

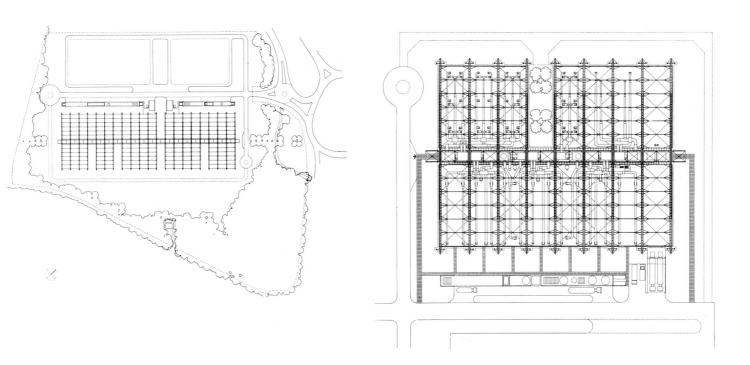

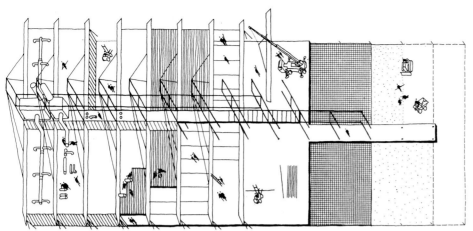

Axonometric showing stages in construction of suspended tension roof; axonometric showing structural system of roof.

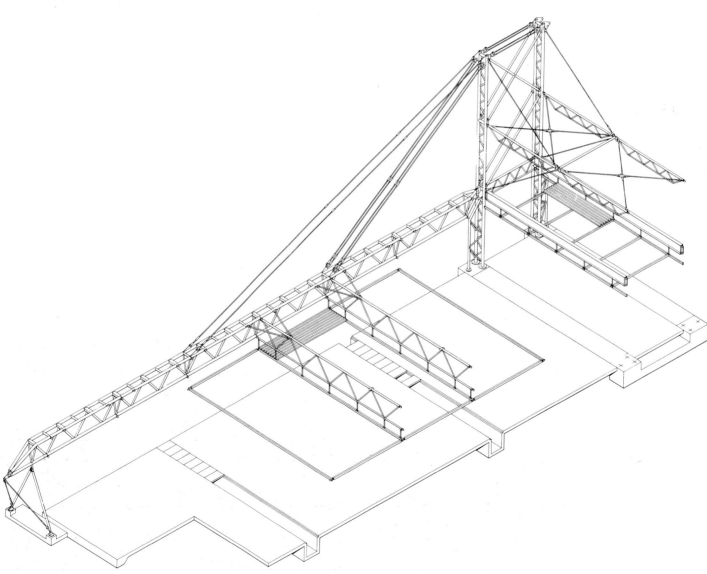

*Detail of elevation showing
structure over internal street;
views.*

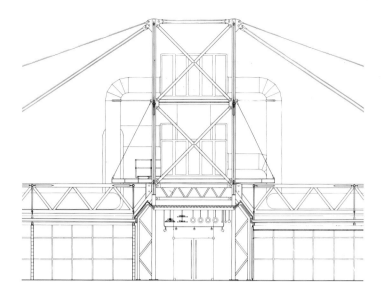

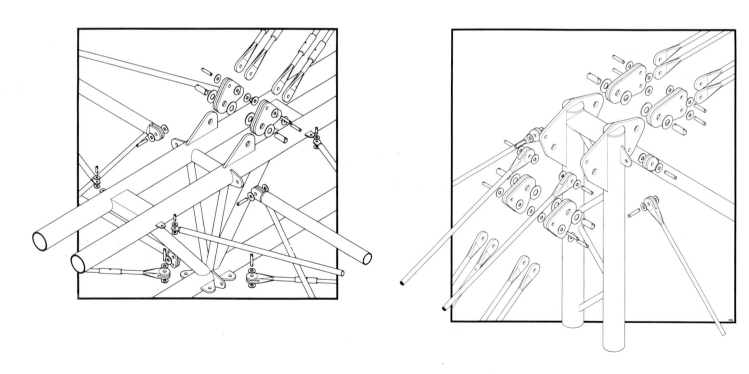

Interiors; section perspective showing servicing.

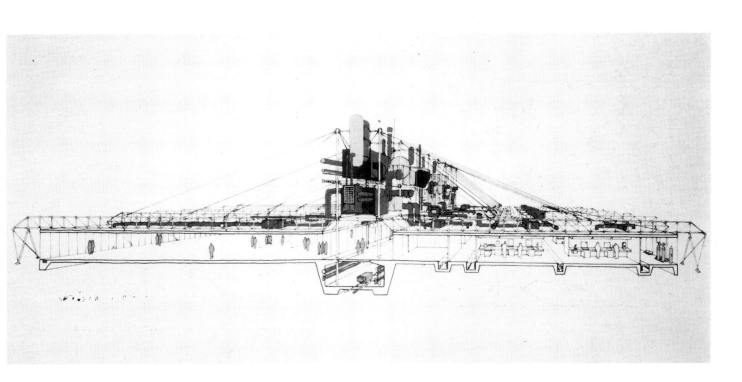

The laboratory and office building for PA Technology, located in the rural setting of an industrial park near Princeton, represents the epitome of Reyner Banham's "well-serviced shed." Built for the same clients who commissioned the Patscentre Research Laboratory in the United Kingdom, this building contains workshop and office spaces that need to adapt in response to a constantly changing research and development program. Accordingly, the building employs a suspended tension structure that allows a virtually column-free interior and carries all its services on the roof. It is a pure "inside-out" building which, says Thomas Hine, "wears its heart on its sleeve—something that makes open heart surgery a lot more convenient" (*Philadelphia Inquirer*, June 12, 1983).

The single-story building is arranged along a central toplit corridor, occupied by common areas and social facilities, with laboratories and offices on either side. The plan of the building is cut back by excising one of the lateral bays to form the main entrance to the building along its short axis, perpendicular to the longitudinal spine. According to Michael Sorkin, the building works via two memorable iconic instruments: "First, the visible, heroicized apparatus of suspension . . . and second, the visible, heroicized apparatus of piped and ducted servicing."

Viewed from afar, the building marks the skyline with its rigorous sequence of sixteen giant red steel A-frames, reminiscent of the all-American "evangelical big top." A yellow structural cradle holds the bulky servicing equipment while large service ducts punctuate the roof at regular intervals. While at Inmos the services are neatly packed into containers, here they are fully exposed. Color coding—silver for air movement, green for water, orange for electrical—creates a more dynamic relationship with the primary structure of the building. The cladding is in translucent Kalwall panels, which make the building glow at night, and a continuous strip of horizontal glazing provides direct contact between the interior and the exterior.

The structure has been pared down to a bare minimum. As the engineer Peter Rice notes, the elements have been designed to enforce "visual" as well as structural stability, ensuring that the innate logic of each component is obvious to the naked eye. Pairs of steel beams spanning twenty-six meters are supported from the A-frame with tie rods pin-jointed with off-the-shelf circular elements—that "wonderful wacky order of giant washers" described by Sorkin. Tie-down columns at the outer ends of the beams act in both tension and suspension. The platforms carrying mechanical equipment are suspended between the A-frames and provide longitudinal bracing.

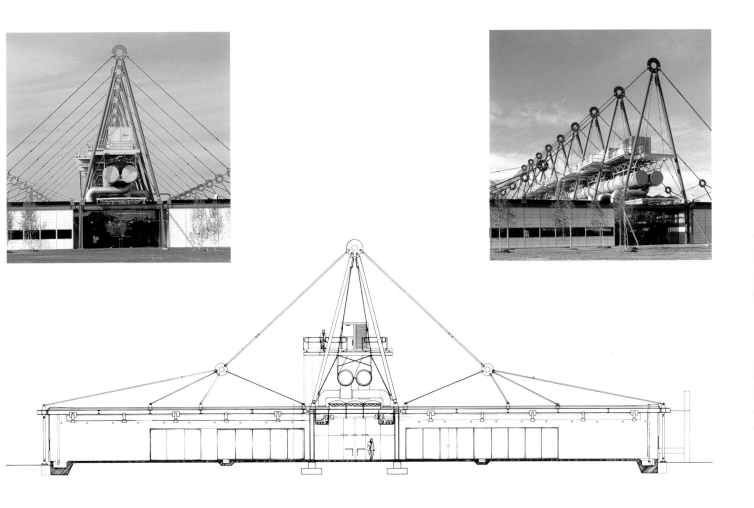

Ground floor plan; view.

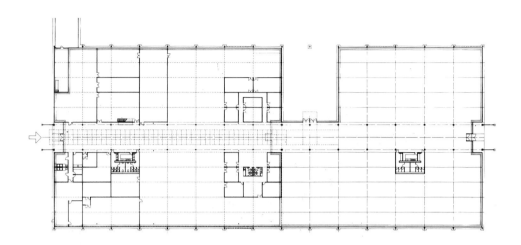

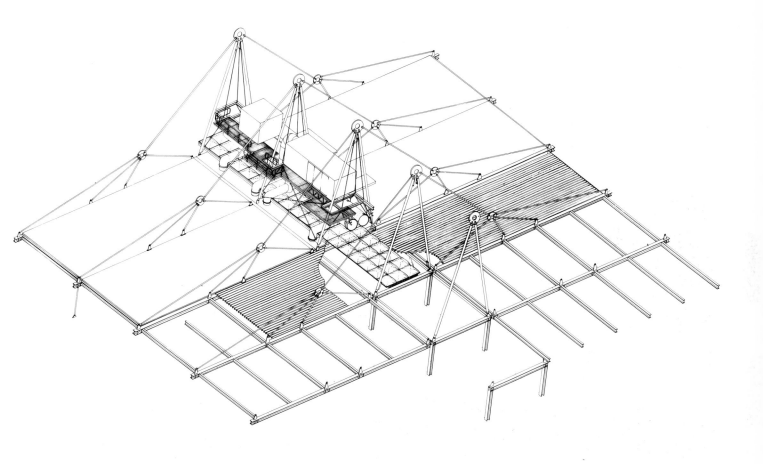

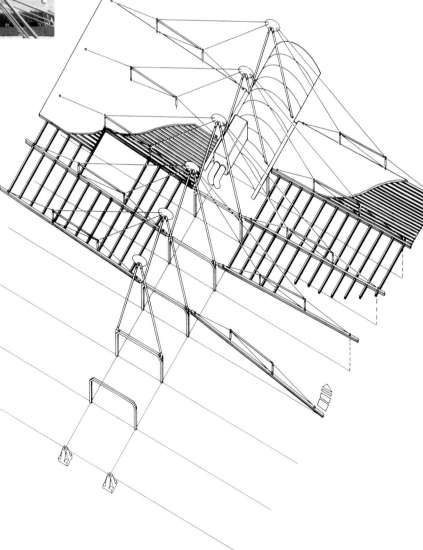

Detail of circular elements; axonometric showing roof elements.

Interiors.

The vaulted car showroom is a modest but important unbuilt project that marks a shift toward greater formal cohesion in the practice's oeuvre. Located near Orly airport outside Paris, the design exploits its structural form to make a strong visual impact on an otherwise indifferent environment adjacent to a highway. The shape itself becomes an advertisement of the building's activities.

The building is essentially a section of a drum, closed at one end and open at the other, that emerges out of the ground. Half the building is fully enclosed and used for the sale of new cars, while the other half acts as a semiprotected shed for auctions of used cars. These seemingly similar activities, which require very distinct environmental conditions and character, are unified under the vast curved roof.

The horizontality of the gentle curve is punctuated by four parallel rows of inclined masts that mark the building's presence and express its structural order. A giant glass wall along the main entrance facade exposes the interior to the outside world, mirrored by a second glazed surface along the central axis that separates the two functional zones. Inclined glazed walls at ground level provide lateral views and daylighting. A mezzanine structure contains offices and support facilities, while parking and service bays are located at basement level.

The curved roof diaphragm is supported by eighteen circular arches spanning one hundred meters at twelve-meter centers, creating a maximum internal height of fifteen meters. Each pair of arches is attached by tie rods to the top and bottom of four intermediate masts which provide stability.

Model; preliminary sketch; section.

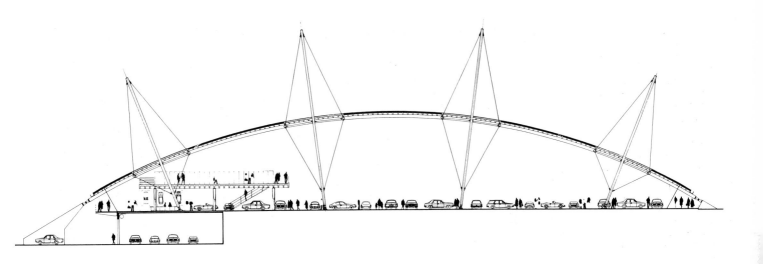

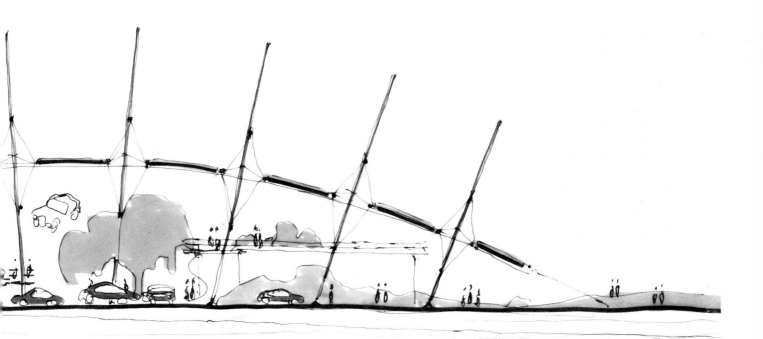

Reyner Banham celebrated the arrival of Rogers' Lloyd's Building as "the new monochromatic and monumental version of High Tech . . . [which] doubtless marks a further stage in the ongoing epic of Late Modernism, the style that was supposed to die" (*Architectural Review*, October 1986, 55). The reason for the falsity of this prematurely reported death was that modernism had been construed as *only* a style, rather than a style supported by a whole complex of attitudes toward design and society. Lloyd's recombines a number of loose threads by rediscovering the important act of "putting buildings together" which, for Banham, was one of the underlying causes of the failure of the modernist project. To his mind, the importance of Lloyd's in the history of modern architecture is that it is "a fairly shocking reminder of the kind of architectural quality that ought to be part of the Modern heritage."

Given its location at the heart of London's most traditional and historic core, Lloyd's, more than any other building in postwar Britain, has confronted the establishment with the potential of contemporary architecture. A radical enclosure for one of the country's most conventional institutions has drawn criticism and praise, yet ten years after its construction, it has become a familiar landmark with its floodlit blue cranes and shining steel surfaces setting a backdrop for St. Paul's Cathedral. "Spurning classicism, or indeed any other compositional control and repose, Richard Rogers Partnership has created a latterday Neo-Gothic edifice—though top-heavy rather than delicately pinnacled" (Peter

Buchanan, *Architectural Review*, October 1986, 41).

Begun in the seventeenth century as a coffeehouse where syndicates of insurance underwriters grouped around tables to exchange business, Lloyd's is now one of the world's great financial institutions, keeping its original basis of operation as an insurance market. Based in the heart of London, Lloyd's has expanded dramatically over the years. The new building by Rogers is in fact the third purpose-designed headquarters in fifty years. One of the main requirements of the brief was that the new building should serve them for at least the next fifty years. To do that, the building had to be able to adapt and its components able to be updated on different time scales. The basic structure was designed to last in excess of fifty years; the air conditioning at best will last twenty years; the communications networks perhaps five. As for the layout of the office floors, they have already been rearranged several times since the building was completed in 1986 as syndicates expand, contract, or amalgamate in response to the fluctuating fortunes of the insurance business.

The Rogers response to the brief was unambiguous: a doughnut plan surrounding a central atrium providing completely unencumbered floor space with all vertical communication, service ducts, and toilet pods pushed outside the main building envelope. Externally there are six independent service satellite towers. Given the complexity of the brief and the intricacy of the site, the design has maintained the clarity and directness of a diagram: a literal interpretation of Louis Kahn's

"served" and "servant" spaces. The placement of all services on the outside of the building, in neatly packed silver boxes above the service towers, is a clear statement of functional and planning logic.

Face-to-face contact between brokers and underwriters is the essence of the insurance industry, even though a large amount of business is conducted through in-

formation technology. The central mechanism of Lloyd's is the Underwriting Room, which occupies the ground floor and the first three galleries around the atrium. In these spaces each syndicate or group of insurance underwriters has its own "market stall" or box. Each syndicate rents a plot in the room and arranges the various components of the box (benches, worktops, video display terminals,

telephones, and so on) to suit its particular requirements. Just like everyday street life, a good "address" and a good location are essential ingredients of good business. Rents are high and, like any marketplace, success depends on the proximity and visibility of the traders.

The Underwriting Room is a densely populated "omniplatz": a fully flexible, highly serviced, open-plan space that occupies the spatial and programmatic heart of the building. Rising the full twelve-story height of the building, the room is a heroic space that creates the same sense of scale-lessness as the open sky. It is the perceptual and physical condenser that gives identity to an otherwise loose organization of competing groups and individuals. From the room you can see everything.

From the boxes and most corners of the building you can see the room. Yet, as Peter Cook notes, "Hardly a whisper of its presence was displayed to the outside world: but from within it is a Super Space . . . An escalator is so designed that it becomes a delightful object, the schoolboy's dreams of yellow Meccano, the visionary's dreams of symbiosis between animal and machine and the urban-

ist's dreams of the vertical street all come together" (*Architectural Review*, October 1986, 49).

Lloyd's rises from six to twelve stories and is surrounded by lower buildings of historical interest, including the nineteenth-century cast-iron Leadenhall Market. Even though the building is effectively concealed, its siting in a dense, neomedieval urban context exaggerates its monumental

93

impact not only in physical but in intellectual terms. It causes the passerby to confront the passing of time. There is no blurring of edges between past and present engendered by so many polite, pastiche designs of the postmodern era. Yet the sense of scale and grain of the architectural details (dimensions, texture, and manufacture of the structure and steel cladding) integrates the building with its incongruous surroundings.

Much of the grain is given by the detailed design of the impeccably finished concrete structure. But the design had originally been conceived by Peter Rice and his team at Ove Arup & Partners as a steel structure to facilitate off-site construction, as well as speed and precision of assembly. Stringent fireproofing requirements suggested a concrete solution, leading to "a steel building made of concrete"; a highly crafted hybrid "at times confusing and unresolved," according to the engineer Tony Hunt. A kit-of-parts system for the formwork was adopted using plastic-faced plywood that gave the extremely high level of finish. The structure is a two-way spanning system with prestressed inverted U-beams transferring the load from floors onto perimeter columns. A separate precast bracket cast into the smooth, round columns resolves the complex connection between beams and columns, giving the concrete a sense of the mechanical expressiveness of steel (reminiscent of the Pompidou gerberettes). A second precast yoke transmits the load from the U-beam to the brackets. The bottom surface of the concrete floor grid is exposed, providing

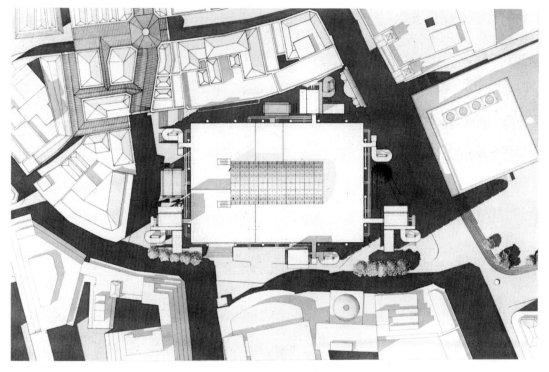

housing for the circular light fittings at ceiling level.

The concrete columns extend the full height of the atrium to the springing of the barrel vault, serving as main supports for the curved steel latticework, with cast-steel four-limbed brackets acting as a point of transition between concrete and steel. All cladding panels, linings, and duct sleeves are in stainless steel. The glazing system is a technical wall that not only keeps out the wind and rain but also acts as an air duct and insulation. The cavity between the double-glazed external skin and the single-glazed lining carries the extract air from the ceiling void down to floor level. This is no sim-

ple curtain wall but a collection of infill components at each level. The translucent glass wall, composed of a grid of small lenslike pimples, creates a continuous wall of light that reveals the lasting influence of Pierre Chareau's Maison de Verre on the key members of the design team.

In hindsight, it is interesting to note that Rogers' submission to the limited design competition won the day by simply setting out a series of strategic options for the client, rather than submitting a highly polished architectural solution. In this sense, Lloyd's is representative of the Rogers approach. It is a statement of strategic simplicity, highly charged with symbolic content.

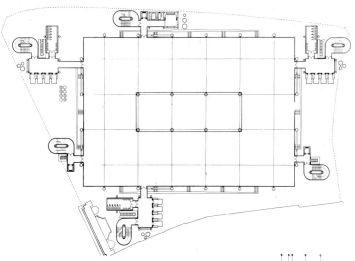

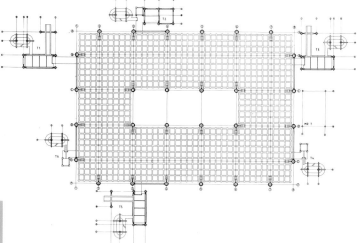

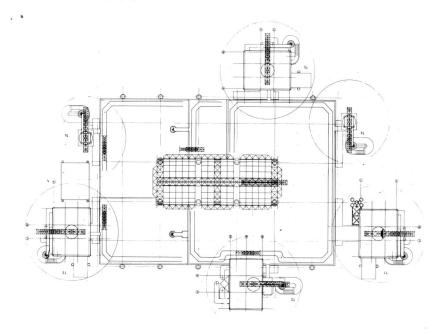

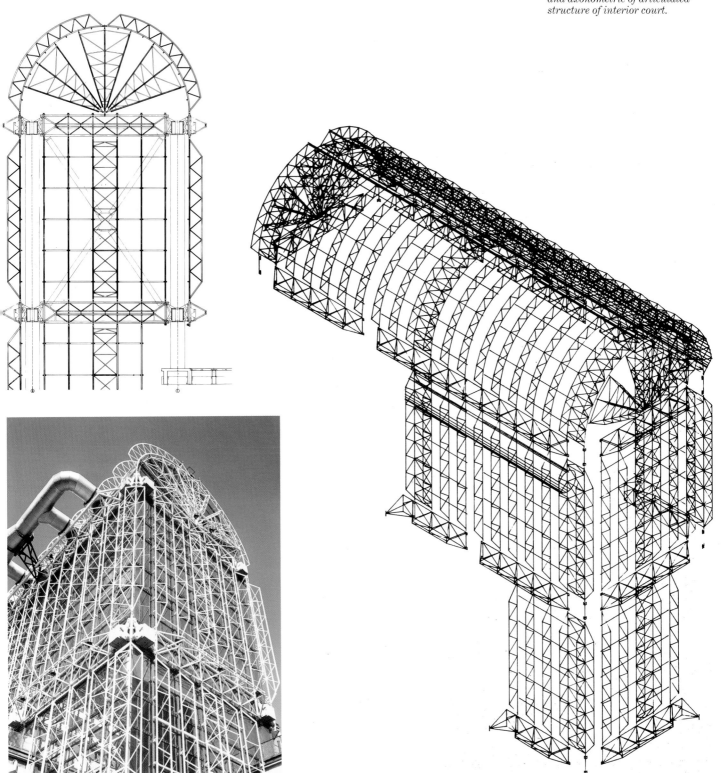

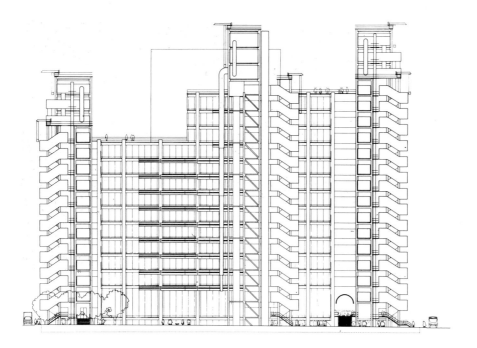

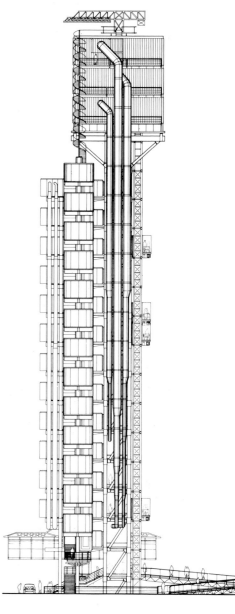

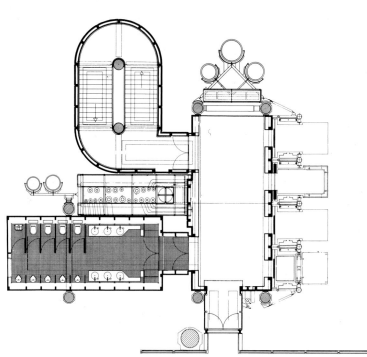

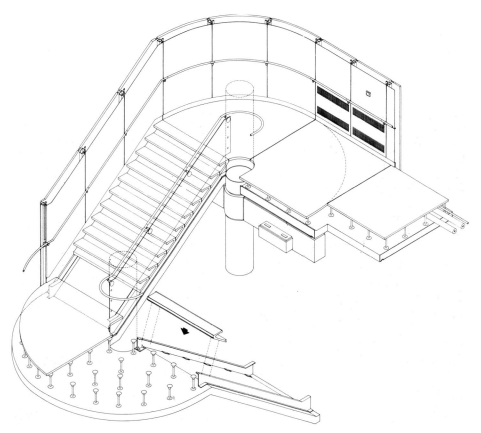

Interior court; sections.

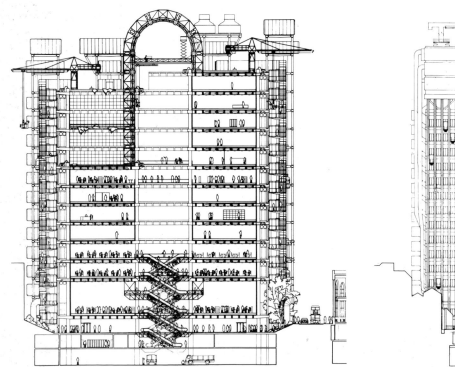

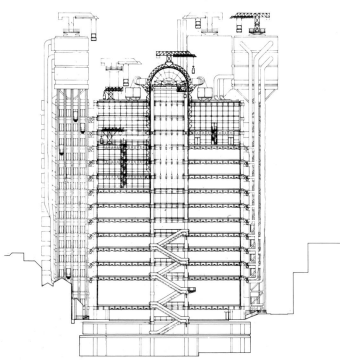

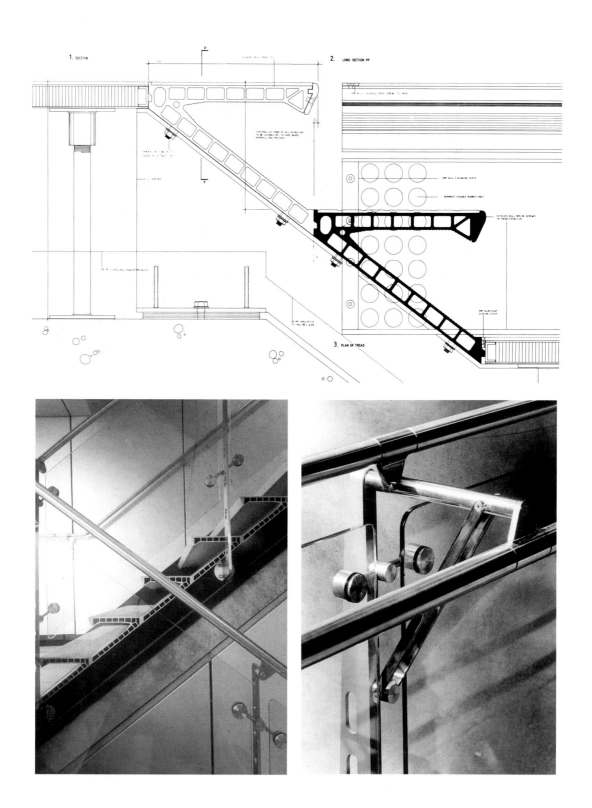

Construction detail; stair details.

View and elevation of outside elevators.

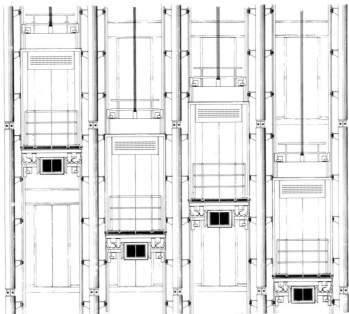

*Details showing lighting and
servicing solutions; interiors;
axonometric showing ground floor.*

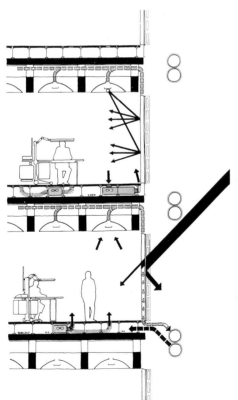

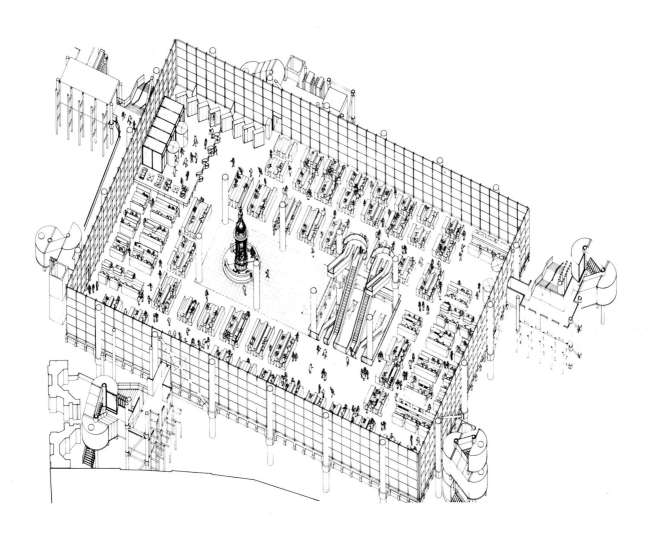

Central to Rogers' design approach is the belief in the integration of old and new. The vibrancy and liveliness of the inner city has, throughout history, depended on the balanced juxtaposition of the modern and the traditional. (Piazza della Signoria in Florence and the Place Beaubourg in Paris are good examples.) Similarly, old buildings can be given new leases on life through sensitive refurbishment and adaptation. This is the case of the late-nineteenth-century Billingsgate, a landmark brick building facing the Thames River in London which by the early 1980s had become redundant as a wholesale fish market.

The conversion from a fish market to a dealing facility for a major financial institution effectively saved the building from demolition. The brick-and-stone exterior with a ground-level arcade has been restored to its former glory, providing the client with the necessary institutional gravitas. The interior has been transformed into a highly serviced envelope that can accommodate the most advanced forms of telecommunications and equipment, including over one thousand computer screens and miles of cabling. The need to integrate the building services within the structure was therefore a major design concern. All services have been concealed in a fifty-centimeter-deep raised floor which rests on new concrete slab, while freestanding, compact air-conditioning units—dubbed the "Braun shavers"—are set against the lateral walls of the main hall.

The basement vaults (formerly the ice stores) and upper-level Haddock Gallery (for smoked fish) with its distinctive,

translucent curved timber roof have been transformed into fully serviced spaces that retain their original character. A new mezzanine gallery, running the full width of the building, is suspended from above with white-painted steel hangers, adding circulation and office space at the heart of the building. The new floors are supported by columns that stand against, but do not touch, the existing wall. At Billingsgate, there is no confusion as to what is old and what is new. The old has been faithfully restored. The new is uncompromisingly new.

The design seeks to maintain the original ethos of the toplit market hall by maximizing the penetration of natural light from the roof and the side walls. A screen of frameless glass—2.5 centimeters thick—is set behind the external arcade, giving the classical building unexpected transparency from the street yet acting as a highly effective buffer from traffic noise. The original lantern roof has been sealed with prismatic glass that reduces glare and solar gain, yet allows sufficient indirect natural light within the spacious working environment.

Building before and after conversion.

*Plans of ground floor and lower
level; interiors.*

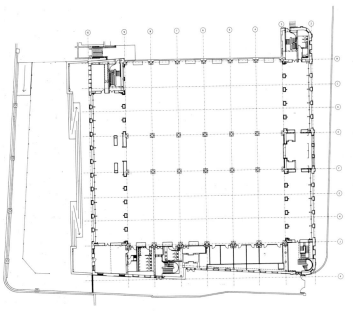

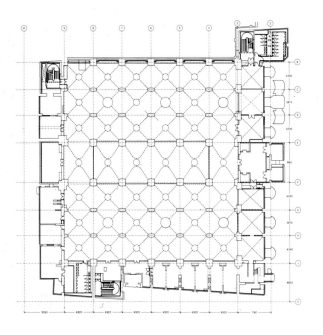

Interior; section; lower-level vaults.

Detail and view of suspended mezzanine gallery.

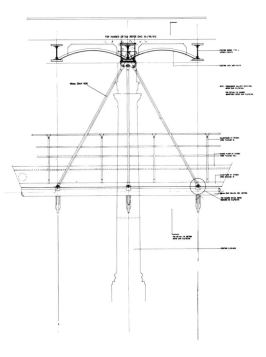

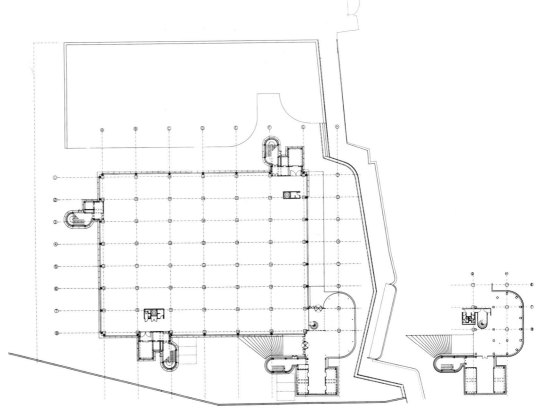

The Reuters Data Centre, located in the industrial hinterland of London's Docklands, is a container of sophisticated computer equipment, "a celebration," as one commentator put it, "of British telecommunications technology as Salisbury Cathedral was of British construction ingenuity and daring in the 13th century" (*Independent*, December 30, 1989). Despite the highly refined quality of its finishes and detailing, the building is an appropriately muscular response to its fragmented and exposed surroundings along the Thames River.

The design extends the Lloyd's model of "served" and "servant" spaces to its natural limit, and it is planned with considerable economy and restraint. All vertical circulation is placed on the perimeter—in four staircase and elevator towers—leaving a clear floor plate that can be adapted to different uses. The cladding system has been designed to accommodate a range of fully insulated solid or glazed panels that can be easily interchanged to suit changing functions of the building. The structural grid is extended at roof level, creating a steel cage that visually defines the services and telecommunications equipment, including an array of satellite antennae.

The building exterior, minimally articulated to reflect the variation in internal functions, forms a subtle, almost classical arrangement of the facade with a base, middle, and top. The lowest floors, containing mechanical equipment, are concealed behind giant aluminum louvers. The intermediate floors, with their stacks of humming data-storage computers, are clad in dark gray panels. The upper floors, which contain offices, are fully glazed. The volume of the building, with its dark aluminum skin, acts as a visual counterpoint to the shimmering vertical towers, which reflect the changing patterns of light along the Thames River. The design of the facade reveals the fine grain of the building, with shadows cast by the horizontal stiffening webs across the vertical glazed surfaces.

The entrance is ingeniously placed between the main vertical circulation tower and the body of the building, creating a strong visual axis with the Thames River.

Transparent glass-and-steel flying balconies, which connect the elevators to the offices and computer areas, allow staff to enjoy views, while also providing visual relief and emphasizing the patterns of horizontal movement within the building. A freestanding pavilion with a curved glass prow and metal brise-soleil, containing a health club and staff restaurant, extends the architectural vocabulary of the main building in a language reminiscent of one of the few modernist masterpieces in Britain, Erich Mendelsohn's De la Warr Pavilion.

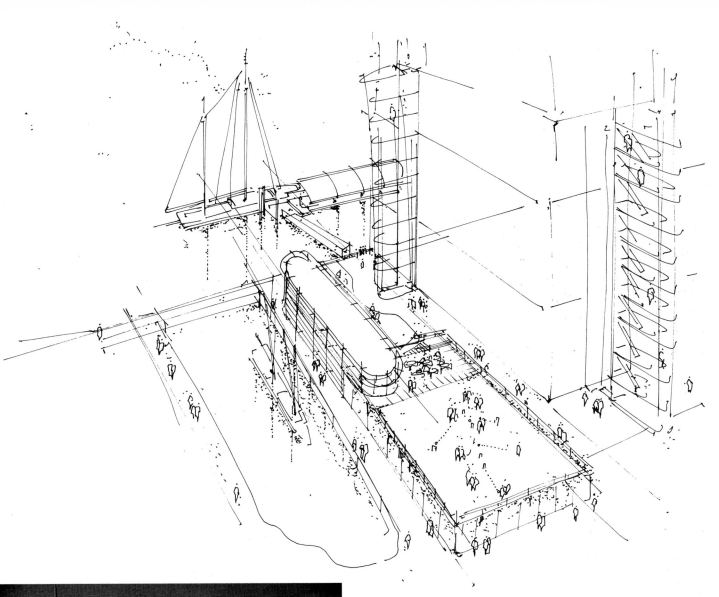

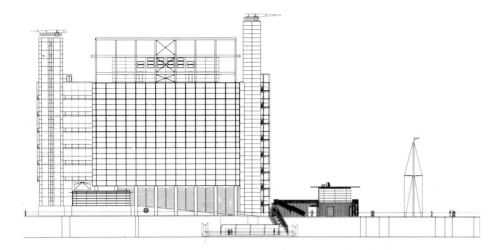

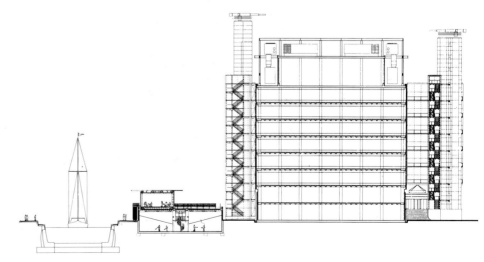

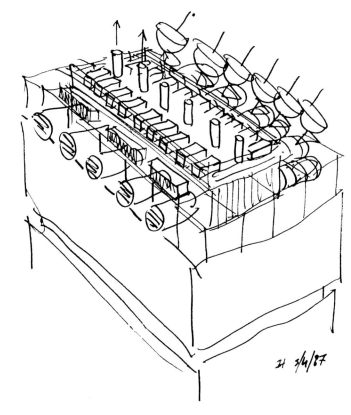

View from below; preliminary sketch; detail of restaurant brise-soleil.

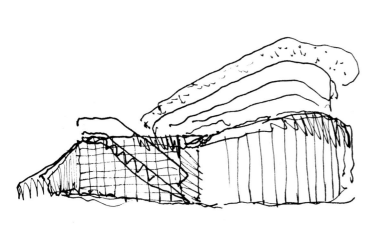

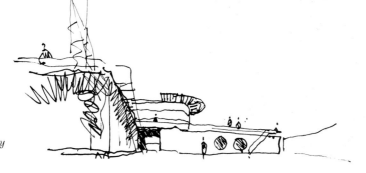

Views of service tower; preliminary sketch of roof structure.

Office and Residential Buildings for Daimler Benz, Berlin, 1993–98

Working within Renzo Piano's urban framework for the Daimler Benz site (a subsection of the Potsdamerplatz master plan), the Rogers practice has designed a series of mixed-use buildings along Linkstrasse that respond to the given urban constraints (eaves level of 27 to 29 meters and footprint of 54.9 by 52.6 meters).

The office buildings make a pioneering contribution to the design of energy-conscious working environments. The eight-story buildings (with retail at ground, first, and basement levels) are organized around a full-height inner courtyard that opens toward Linkstrasse, creating a generous entry sequence and introducing

daylight into the offices. The atrium plays a key role in the energy strategy of the building, drawing out stale air. A strongly articulated roof defines the horizontal cornice level while a funnel-shaped window exposes the atrium to the street, bringing additional daylight to the offices. The buildings are designed to provide 100 percent natural ventilation, with transparent glass insulated cladding on all sides providing views and good daylighting within.

Model; facade drawing; perspective.

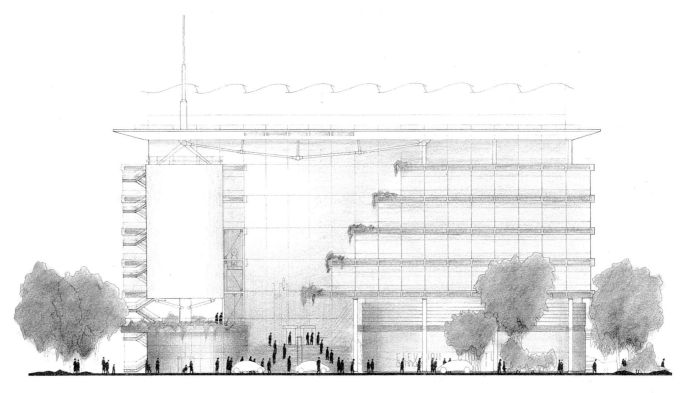

Model in context; typical plan.

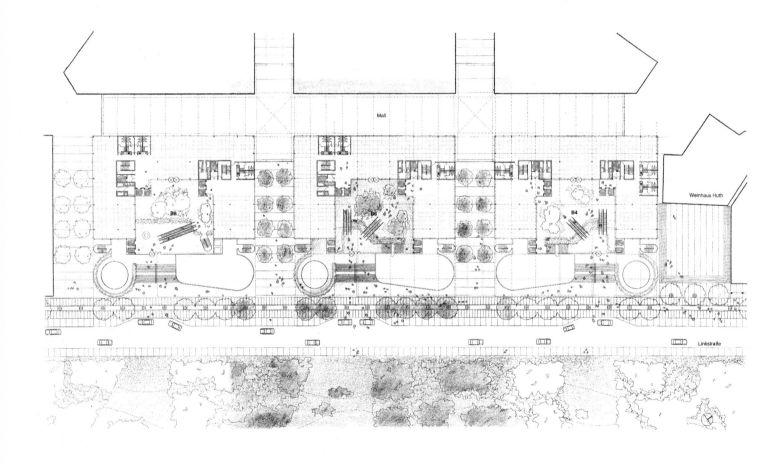

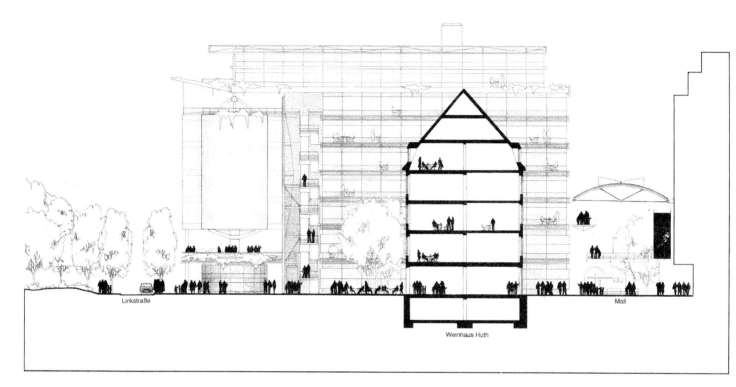

Linkstraße

Weinhaus Huth

Mall

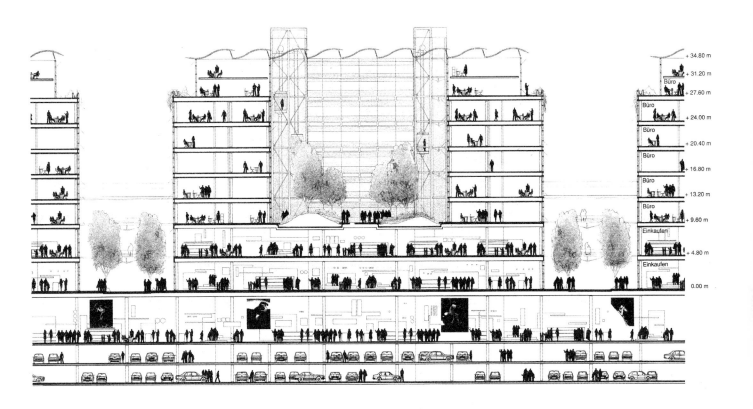

+ 34.80 m

+ 31.20 m

Büro

+ 27.60 m

Büro   + 24.00 m

Büro   + 20.40 m

Büro   + 16.80 m

Büro   + 13.20 m

Büro   + 9.60 m

Einkaufen   + 4.80 m

Einkaufen   0.00 m

views

The office headquarters and studio complex for Britain's independent television company, Channel 4, is in the very heart of London, within sight of the Houses of Parliament and Westminster Abbey. In tectonic and aesthetic terms, the competition-winning design is a direct descendant of Lloyd's, but its response to the site reflects the formal urban concerns exemplified by the Potsdamerplatz master plan for Berlin and the Law Courts in Bordeaux.

The building is a set piece of urban theater within a tight inner-city site. Two linear office blocks define the edges of the site, embracing a soft, landscaped garden that acts as a visual focus to the building, providing much-needed public open space to this congested part of the city. Two residential structures, designed by other architects, complete the geometry of the mixed-use urban block.

The main entrance to the building is placed on a diagonal, creating an organic knuckle between two orthogonal limbs. A glass-and-steel canopy over a lightweight bridge, supported by steel cables from red cranelike supports, penetrates the inclined glass atrium. From the bridge, the drama of the building unfolds. One can see straight through the lobby to the garden or look down

through a glazed umbilicus into the bowels of the building. To celebrate the public nature of the building, the entrance is flanked by a tall vertical shaft animated by glazed elevators that expose the life of the building to the outside world. Horizontal movement similarly occurs near the external face of the building (between the offices and the sloping canopy) and on linking glass-and-steel bridges, thus adding to the liveliness of the facade when viewed from the street.

The curved linking element on the courtyard elevation contains executive offices with a generous south-facing terrace at the upper level. At the entrance level, the double-height curved staff restaurant area, which acts as the main public focus of the building, extends to an outdoor seating area overlooking the garden. The linear blocks, clad in horizontal bands of glass-and-steel integrated panels, contain conventional office spaces, while a television studio and viewing theater are at basement level. The vertical shaft is topped by a telecommunications mast, steel flues, and a technical plant (neatly wrapped in steel boxes) while all main structural elements are painted the same dark red as San Francisco's Golden Gate Bridge.

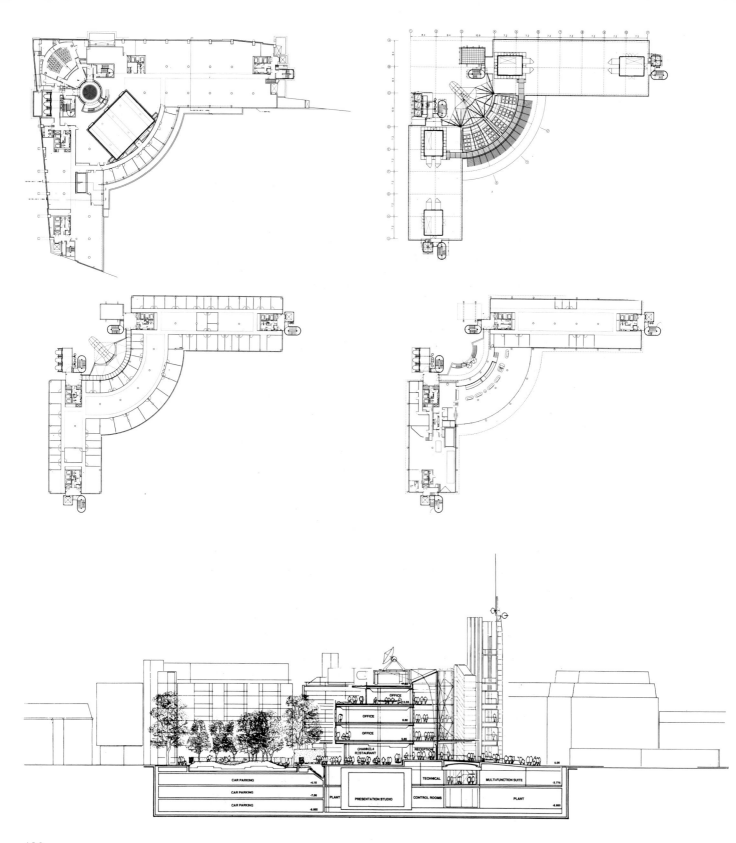

Plans; section; model.

Entry facade at night.

*Curved garden facade; elevation
showing windows.*

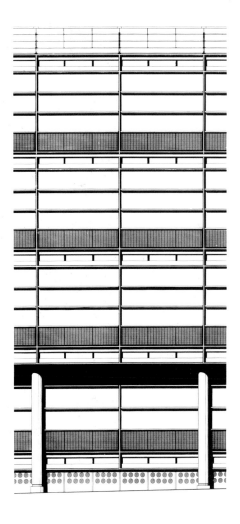

*Entry facade; axonometric showing
linking element; central light well.*

The triangular, freestanding site occupies a prominent position in central Berlin on axis with major urban routes and adjacent to a public park. The ground level is conceived as a public plane that establishes continuity with the surroundings, encouraging through movement of pedestrians from all directions. A two-level, part-open, sunken passageway extends the building's public zone underneath the main road, creating a direct route to the park, which is animated by shops and commercial activities. The building is arranged symmetrically around its short north-south axis, with two narrow lateral bays and a wide central bay defined by two vertical circulation towers. Horizontally, the building is divided into an upper and lower section by a double-height setback forming an indented cornice at ninth-floor level. The upper and lower sections are further differentiated by a variation in the grain and scale of the glazed cladding panels, while a double-height colonnade at ground level underlines the classical tripartite arrangement of the facade with a base, middle, and top.

A glazed atrium rises the full height of the central lower section of the building, forming a giant entrance porch with a cantilevered glass-and-cable canopy that marks its presence and frames views across the park. Hotel and shopping areas are arranged around the atrium, while naturally daylit offices can be accommodated at all levels of the building. The main circulation and service elements are clustered around the twin exposed steel truss masts. A cantilevered high-level viewing platform at the top of the taller

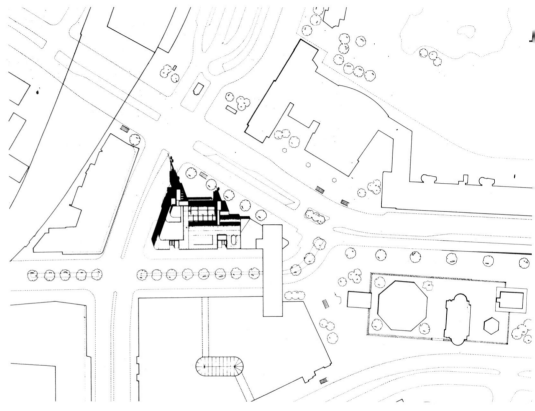

mast emphasizes the distinctive razor-sharp edge that marks the building's presence in the urban landscape.

With the clear enjoyment of the formal interplay of expressed vertical elements and highly articulated glazed facades, the Zoofenster office building in Berlin synthesizes the recent strand in Rogers' oeuvre that finds inspiration in Soviet constructivism and Mendelsohn's expressionism.

Model; preliminary sketch; elevation and sections.

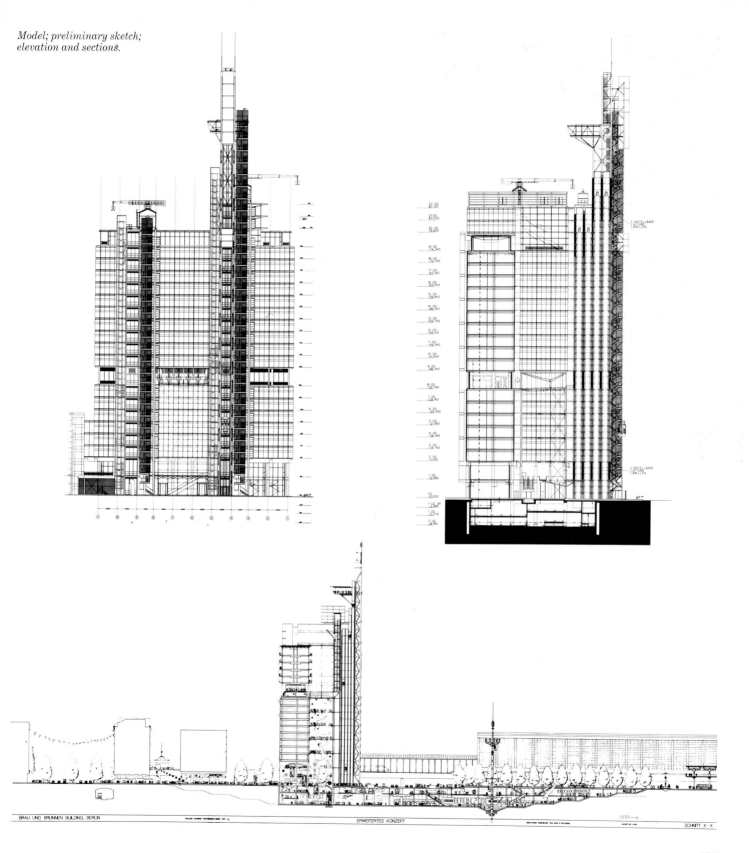

BRAU UND BRUNNEN BUILDING, BERLIN

ERWEITERTES KONZEPT

SCHNITT X - X

135

Model; elevation of service tower.

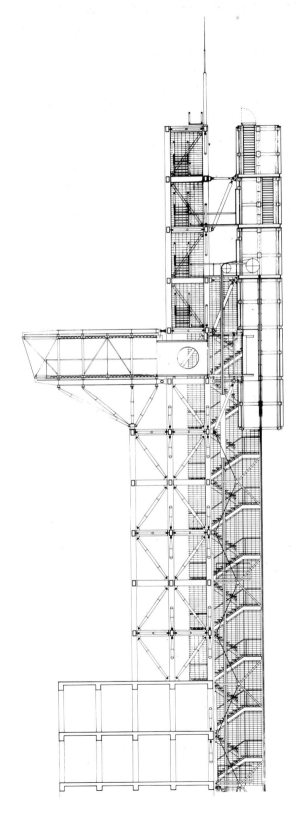

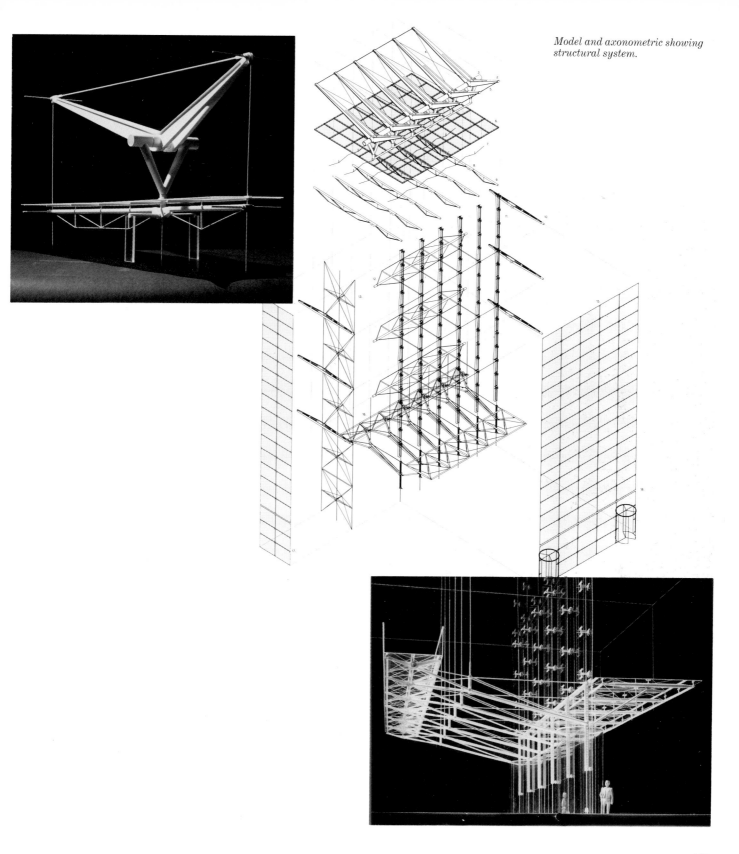

137

Inland Revenue Headquarters, Nottingham, United Kingdom, Competition, 1991

Site plan; model; perspectives and plan showing integration of surrounding environment.

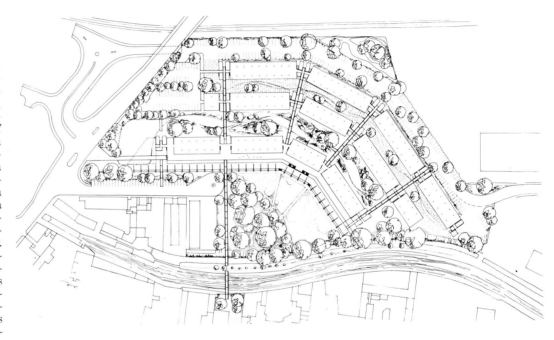

Rogers' competition entry for the headquarters of a national bureaucracy fully exploits the architectural potential of passive environmental control. In many ways it is the practice's most coherent synthesis to date of environmental, urban, and architectural concerns. Located in the northern British city of Nottingham, the site is defined by a steep ravine dominated by Nottingham Castle to the north and a noisy main road to the south. Gently curving parallel blocks form a "cupped hand" that embraces a new park and the canal, emphasizing views of the castle and screening noise from the road and railway. The external envelope, with its sinuous curved roof, effortlessly follows the topographical boundaries of the site, recognizing the importance of views from above. The profile of the glazed roof-facade plays an active role in generating the natural air flows that determine the environmental logic of the building.

The building complex, which contains offices with recreational, conference, and social facilities, is conceived as an urban network of streets and public spaces that are fully integrated with the natural landscape. The southernmost building is composed of two linear office blocks united by an internal glazed atrium that forms a central spine, reminiscent in its spatial character and geometry of the earlier Coin Street project in London. A lower "social block" contains the main public facilities overlooking the park with glazed bridges linking back to the main office areas. A hierarchy of spaces is established from the atrium gardens to the landscaped zone between the parallel rows of buildings through to the semipublic gardens.

The building form and the stack effect of the atrium encourage natural ventilation, while orientation maximizes the potential for low-energy solutions to control solar gain and heat loss. With its patchwork of solid, translucent, and clear elements, the roof-facade is designed as a fully responsive skin that adapts to changing orientation and conditions of exposure. The floor plates are set back from the external skin to create a naturally ventilated perimeter zone that obviates the need for air conditioning. Water plays an important role as a landscaping feature but also contributes to the passive cooling and humidification within the main atrium space. As a result of these innovative passive environmental controls, the building would require relatively low levels of energy, reducing demand by nearly 30 percent compared to a typical office building.

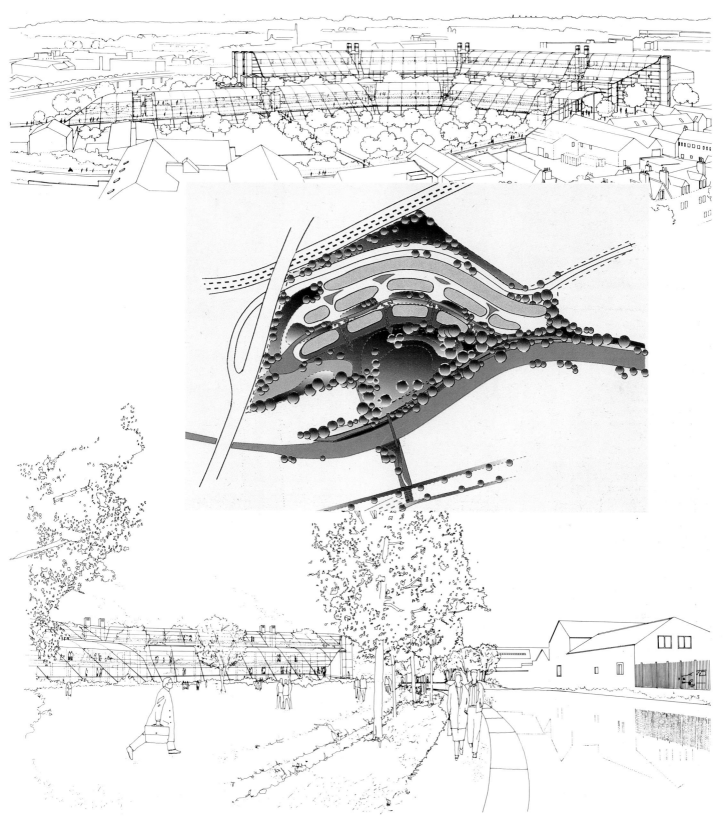

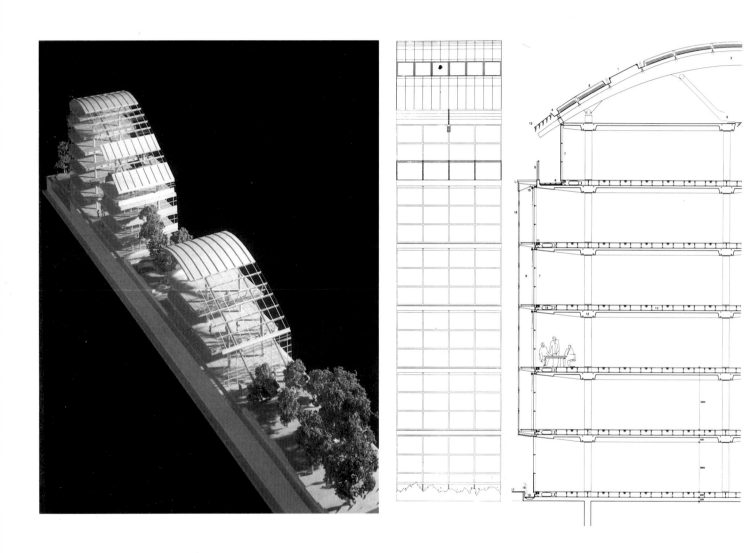

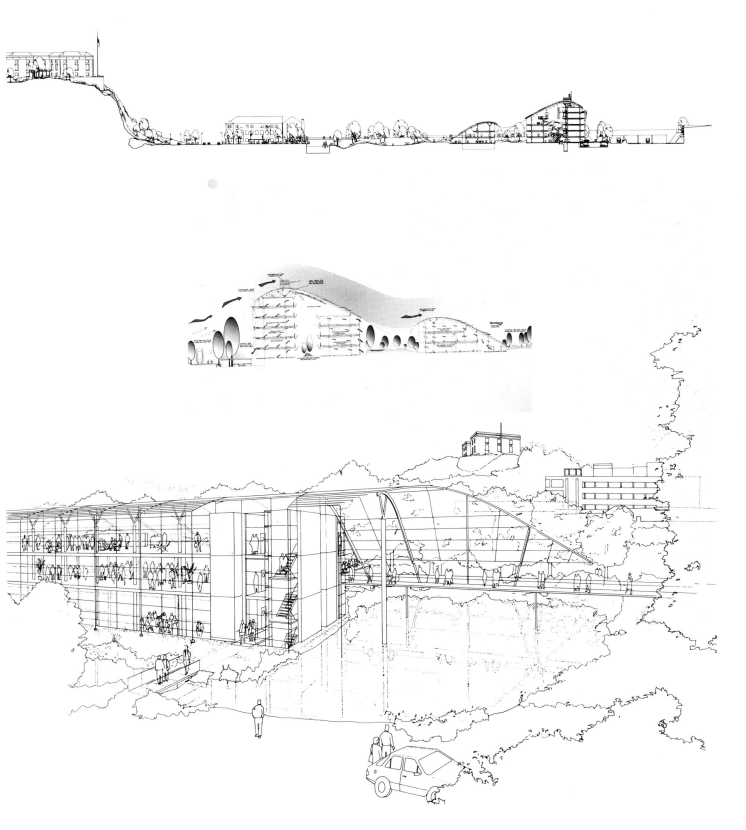

141

Designed as the headquarters for a major Japanese bank in the City of London, the leading financial center in Europe, the building is designed to reconcile a number of apparent opposites: east versus west, public versus private, old versus new, modern versus postmodern, and so on. The site is a complex synthesis of the history of planning in London. To the south lie the remains of ancient Roman London and the dense medieval street pattern centered on Christopher Wren's St. Alban tower. The area to the north was devastated by bombs during World War II. In the 1960s a six-lane urban highway (London Wall), lined by the notorious concrete tower slabs of the Barbican, was built on the immediate fringes of the site. And finally, in the 1980s, a highly decorated office tower designed by Terry Farrell was built over London Wall.

The Rogers scheme reinterprets these dissonant urban conditions by placing the new building at a diagonal to the surrounding streets. The triangular plan is softened by a generous curve between Wood Lane and London Wall. A diagonal pedestrian route traverses the entire building, turning an intrinsically private brokerage house into a public galleria that contributes to the life of the city. The glazed axis focuses on Wren's St. Alban tower and gives new meaning to this isolated historic monument.

The building is designed with a steep stepped section that rises from six stories (relating in scale to the smaller buildings to the south) to thirteen stories as it reaches London Wall and its neighboring office towers. As one moves across the building, the

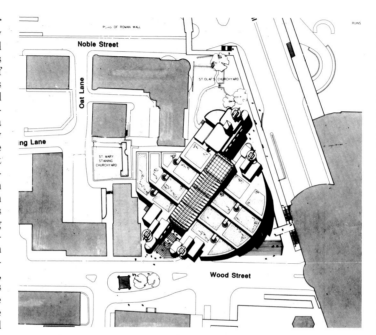

glazed roof rises dramatically above the galleria, which is further animated by exposed elevators placed at both ends of the public space. The setbacks allow south-facing terraces on the upper floors on either side of the glazed galleria roof, while a colonnade mediates the changes in level in the lower parts of the building. The internal offices benefit from natural daylight from all aspects, including views and light from the internal atrium.

In planning terms, the design is an evolution of Lloyd's with vertical circulation placed outside the main volume of the building. Nonetheless, the different elements are integrated by the sweeping curve of the building that gives a clear urban definition to the site and introduces a sense of order to a highly confused architectural setting.

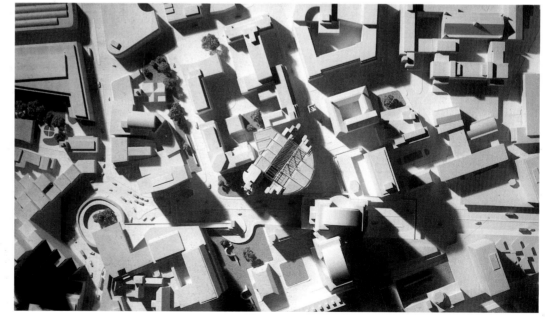

*Typical plan in the principal
volume; model.*

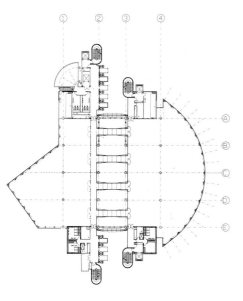

Renderings of entrance with
canopy; model; sections.

Kabuki-cho Tower, Tokyo, 1987–93

One of a series of projects for commercial buildings in Japan (with the Tomigaya and Iikura schemes), the Kabuki-cho Tower was designed at the height of the economic boom, when land values in central Tokyo outstripped the cost and value of buildings. The lack of aesthetic controls and stringent anti-earthquake regulations further compounded a fairly unorthodox context. Only an experimental, constructional architecture could turn these constraints into an architectural opportunity.

The mass of the building is located toward the rear of the site, a tall tower stepping back as it rises to its ten-story height to avoid casting shadows onto the street. A cantilevered metal balcony at the fifth-floor level marks the change in pace between the four-story inclined glazed atrium and the upper four levels, which define the vertical plane of the building. A glazed roof over the basement restaurant brings daylight deep into the building, capturing commodities rare in central Tokyo: space and light. At night the glazed atrium glows, projecting light through the green glass curtain walls.

The concrete-covered steel frame is clad in glass, suspended by a filigree of steel components that supports a sophisticated sun blind mechanism, one of the more advanced environmental features of the building. The neutrality of the structure is contrasted to the vivid orange of the metal cladding of the lift tower and the glazing which is shaded by brightly colored stretched fabric blinds.

146

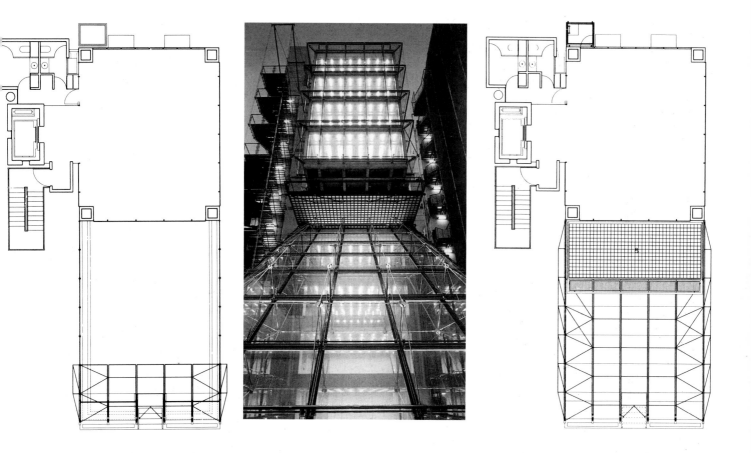

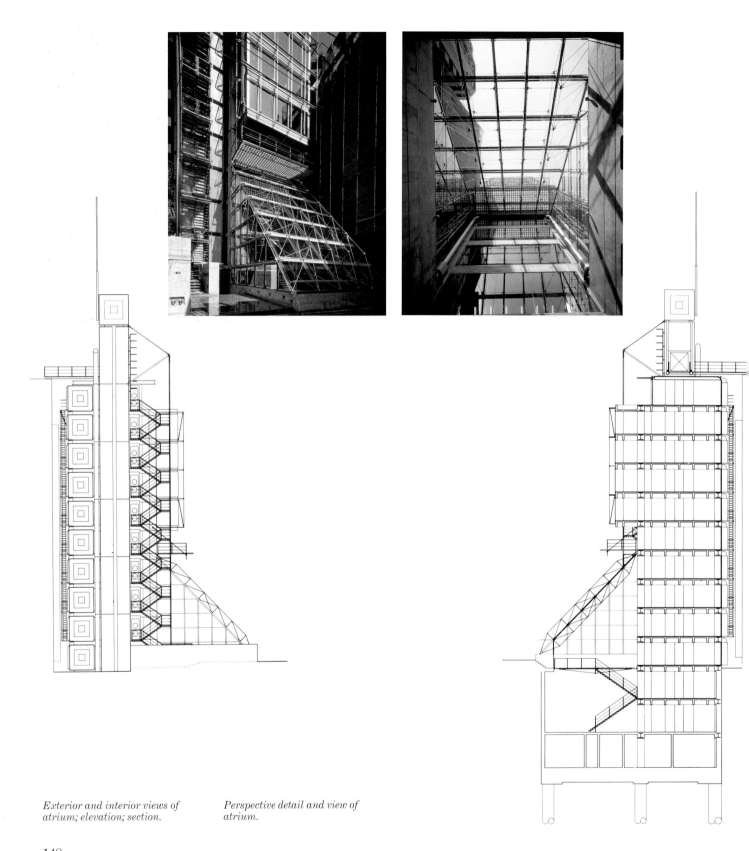

Exterior and interior views of atrium; elevation; section.

Perspective detail and view of atrium.

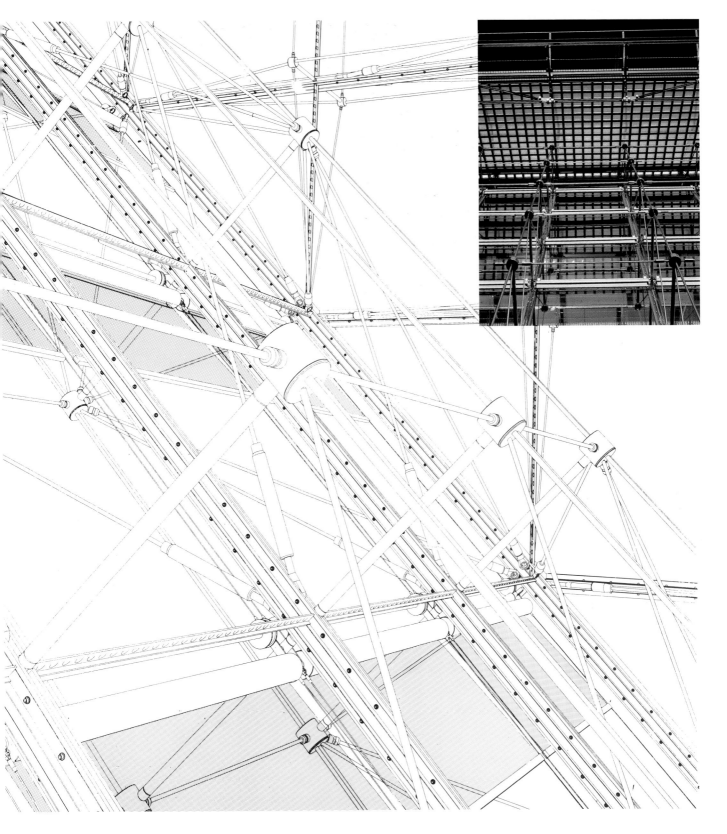

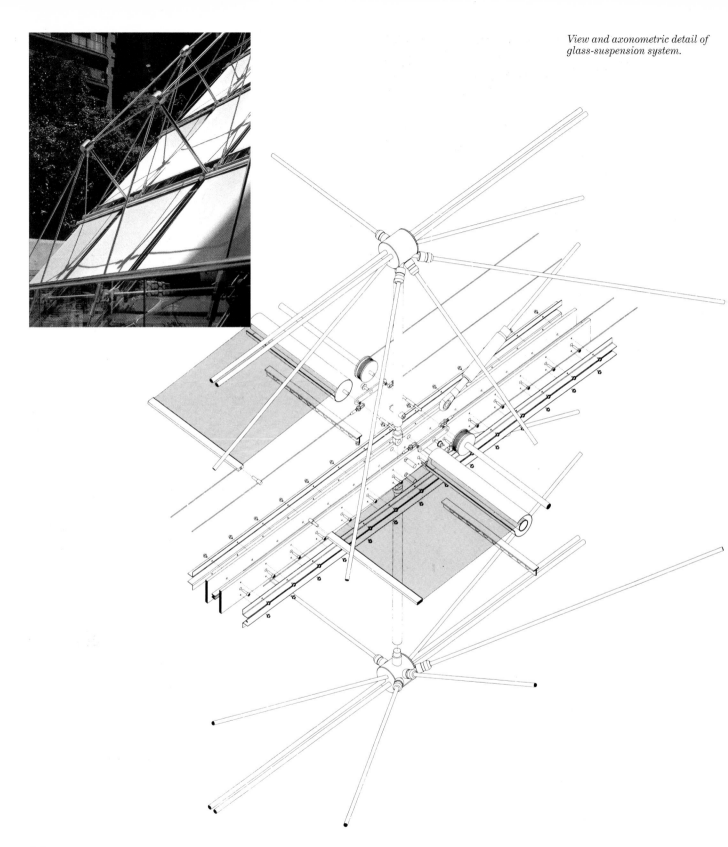

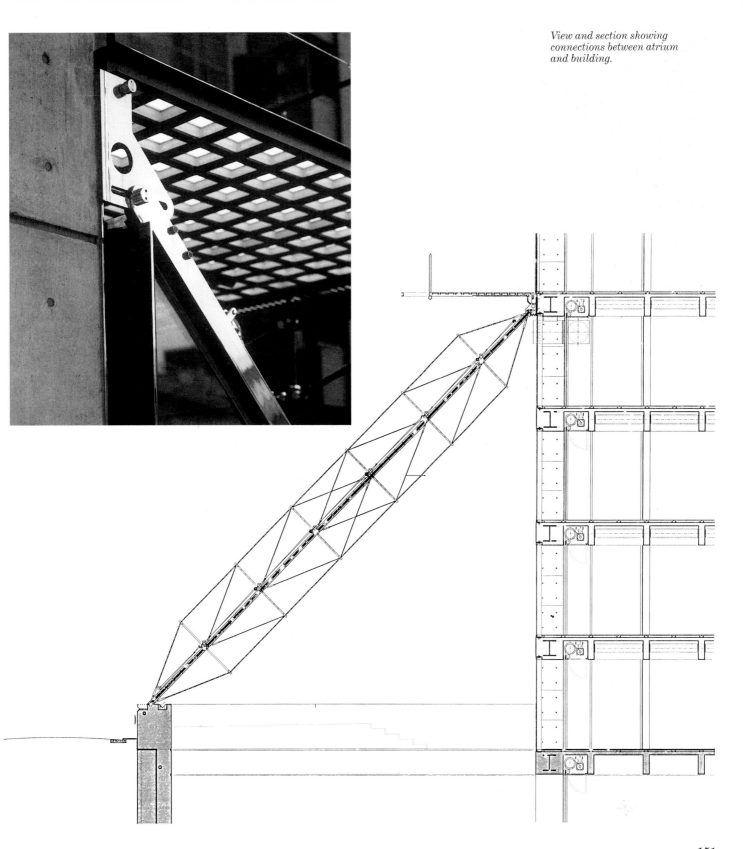

*View and section showing
connections between atrium
and building.*

The original design for the Tomigaya Exhibition Space (Tomigaya I) is a sophisticated response to the constraints and permitted density of the site. Placed in an awkward triangular corner site, at the meeting point of two major roads in central Tokyo, the building maximizes its visibility with an all-glass enclosure that becomes a showcase for people and objects. The building contains only three permissible fixed office floors, while adjustable mezzanines provide extra office space or flexible exhibition space. Inclined vertical steel trusses double up as a crane structure, a giant Meccano set that lifts large objects into a mega-showroom at the heart of the city.

Following a reassessment of the demand for this type of building, the clients requested a redesign. The practice used the opportunity to develop Tomigaya as a low-energy building prototype, a three-dimensional manifesto of the firm's environmental beliefs. The basic premise is that the external climate is continually changing, hour by hour, day by day, season by season. Yet most buildings are insensitive to these changes. They remain static and dumb rather than interacting dynamically with the environment to exploit free energy and create comfortable living and working spaces.

The new building, known as Tomigaya Turbine Tower, is designed as a total energy system where every aspect is fine-tuned to achieve low running costs and to reduce services plant and equipment to a minimum (thereby reducing loads on the structure and increasing the amount of usable space for the client). The facades are designed to change like a chameleon to provide the appropriate environment within. The northern facade is a composite of clear and diffused glass and opaque panels that provide insulation and daylighting as well as external views. The heavy concrete structure is fully exposed, acting as a thermal mass that absorbs heat gain and moderates the building's internal environment. Water is placed at the basement levels to provide natural cooling during peak summer months and warming of cool air during the winter. The transparent south-facing elevation is designed to shade high-angle sun, which is reflected to provide useful lighting inside the building.

The distinctive building form (with a lozenge-shaped main volume and a freestanding vertical tower) is explicitly designed to maximize the potential of wind power as a source of the energy. The curved facade accelerates the speed of wind between the main volume and its vertical core, driving a turbine that generates electricity. The energy is used by the building, and any excess energy is stored or supplied into the main grid. Wind tunnel tests suggest that on an average day 130 kilowatts per hour could be generated by the building's innovative energy-generating system. The vertical tower element works as a chimney under the action of the sun and wind, extracting stale warm air from the building.

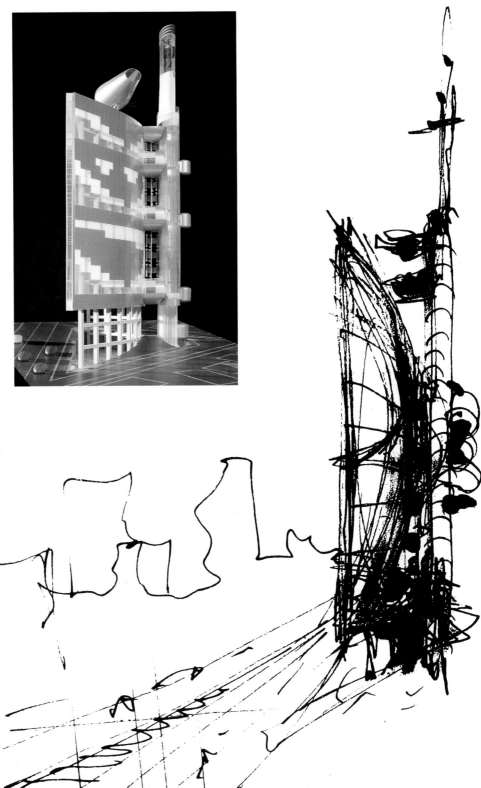

Principal elevation; model;
preliminary sketch.

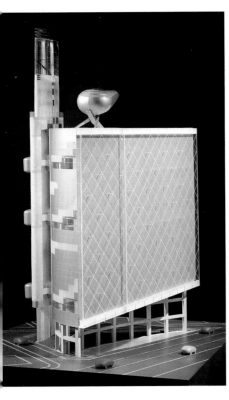

Analyses of air flow; Meccano model.

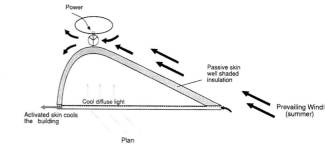

Power

Passive skin well shaded insulation

Prevailing Wind (summer)

Cool diffuse light

Activated skin cools the building

Plan

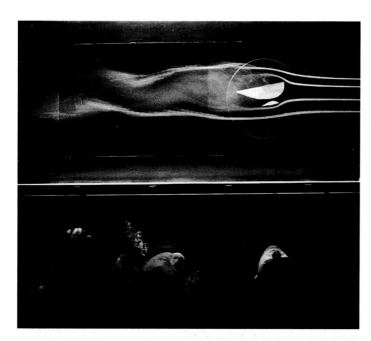

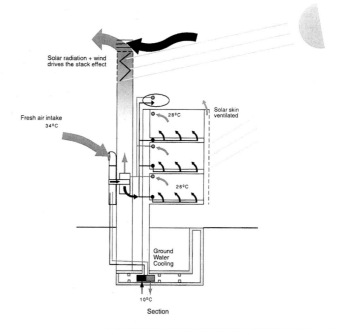

Solar radiation + wind drives the stack effect

Fresh air intake 34°C

28°C

Solar skin ventilated

26°C

Ground Water Cooling

10°C

Section

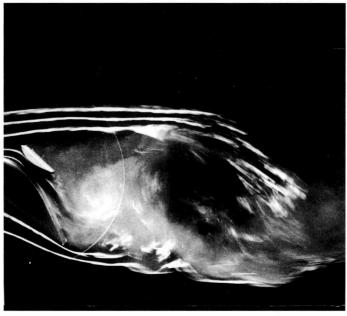

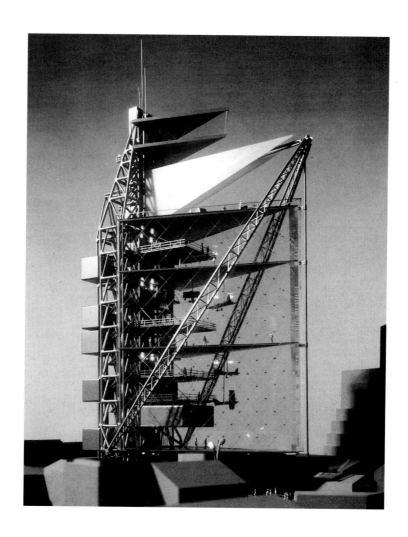

Lloyd's Register of Shipping, Liphook, United Kingdom, Competition, 1993

The competition-winning entry for an office and training complex is set in an area of outstanding natural beauty amid buildings of historic interest. The new buildings are broken down into identifiable units to minimize the impact on the surroundings and to maximize flexibility for the client, a large corporation with changing needs and requirements. The solution is based on a spiral arrangement of individual elements set in a campuslike environment, enclosing a sloping horseshoe-shaped park that acts as the formal front lawn to the complex.

A linear spine building containing the main entrance and public facilities is placed on axis with the "historic avenue" on the site. The distinctive curved section forms a visual canyon that invites visitors into the building. Four shorter office pavilions, set at tangential angles to the parkland, are linked by a sequence of open courtyards that form a walled enclosure around the edge of the parkland meadow. Car parking is concealed within rows of planting in the narrow field behind the spine building to avoid compromising the natural or historic landscapes. The plan form and sections of the individual buildings respond to the different landscape conditions of the park, woods, and fields. The swooping curve of the roof, for example, extends the slope of the parkland meadow and assists natural ventilation within.

The wing buildings are arranged on two levels of offices overlooking a generous double-height zone enclosed by the curved roof structure. Views from the upper-level offices are through a band of horizontal slatted strip windows with external blinds that maximize daylight but control solar gain. The spine building has a similar section with a data center at basement level and public facilities, including a library, within the curved double-height space overlooking the landscape.

The curved roof structure, which doubles as facade along its southern aspect, maximizes environmental performance of the external skin and allows internal airflows to circulate along the internal perimeter of the building. The roof is designed with a matte gray finish, and the glazed facade is set back from a deep overhang underlining the building's low-key presence on the site. The flat portions of the spine building's roof will be covered in grass to integrate it with the landscape. The cladding will be in clear glass to reduce the need for natural lighting with opening windows to admit fresh air and to cool office spaces in the summer.

The design builds upon the historic English landscape tradition, integrating the best of nineteenth-century innovative glass and iron design (such as Kew Gardens) with the current concerns about environmental performance and energy conservation. There is a strong resemblance to earlier projects by Team 4 for Wates Housing (1965), where a series of stepped terraces is built into the natural vegetation on a sloping countryside site, and the sketch proposals for a research center in East Anglia, where a hybrid tension structure is built into the surrounding green area.

Site plan; sections; model.

*Perspective showing entrance to
spine building; axonometric section
showing materials.*

*Sections showing environmental
aspects of design.*

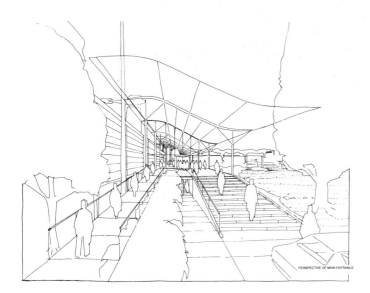

PERSPECTIVE OF MAIN ENTRANCE

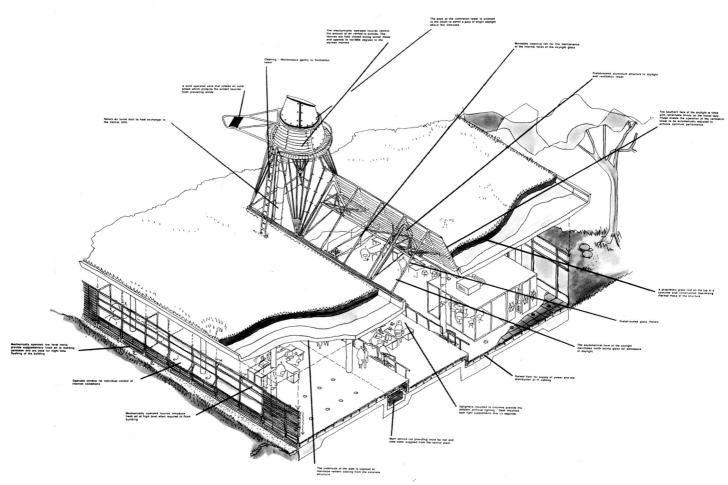

158

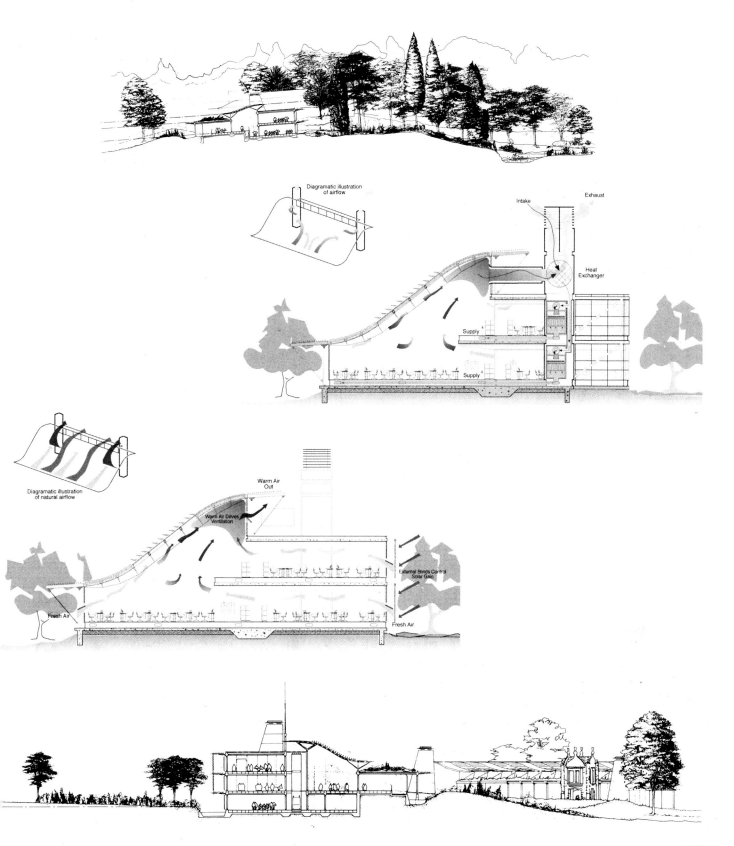

Diagramatic illustration of airflow

Intake   Exhaust

Heat
Exchanger

Supply

Supply

Diagramatic illustration of natural airflow

Warm Air
Out

Warm Air Drives
Ventilation

External Blinds Control
Solar Gain

Fresh Air

Fresh Air

159

Public Buildings and Infrastructure

Centre Georges Pompidou, Paris, 1971–77

The Centre Pompidou is one of the most public and most controversial icons of contemporary architecture of the late twentieth century. The building was hailed as a major architectural statement of the expectations of the modern movement in the early 1970s. It has, in effect, become a manifesto of late modernism with its commitment to the public realm, the integration of design and technology, and the unflinching belief in total flexibility. The very nature of its program (a centralized palace of culture that consumes 10 percent of the national culture budget), let alone the radicality of the proposal, has been the subject of much criticism and debate which still animates the cultural world. The recent competition for the new Tate Gallery of Modern Art in London, for example, referred to the Centre Pompidou as *the* archetype of the urban museum of the postwar period. Whatever its strengths and weaknesses, the building has proved a phenomenal public success attracting some thirty thousand people a day (though the brief estimated ten thousand), more than one hundred million visitors since its completion in 1976.

Reyner Banham emphatically pronounced the Centre Pompidou "the only public monument of international quality the '70s has produced" and applauded the design for challenging "Le Corbusier's increasingly geriatric understanding of monumentality as mere mass and impenetrable substance" (*Architectural Review*, March 1977, 277). Alan Colquhoun instead criticized the building and its program for the "attempt to combine 'modernity' and traditional institutionalism, populism and gigantism," noting that the "uncompromising audacity of the solution was achieved at the expense of making the building into a vast self-sufficient block, inserted rather crudely into the city fabric" (*Architectural Design*, 1977). Kenneth Frampton has described the building as a "case of under-provision of wall surface and over-provision of flexibility" (*A Critical History of Modern Architecture* [London, 1980], 284), while Peter Cook and many others hailed it as the perfect machine of its time. Monument or antimonument, the debate still continues. As Reyner Banham presciently noted in 1977, "If that fixed image can retain its present power until, say, the century's end, Centre Pompidou will prove to have succeeded in one of the most teasing but central tasks that were in the unwritten programme (*pace* Giedion) of the Modern Movement."

The Competition

The competition entry for the Plateau Beaubourg Centre Paris (as the project commissioned by President Georges Pompidou was then called) was put together rather hurriedly in the spring of 1971 by the relatively unknown and untested team of Richard Rogers and Renzo Piano. At that stage of their careers (Rogers was thirty-eight years old and Piano thirty-four), they had built a few buildings independently but, as a team, had only realized a small rooftop conversion for an office in Aybrook Street in London, affectionately known as the "Yellow Submarine."

The jury for the competition, which attracted 681 entries from forty-nine countries around the world, was chaired by the eminent builder-engineer Jean Prouvé, whose innovative approach to design and construction was in tune with Piano + Rogers' design philosophy. Other members included Philip Johnson, who as a tutor had been rather critical of Rogers' work at Yale University in the early 1960s; the modernist Brazilian architect Oscar Niemeyer, who was ideologically opposed to Piano + Rogers; and the Dutch curator Willi Sandberg, who had been immensely influential in contemporary thinking about museum and gallery design. Sandberg played an important role in recognizing the liberating potential of the Piano + Rogers approach, which avoided the trap of institutionalization so typical of such organizations. Significantly, the jury report noted, "The winning project's simplicity is striking . . . It is not simplistic. It is lucid."

The opening statement of the Piano + Rogers submission was typically candid and bold: "We recommend that the Plateau Beaubourg is developed as a 'Live Centre of Information' covering Paris and beyond. Locally it is a meeting place for the people." It was the only entry in the competition to leave more than half of the site empty for a large public piazza. Twenty-five years later, both Richard Rogers and Renzo Piano acknowledge that the most significant victory of the project was the creation of the open public space that has transformed the entire area, contributing to the regeneration of the surrounding Marais district.

The recent plans for refurbishment of the entire complex by Piano have been welcomed by Rogers as a sign of the robustness of the original conception. It is an acknowledgment that the building, as originally planned, should be in a state of constant change, that it can be adapted to accommodate changes in the administration and dissemination of mass culture. After all, their original submission hinged on the concept of flexibility and efficiency inspired by Buckminster Fuller, as stated unambiguously in their competition document: "The building offers maximum flexibility of use. Total uninterrupted floor space is achieved by limiting all vertical structure, servicing and movement to the exterior . . . All lifts and escalators are clipped onto the facade and can be changed if the intensity of use increases or the positions of the departments or their entrances are changed."

The original competition design envisaged two structural walls within which hung sections of floor that could be raised and lowered to provide flexibility. Within each floor deck was a standardized servicing system that connected through the rear to the service plant on the roof. A live information wall was supposed to be clipped onto the facade overlooking the piazza, carrying electronic messages on cultural events relating to the center and beyond. The idea of moveable floors was discarded almost immediately because of time and technical constraints. The live information wall was also dropped due to lack of funds (even though the fixings have been incorporated into the structure), reflecting a growing political concern that such a powerful form of communication could ultimately work against the interest of the status quo.

Aerial view.

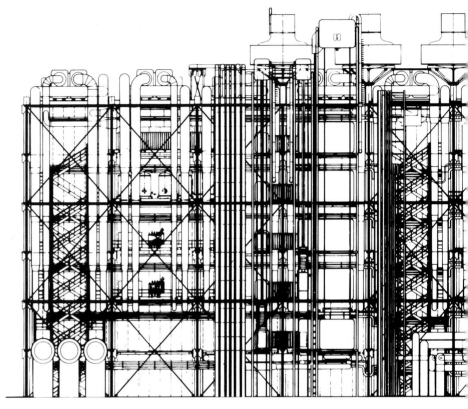

Organization and Structure

Functionally, the Pompidou is a large, simple loft building. Floor trusses, three meters in depth, span the full width of the building from east to west, creating six levels of vast column-free interiors (the size of two soccer fields, 169 meters by 48 meters). The glass skin runs clear and uncompromised behind the columns. The building is divided lengthwise into thirteen bays, 12.9 meters wide and with 48-meter clear spans. These bays are supported on lattice trusses suspended between the "gerberettes" whose outer ends connect with the vertical ties. The cast-steel gerberettes (named after the German bridge engineer Gerber) are cantilevers that minimize deflection of the main structural trusses. The structure is conceived as an adjustable scaffolding framework where every detail shows its function. There are no expansion joints, and the whole building has been designed as a single structural entity.

Though the depth of the trusses clearly limits the floor-to-ceiling height, they are skillfully designed to meet the vertical structure. At their extremes they are brought up to a pin joint in the plane of the external skin and supported by the short ends of giant gerberettes. The gerberettes pivot on pin joints on the main supporting columns, while outward cantilevers are tied down by vertical and diagonal braces. The use of a cantilever solution generates a zone of space between the structural columns and the external bracing substructure which accommodates the services on the street side and the horizontal circulation ducts on the piazza side. The escalators instead project clear of the structure not only to produce a more dramatic visual effect but also to obviate restrictions of local fire regulations.

Piano recognizes that the Pompidou is not the high-tech tour de force that it is made out to be. He notes ironically that the process of getting the vast steel trusses to the Beaubourg site from La Chapelle station required greater advances in technology than the erection of the building. It is a view echoed by Laurie Abbott, who compares the cost, speed, and efficiency of the Pompidou unfavorably with the Japanese battleship *Yamamoto*, a pure state-of-the-art construction, twice as big as Pompidou but built in under one year for a quarter of the cost.

Assembling the Team

After their unexpected victory, Piano and Rogers set about assembling a team for Europe's largest cultural project. They contacted old friends, or friends of friends, who would understand the underlying principles of this radical project. Rather than forming a team of experienced specialists (who would have inevitably pushed the project toward a more conventional solution), they looked for practicing converts. Hence, Mike Davies, happily engaged in the design of experimental structures on the west coast of the United States with Alan Stanton and Chris Dawson, received a midnight phone call asking them to join the team in Paris the following week. John Young, who had proven his immaculate skills at detailed design in the Reliance Control Building by Team 4, wa immediately co-opted togethe with the brilliant but nomadi Laurie Abbott, who became th overall coordinator of the projec Marco Goldschmied, who had pre viously joined the practice in Lon don, had developed a special inter est in management and strateg that was to prove invaluable in project of this scale and content Thus, the core team (Rogers Davies, Young, Goldschmied, an Abbott), which still leads th Rogers practice today, was conso idated in the early 1970s by th Pompidou project. Mike Davie went on to oversee the design an implementation of the IRCAM center, sunken into the adjacen plaza to benefit from maximun sound insulation.

Peter Rice, one of the young est members of the Ove Arup &

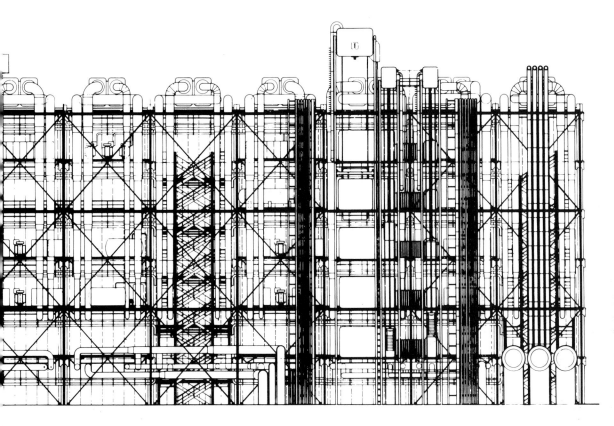

Partners engineering team (led by Ted Happold, who had personally frog-marched Piano and Rogers into doing the competition), found his natural role as magician, technician, and problem-solver, playing a key role in the evolution of the project for years to come. Gianni Franchini, Shunji Ishida, and other members of the team played equally important roles in the early design stages of the project. The team itself is emblematic of Piano and Rogers' approach to architecture. Today it still informs the modus operandi of the two partners' respective practices. It reflects their enduring belief in architecture as an interdisciplinary activity, where built form arises from an understanding of programmatic, technical, social, and environmental issues, rather than a formal a priori.

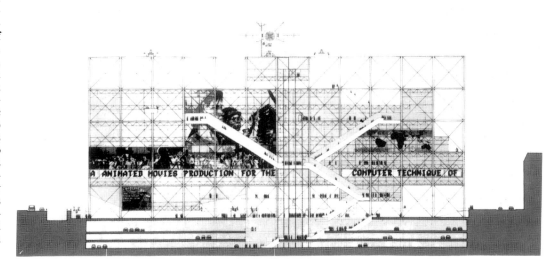

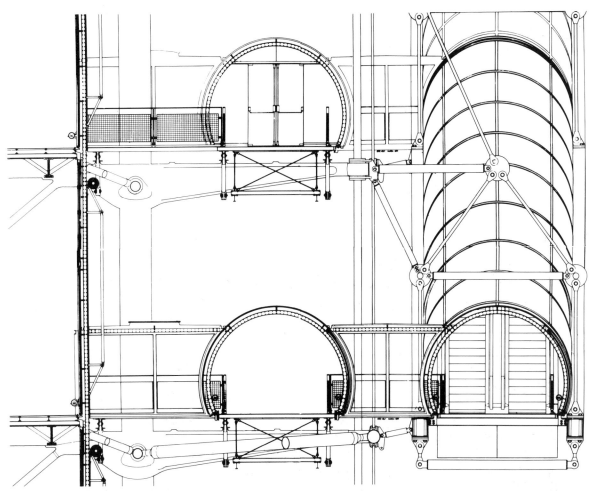

View of corner; perspective/section;
section.

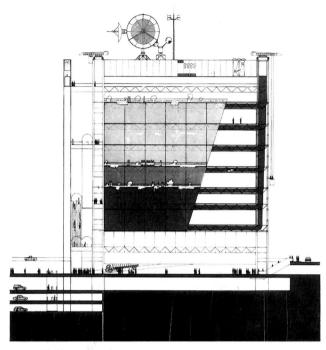

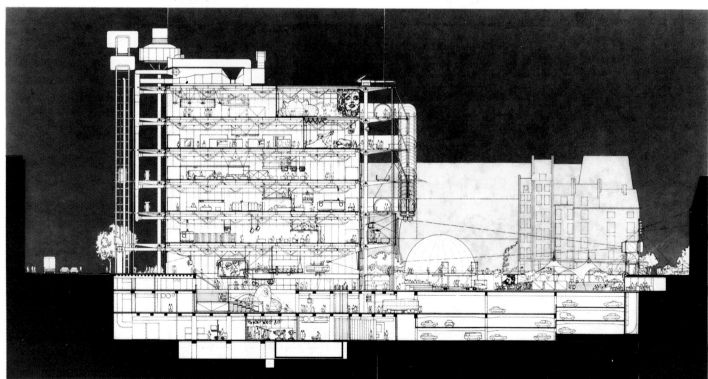

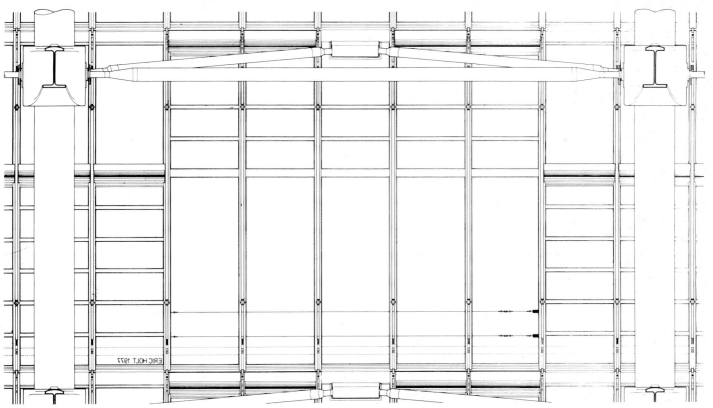

ERIC HOLT 1977

Rear facade.

Sections and details of gerberettes.

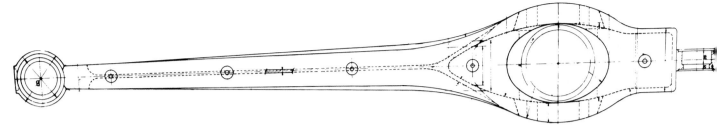

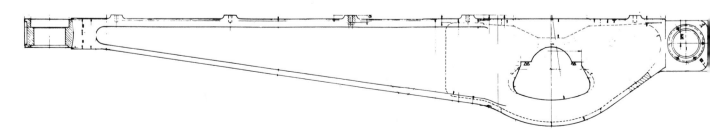

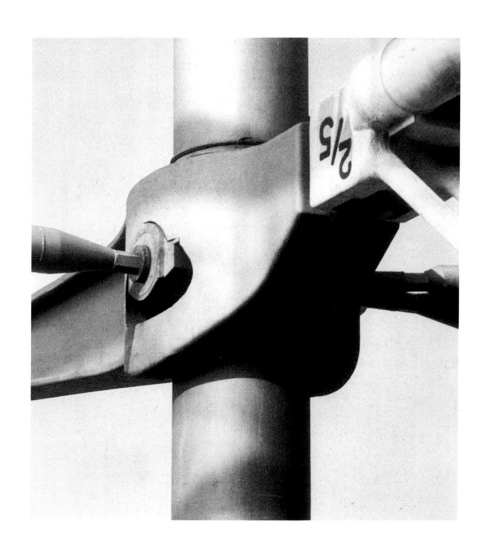

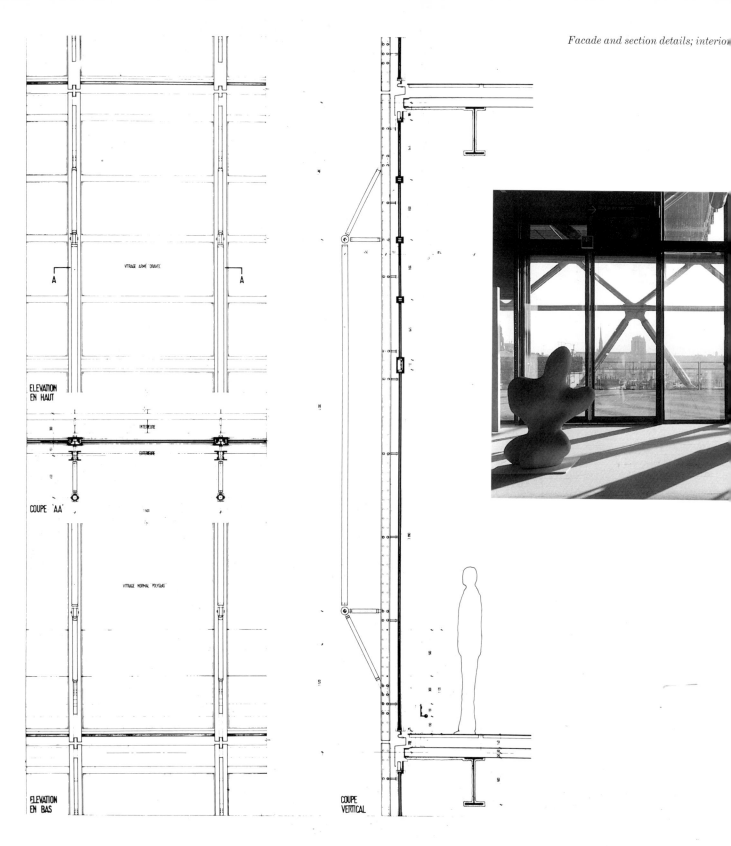

ELEVATION
EN HAUT

VITRAGE ARME DRAVEL

A ———— A

COUPE AA

VITRAGE NORMAL POLYGLAS

ELEVATION
EN BAS

COUPE
VERTICAL

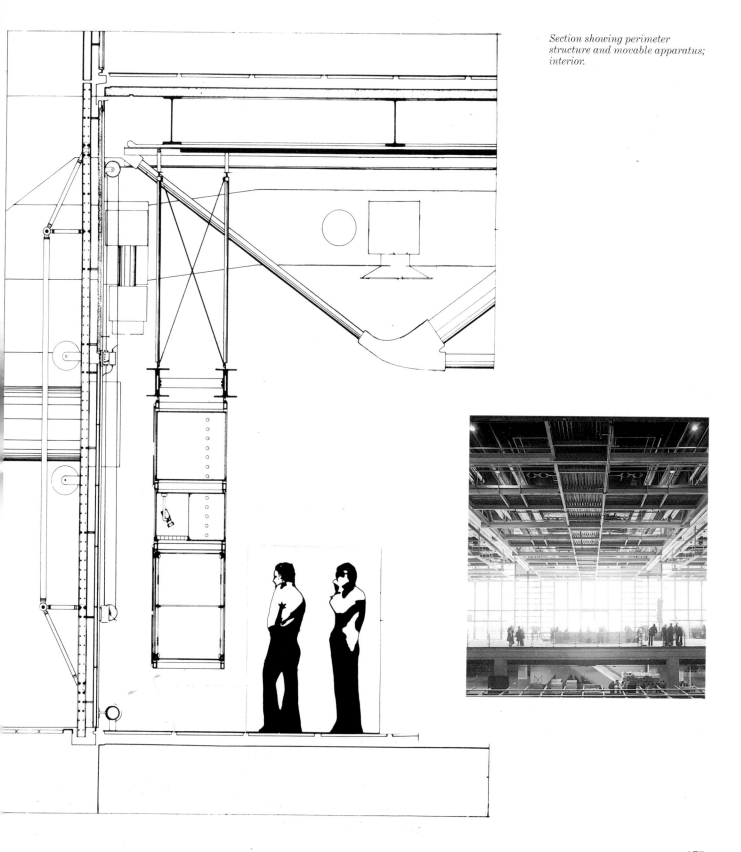

Section showing perimeter
structure and movable apparatus;
interior.

Interiors.

Tokyo Forum, Tokyo, Competition, 1990

Site plan; preliminary sketches; lower-level plan; schematic diagrams of roofs.

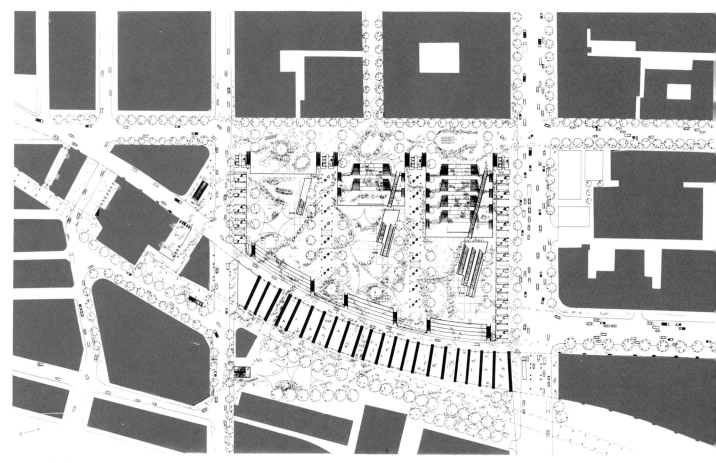

Nearly twenty years after the radical insertion of the Centre Pompidou into Paris, the Rogers office took the opportunity of developing an equally radical proposal for Tokyo. The name itself, "forum," seemed tailor-made for Rogers' urban philosophy: a place where people meet, talk, and celebrate their membership in collective, democratic life. Yet in Tokyo, with its high density and nearly frenetic levels of street life, this project took on a new, more focused meaning.

The Rogers design is a highly polished three-dimensional diagram of the brief, which required three auditoriums, conference and exhibition halls, and large areas of indoor and outdoor public space. The three halls are suspended in "polished steel capsules" hanging from a giant exoskeleton, a framework of steel trusses that casts a net over an entire block in Tokyo.

Beneath the grand halls, acres of protected open space continue and extend the public realm of the surrounding streets providing a setting for a rich mix of urban life, with street theater, music, dance, shops, and cafés. Exhibition spaces, restaurants, and parking are placed in four levels below ground, while conference rooms and reception facilities are housed on the roof among gardens with spectacular views of the city. Observatories with viewing platforms are placed on the upper levels of the four giant pylons that mark the Tokyo skyline.

The auditoriums are connected to the new ground plane with giant transparent escalators that contribute to the sense of urban theater. More refined and more architectural than the sketch winning entry for the Beaubourg competition in 1971, the Tokyo Forum project reveals a fascination with the concept of architecture as a mechanical framework for human activity, reminiscent of Sant'Elia's and Archigram's futuristic urban visions.

178

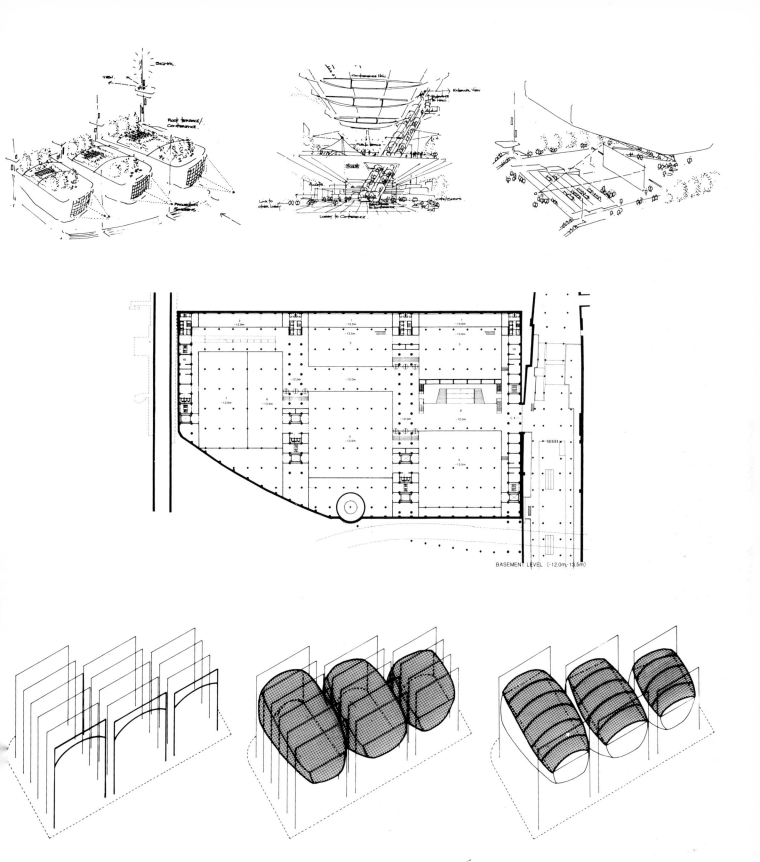

BASEMENT LEVEL (-12.0m,-13.5m)

179

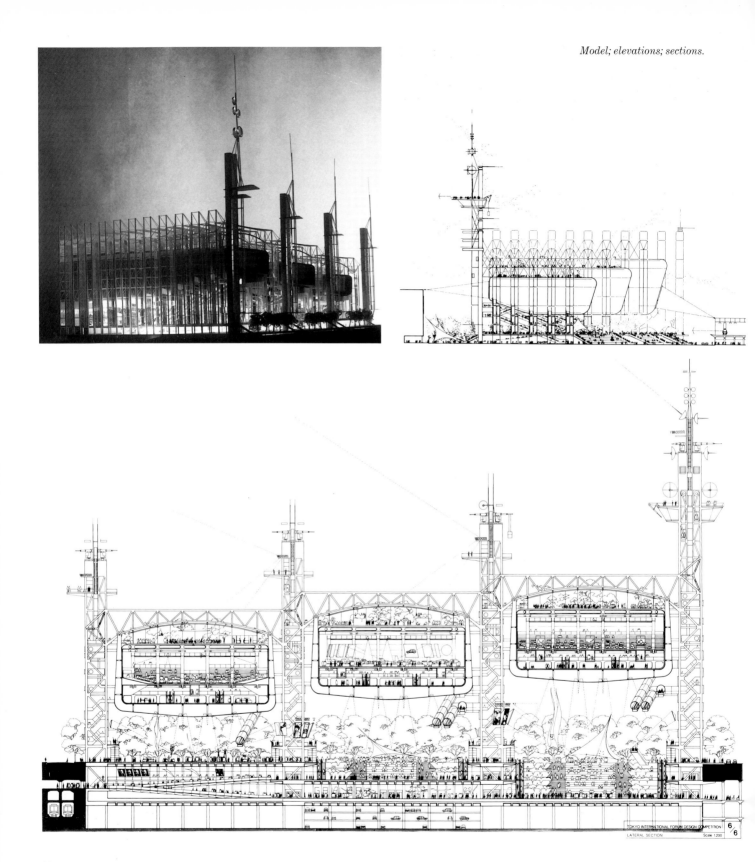

Model; elevations; sections.

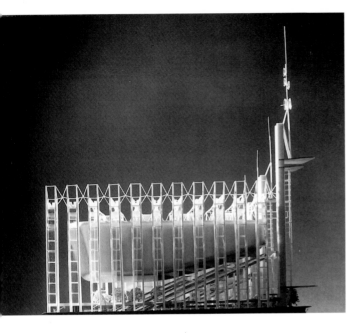

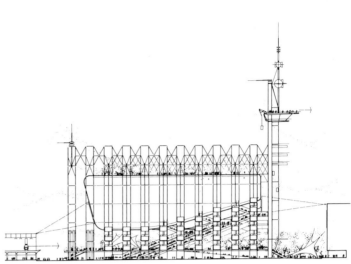

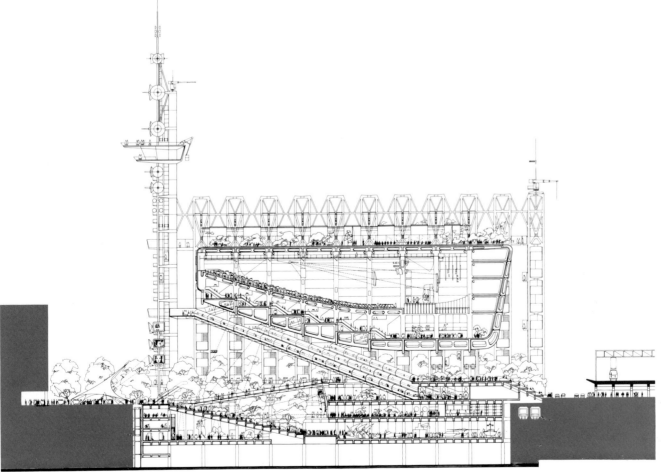

Plans at various levels; detailed plan of an auditorium.

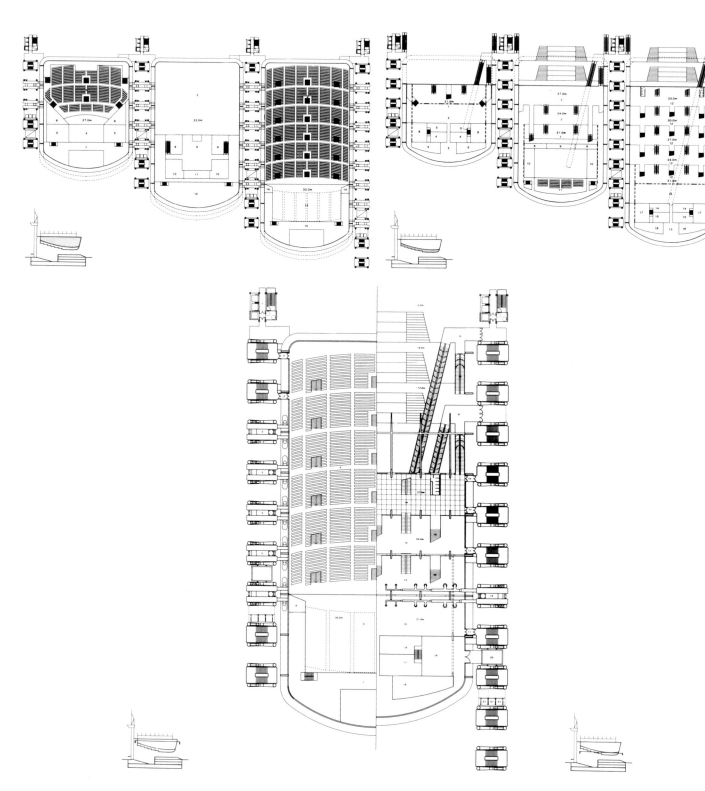

Perspective drawing of an auditorium.

The European Court of Human Rights is a "building in a park" located along the River Ill in Strasbourg. The formal functions of the institution are broken down into distinct components: expressed geometric volumes for the court and commission halls (at the more urban, institutional end of the site) and stepped linear blocks for the offices (at the more tranquil, suburban end). The building has, in effect, a head, a neck, and a tail. The head is fully exposed, with large drums containing the main courts and the public hall. The neck contains meeting chambers within an extruded cylindrical volume. The tail, with its parallel blocks of stepped offices, slides along the river's edge, providing views over the water and the surrounding park.

The entrance to the complex is through the central glazed drum of the public hall: a big circular room encased in glass and overlooking the river. With its sense of transparency, openness, and light, the hall has been designed as an antithesis to the claustrophobic nature of major legal institutions. The two main court chambers are instead enclosed in lightweight drums clad in stainless steel that float above the public hall supported by concrete tripod frames. The engineer Peter Rice, who worked closely with the Rogers team on the project before his death in 1993, played an instrumental role in resolving the complex interrelationship of geometries of the three circular volumes.

The main meeting chambers and support spaces are arranged along the short axis of the building, leading directly to the offices oriented along the river. A landscaped open space, with water features and fountains, occupies the central zone between the office wings. The natural tendency for the Rogers office to build in a degree of flexibility was put severely to the test during the evolution of the project. As a direct result of political events in the early 1990s, the Council of Europe wished to increase its membership from thirty-one to forty-five states, requiring a substantial increase in office space. The design team was forced to exploit the built-in potential for expansion by remodeling the stepped section of the building. The net effect has been to increase the tail of the building by 40 percent and the head by 25 percent without substantially affecting the overall balance of the composition.

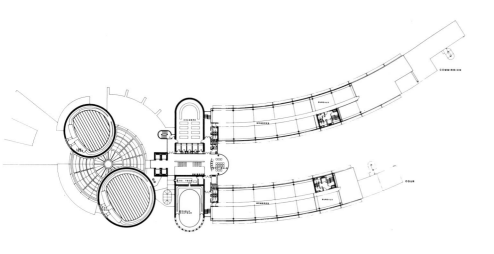

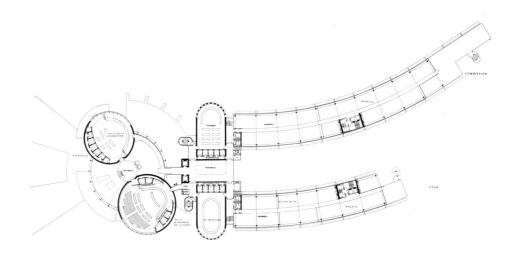

Overall view; preliminary sketch.

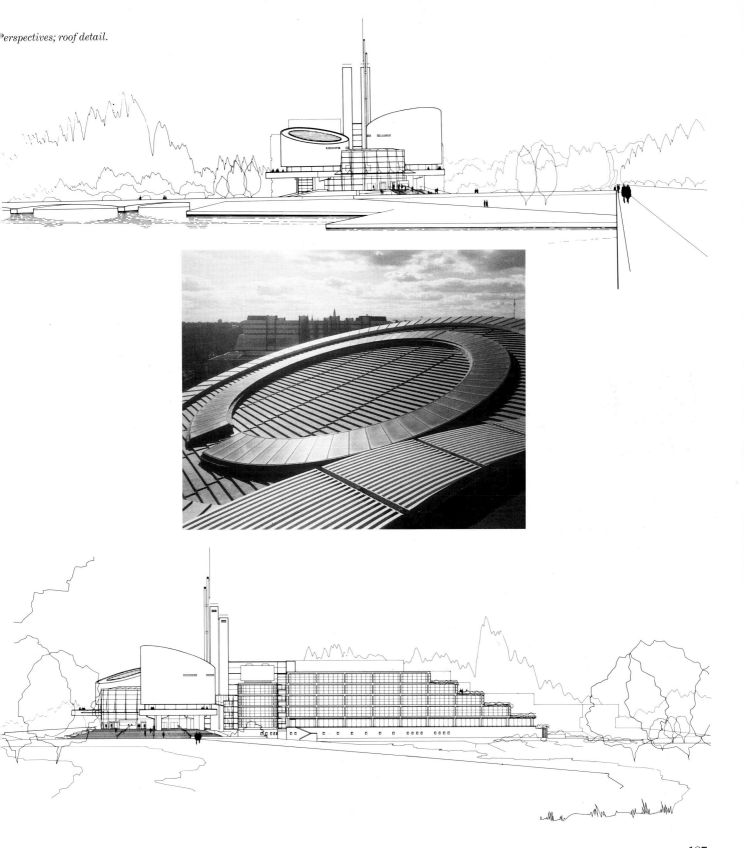

River elevation; model.

Views and perspectives of drums.

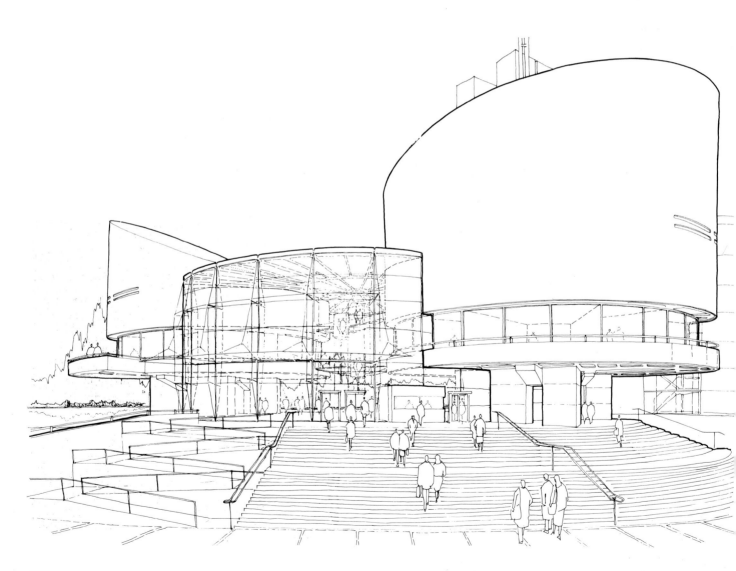

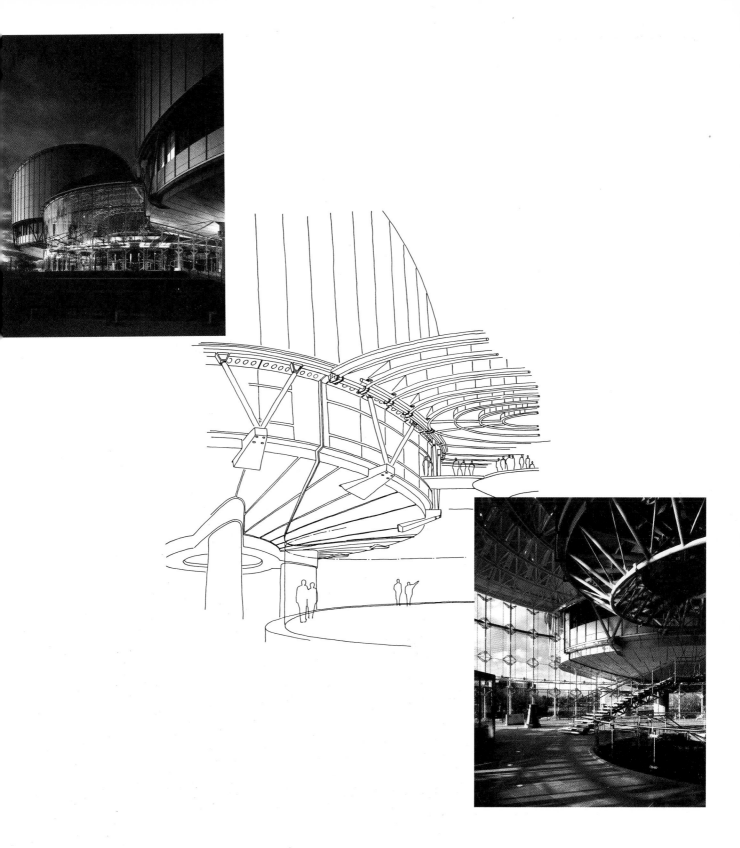

Pump House, Docklands, London, 1987–88

The small cylindrical building is a water pumping station situated in London's Docklands. As a "pure" industrial container for machinery, it is an especially appropriate project for the Rogers practice to explore the potential of "pure" architectural form. Though the building sits in an undistinguished urban context, it occupies a singularly prominent site as a gateway to the new development areas in the Royal Docks and close to the Reuters Data Centre.

Two concentric drums rise twelve meters above ground with twenty-five-meter-deep shafts placed axially to the direction of the water flow. The servicing and operational equipment of the pumping station is neatly contained within the upper portion of the cylindrical drum. All heavy submersible pumps and equipment can be accessed by annular craneways housed in the main pump hall.

All steelwork detailing is heavily articulated to emphasize the building's character and ensure durability of the working parts. The concrete walls are painted in vibrant colors, giving the impression of the glossy enameled finish of ocean liners and oil tankers. The maritime analogy is further reinforced by circular windows, twin exhaust funnels, steel balustrades, and the curved curtain wall (made up of fine metal grille and translucent polycarbonate panels) that forms a prow to the building, creating an appropriate visual contrast to the heavy construction of the drum.

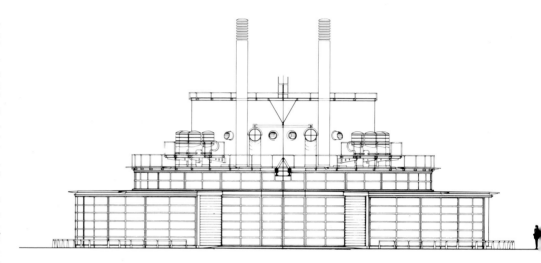

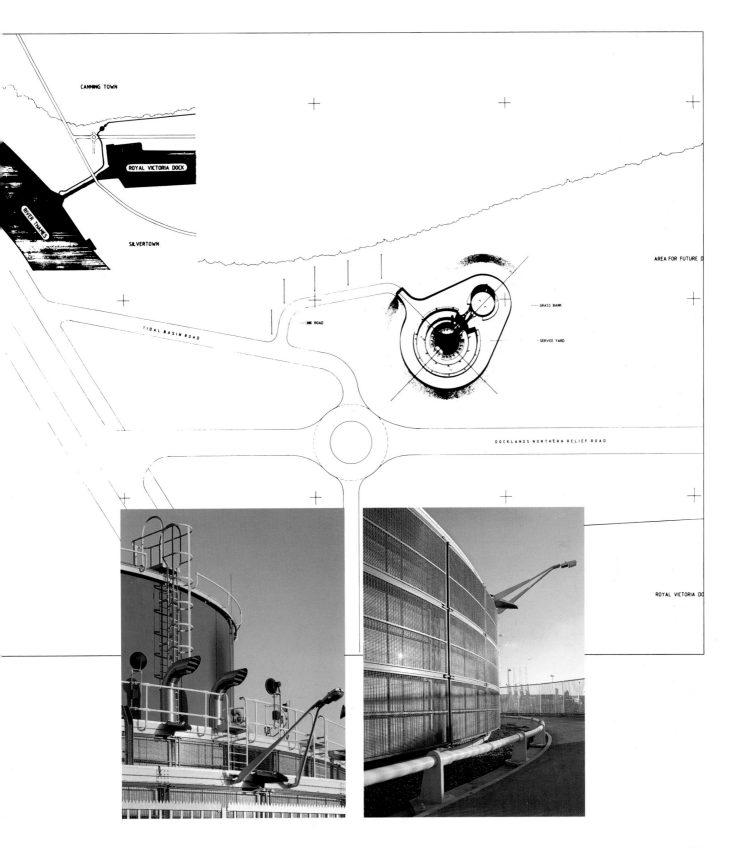

CANNING TOWN

ROYAL VICTORIA DOCK

RIVER THAMES

SILVERTOWN

AREA FOR FUTURE D

TIDAL BASIN ROAD

LINK ROAD

GRASS BANK

SERVICE YARD

DOCKLANDS NORTHERN RELIEF ROAD

ROYAL VICTORIA DO

Interior; plan; elevation; section.

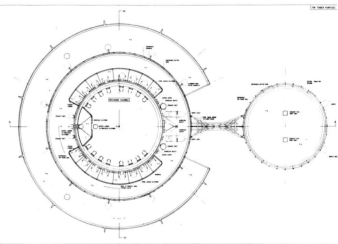

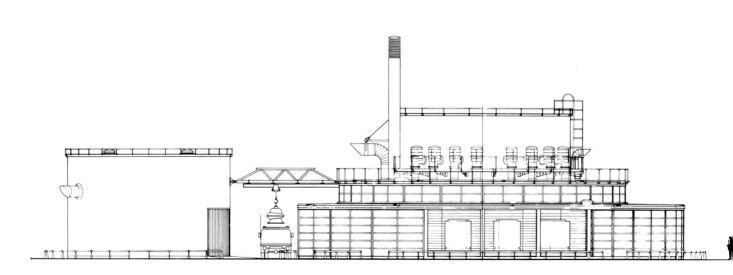

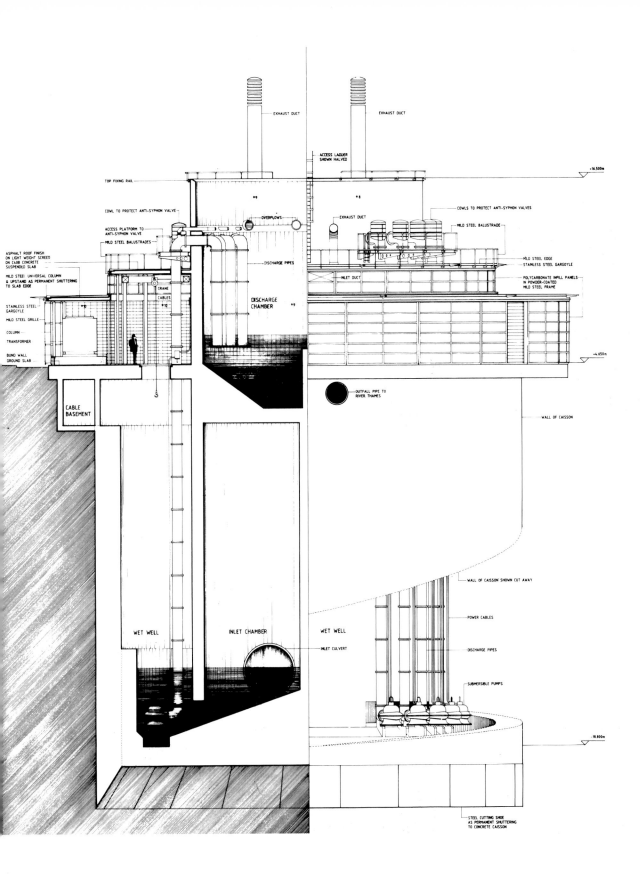

EXHAUST DUCT

EXHAUST DUCT

ACCESS LADDER
SHOWN HALVED

+16.500m

TOP FIXING RAIL

*4

*8

COWL TO PROTECT ANTI-SYPHON VALVE

COWLS TO PROTECT ANTI-SYPHON VALVES

OVERFLOWS

EXHAUST DUCT

MILD STEEL BALUSTRADE

ACCESS PLATFORM TO
ANTI-SYPHON VALVE

MILD STEEL BALUSTRADES

DISCHARGE PIPES

MILD STEEL EDGE
STAINLESS STEEL GARGOYLE

ASPHALT ROOF FINISH
ON LIGHT WEIGHT SCREED
ON C40B CONCRETE
SUSPENDED SLAB

POLYCARBONATE INFILL PANELS
IN POWDER-COATED
MILD STEEL FRAME

MILD STEEL UNIVERSAL COLUMN
& UPSTAND AS PERMANENT SHUTTERING
TO SLAB EDGE

DISCHARGE
CHAMBER

*9

CRANE
CABLES

STAINLESS STEEL
GARGOYLE

MILD STEEL GRILLE

COLUMN

TRANSFORMER

BUND WALL
GROUND SLAB

+4.650m

CABLE
BASEMENT

OUTFALL PIPE TO
RIVER THAMES

WALL OF CAISSON

WALL OF CAISSON SHOWN CUT AWAY

POWER CABLES

WET WELL

INLET CHAMBER

WET WELL

DISCHARGE PIPES

INLET CULVERT

INLET CULVERT

SUBMERSIBLE PUMPS

-18.800m

STEEL CUTTING SHOE
AS PERMANENT SHUTTERING
TO CONCRETE CAISSON

197

Marseille International Airport, Marignane, France, 1989–92

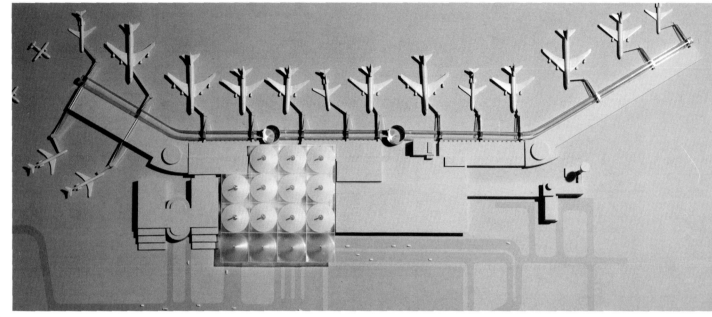

The project is both an extension of the existing terminal building and a master plan for future development of Marseille's international airport in the south of France. The overall plan envisages a linear development of the orthogonal terminal building extending the building at both ends. The extremities embrace the airside taxiing area, reinforcing the central north-south axis of the building. The completed first phase includes a new domestic flight terminal at the eastern end of the complex. The pragmatic planning and controlled industrial aesthetic of the building is a development of the architectural parti of Fleetguard, PA Technology, and the other industrial sheds of the 1980s, yet the softer articulation of the individual components creates a more organic composition.

The central pavilion, to be completed in the second stage of the project, will act as the new heart of the complex, marked by five rows of columns that penetrate the roof supporting a grid of modular concrete cupolas. Inside the building, these floating parasols, which are illuminated by uplighters at night, will give a sense of height and gravitas to the entrance hall. The main "urban" entrance to the terminal is up a pair of inclined ramps that lead directly to the piano nobile at first-floor level, where check-in and departure occur. Arrivals are placed on the upper floor, while baggage handling is at ground level. On the aircraft side, a new high-level glazed walkway, built over the service road, will provide continuity to the northern facade. The so-called tube will be connected to

passarelle structures that project out into the apron, serving both arriving and departing passengers through automatically controlled glazed sliding doors.

While movement patterns of departing and arriving passengers are physically segregated, they are spatially integrated within the single double-height volume of the completed building. The design fully exploits the potential of the curved roof beams of the terminal building, bringing natural daylight to both arrival and departure levels without compromising the quality of space in either. Overhead flying balconies, encased in glass, add a sense of movement and dynamism. The services and air-handling units are placed externally on the roof, which is supported by exposed curved steel trusses. The design

overcomes the restrictive impac of security requirements that s often stifle the spatial experienc in modern airports.

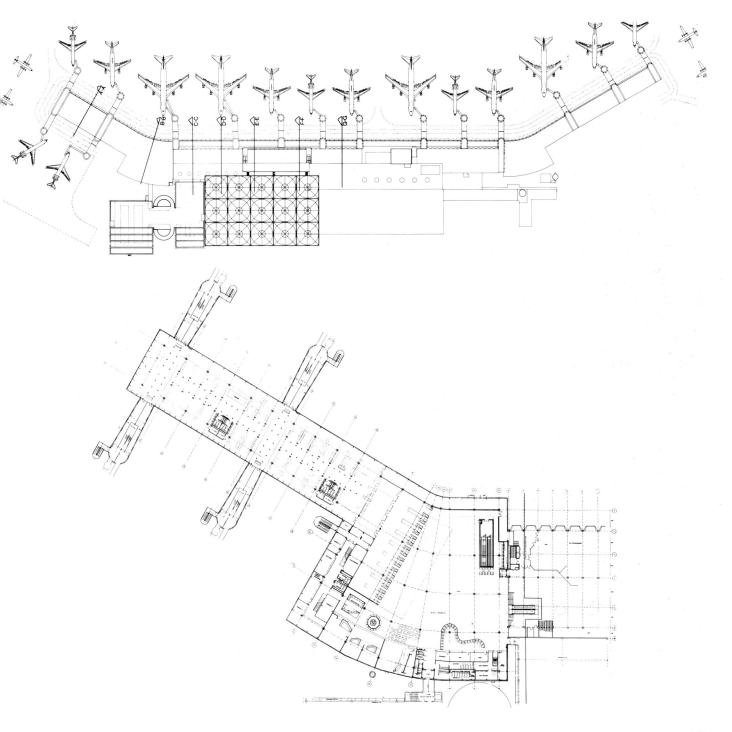

Section through domestic flight terminal; views; elevation of central pavilion.

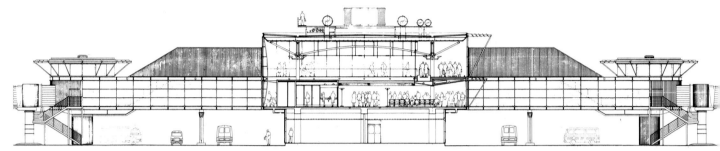

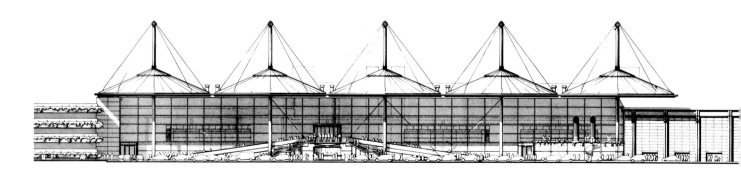

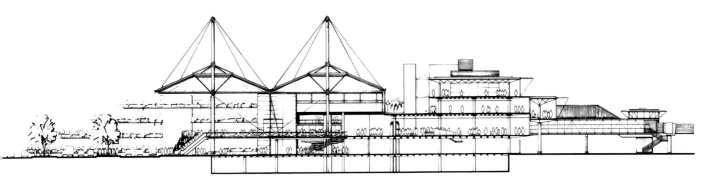

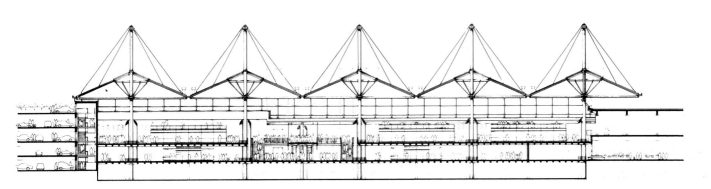

Section; views.

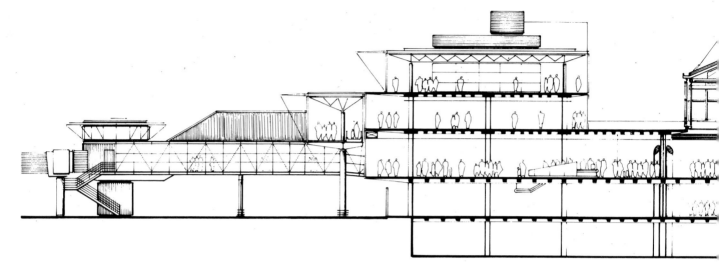

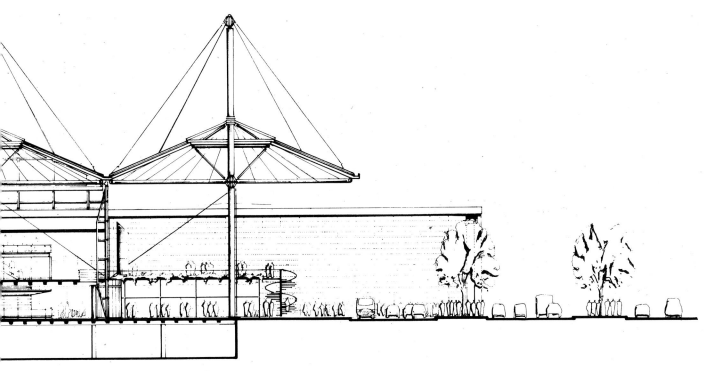

Interiors.

Terminal 5, Heathrow Airport, London, 1989–2016, Competition, 1989

Heathrow Airport, with its four terminal buildings, is one of the world's busiest air transport hubs. Projected increase in demand requires a completely new terminal building that will handle up to thirty million passengers a year by 2016. The design recognizes the changing role of the airport from a functional box into a major urban experience for passengers and non-passengers alike. The critic Deyan Sudjic has claimed that the modern airport, together with the out-of-town shopping center and the business park, is the emerging form of the international contemporary city. As such, the design for this new typology of quasi-urban constructions addresses this shift. The Rogers design for Terminal 5 is both monumental and flexible. It creates the framework for urban theater yet maintains the basic simplicity of the functional box, where passengers can reach their destinations quickly and efficiently.

The practice's successful entry in a limited international competition set out to "illuminate and give meaning to the act of travel" with a building that fits into the landscape and guides the passenger "naturally, clearly, and comfortably" from arrival to departure. The main terminal building is an orthogonal box with a curved waving roof that fluctuates toward the runways. The two linear satellite buildings, with a similar formal configuration, are reached by an underground rail shuttle system. Land-side access to the terminal is from a raised access road between the terminal building and a multistory car park which sits in a bold landscaped park, known as the "parking fields." Deep, toplit vertical shafts contain escalators linking to the rail and underground lines. Access

to and from the airplanes is from the other three sides of the box.

Great care has been taken to reduce changes in level for passengers as they go through the arrival, check-in, and boarding sequence. All departure activities are placed on the main concourse level. Arriving passengers ascend to the lofty arrival and immigration halls underneath the curved glass roof. The apron level is reserved for baggage handling and support facilities. The organization of the plan recognizes the increasing commercial importance of retail in the financial balance sheet of airport management. Duty-free and high-street type shopping has become so successful in large international airports that it is competing with the business of flying as the main source of income. Airports are becoming significant regional shopping centers that attract non-flying customers from a wide area. Accordingly, large areas at concourse level are given over to shopping, food halls, and entertainment areas.

The basic wave form of the roof structure reflects the dynamism of Scandinavian and central European modernism, especially the wonderfully willful organic shapes of Alvar Aalto's Finlandia Hall and Viipuri Library. The main roof structure spans thirty-six meters with inclined tubular struts radiating from concrete supports. The wave not only signals the intention and program of the building but also has clear environmental and spatial benefits. By allowing heat build-up to accumulate on the upper levels on the underside of the curve, excess heat gain does not enter the occupied zones of the building. The temperature in the upper levels is allowed to drift, but the temperature at lower lev-

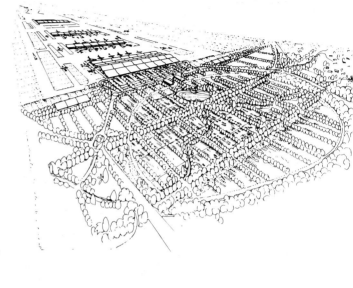

els, where people move and work, remains controlled and constant. The design of the structure has a direct impact on the nature of its environmental performance and running costs, leading to lower levels of air conditioning than might be expected in a building of such scale and levels of occupation. The curved roof also allows natural lighting to reach deep down into the building, while a light-control system minimizes the penetration of direct sunlight. The roof shape also prevents the spread of smoke in case of fire.

The design is a living testament to the "loose-fit, low-energy,

long-life" approach, where structure, space, and environment performance have been integrated into an organic whole that w enhance the humdrum experien of travel. This approach is bei severely tested by the curre stage of "value engineering" th will invariably result in a modifi version of the original competion scheme. Terminal 5 repr sents one of the practice's fir projects driven by energy co cerns which have further evolv in the designs for Inland Re enue, Lloyd's Register of Shi ping, and the master plans for V d'Oise and Shanghai.

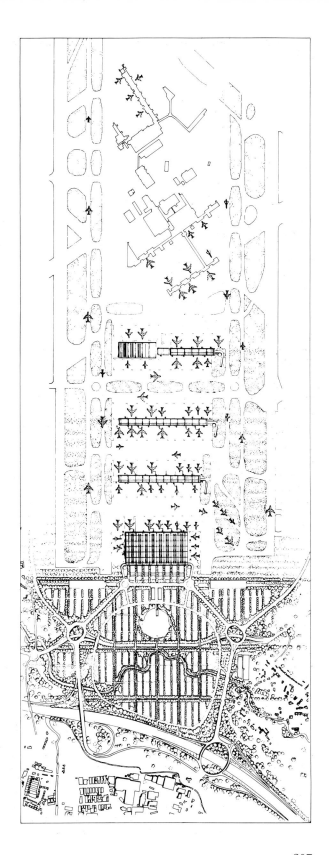

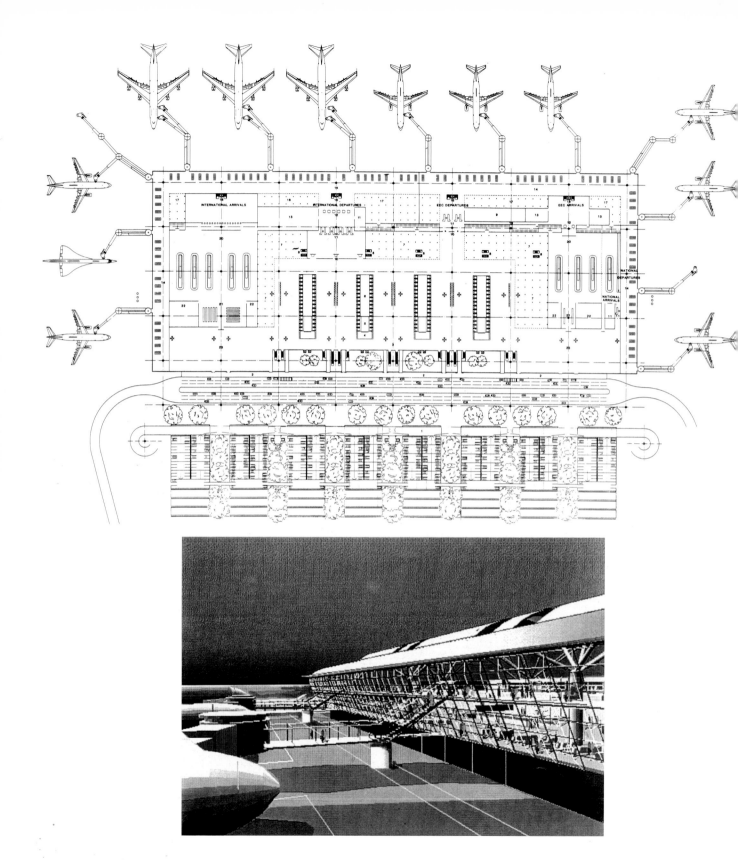

ın of main terminal building;
eliminary sketch; section
rspective; renderings of exterior
d interior.

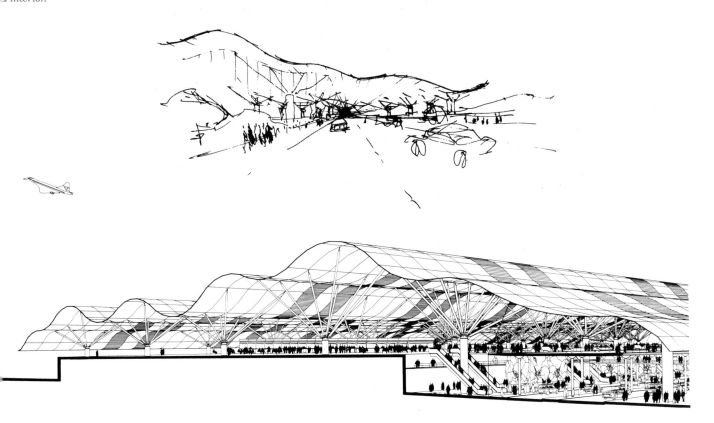

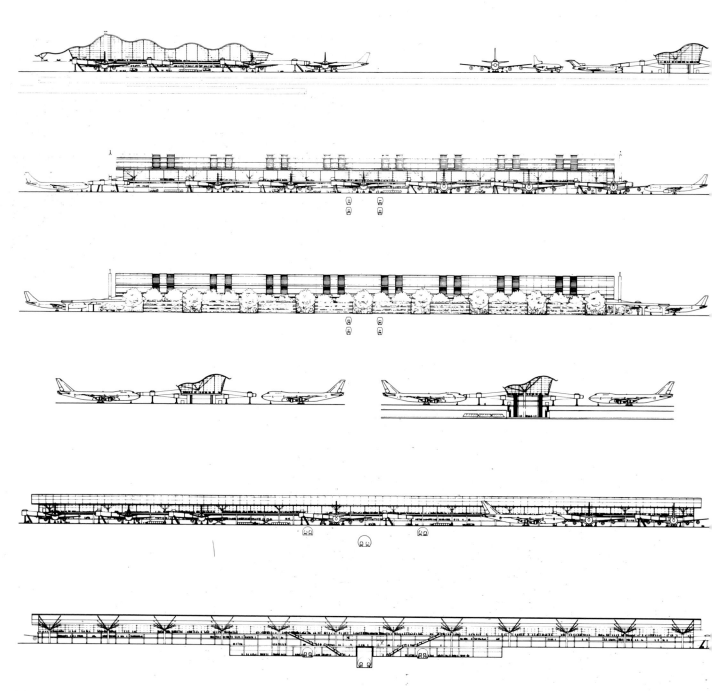

210

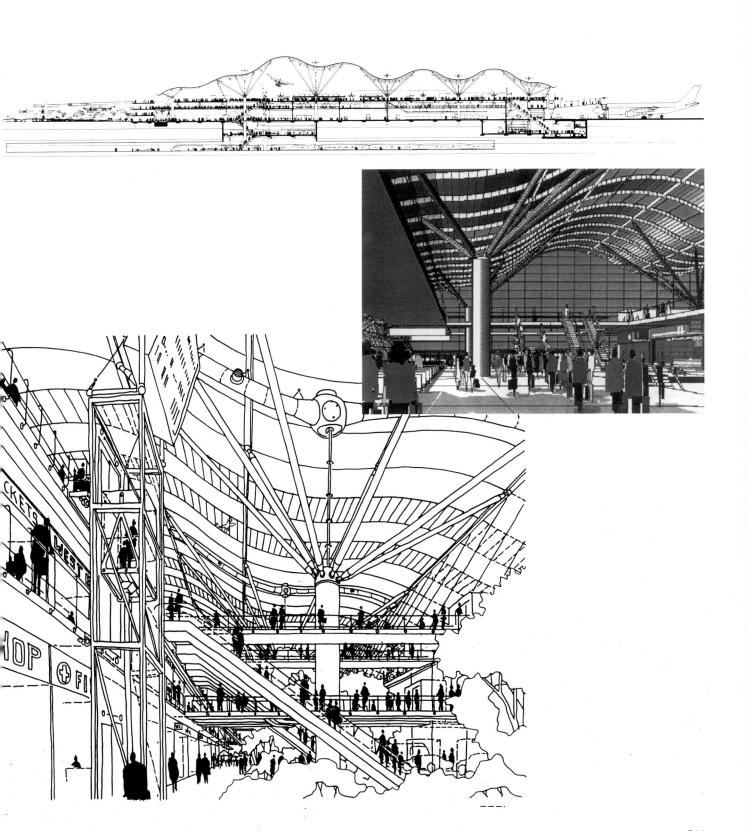

The competition-winning entry for a new complex of law courts is situated at the heart of the historic core of Bordeaux, near the cathedral and town hall. The awkward site is framed by the neoclassical law court building and is traversed by a section of the original medieval walls, complete with moat and bastions. The scheme exploits the public potential of the building by creating a pedestrian concourse that links the new complex with the rest of the city: "With its informality and openness this sequence is an entirely new way of looking (literally and metaphorically) at the administration of justice in a modern democracy" (Peter Davey, "Open Court," *Architectural Review*, March 1993, 51).

A reflecting pool extends and revitalizes the moat, framing the institutional building with water along its most prominent urban edge. While the main public entrance is from a new ramp connecting the site to the city center, the design is completely integrated into the existing structure of streets and buildings, including the old law courts and law school on the south and east of the site.

The new building, set on a heavy stone podium, defines the western edge of the site with an orthogonal block containing judicial offices and cells. A giant skeletal frame rises from the podium with a continuous glazed facade overlooking the soft landscaped heart of the site. The individual courtrooms are enclosed within this frame in seven clearly identifiable volumes, tapering in section and rounded in plan. These irregular toplit shapes stand free within the great glass volume like a row of bottles or wine vats. Supported on pilotis, the entire entrance level becomes a large uninterrupted concourse that flows under the courts, emphasizing the public nature of the building. The design recognizes that, for the majority of users, the space around the courts is as important as the space within.

The courtroom elements were originally conceived as exposed ferro-cement structures. The design team has since explored the potential of stressed-skin systems that offer greater flexibility of construction and greater durability, including a lightweight aluminum honeycomb sheet structure (usually employed in the aircraft industry) with a painted epoxy resin finish, which can be prefabricated under factory conditions and easily assembled on site in individual onionlike segments.

The design for the law courts is a variation on the frame-object theme that has informed a number of the practice's recent projects, including the Tokyo Forum. With its use of irregular forms and natural materials, the project represents a rare investigation into the expressive potential of the organic architecture of Hans Scharoun and Hugo Häring.

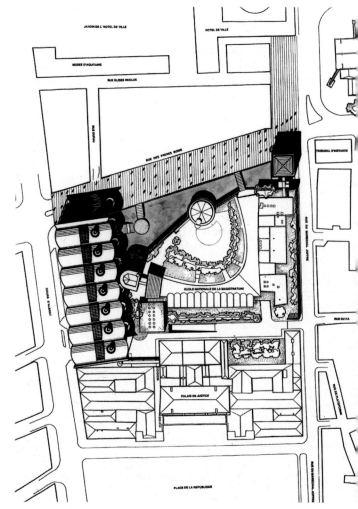

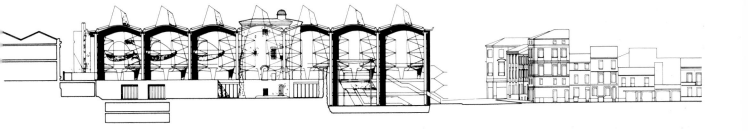

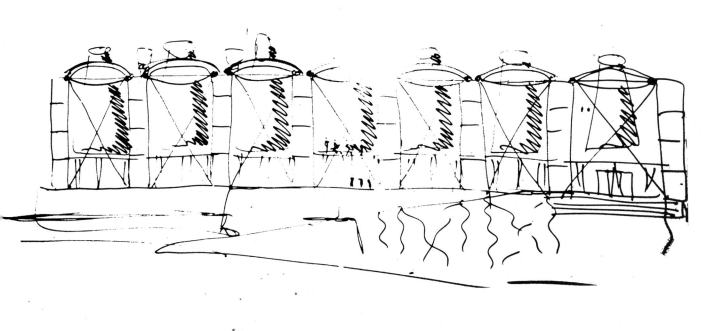

Model; section.

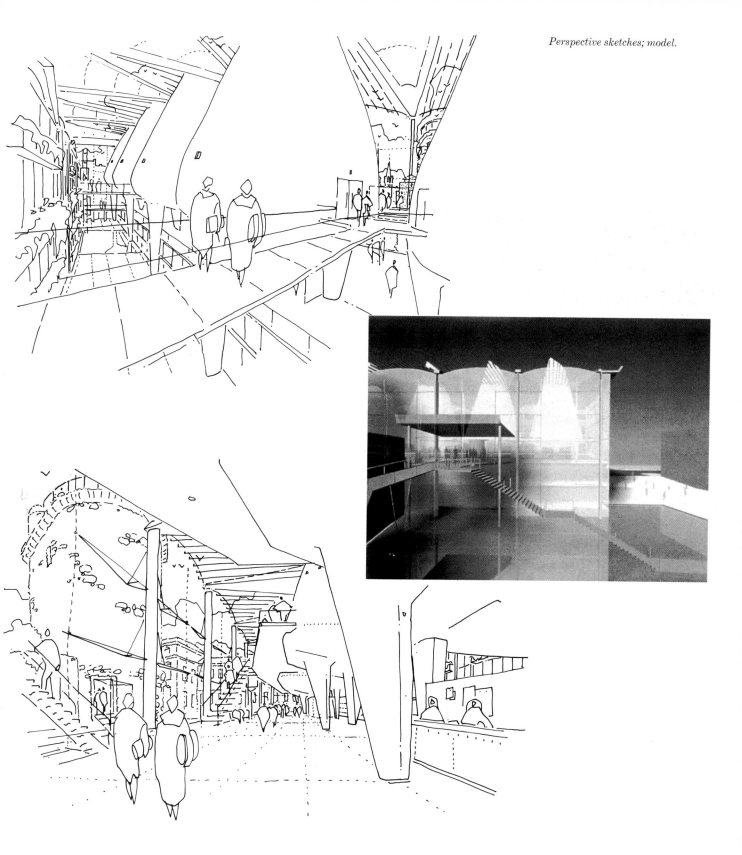

Bahnhof (Underground Station Prototype), Berlin, 1993

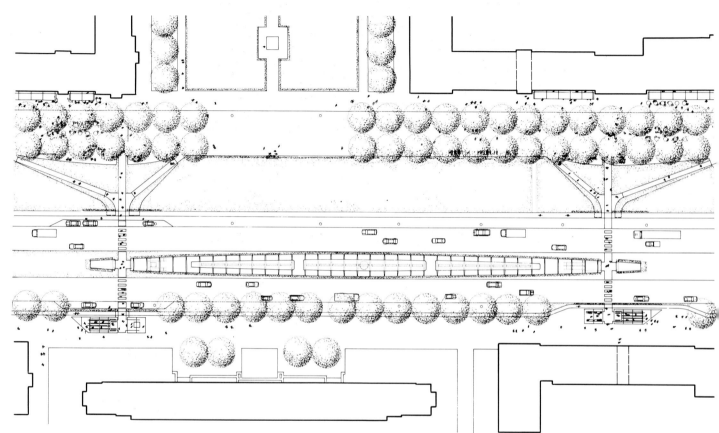

The proposals for a prototypical underground station in Berlin are founded on the principle that the journey between the train, the station, and the city (and vice versa) is a fundamentally urban experience. The stations are thus designed to facilitate movement, visibility, and legibility by exposing as much of the station as possible to views and natural daylight. Given the relative shallowness of the Berlin underground system, the stations are conceived as extensions of the street system with landscaped ramps and staircases leading directly to lower-grade platforms. The platforms are toplit with street-level skylights in long, shallow ellipses that become an integral part of the visual language of Berlin's tree-lined boulevards. At night, the glazed roof of the station glows, reinforcing its presence in the urban landscape. A variety of curved glass shelters housing ticket counters, information displays, and disabled access elevators further extends the presence of the underground, encouraging through-movement and celebrating the efficiency of the city's public transport system.

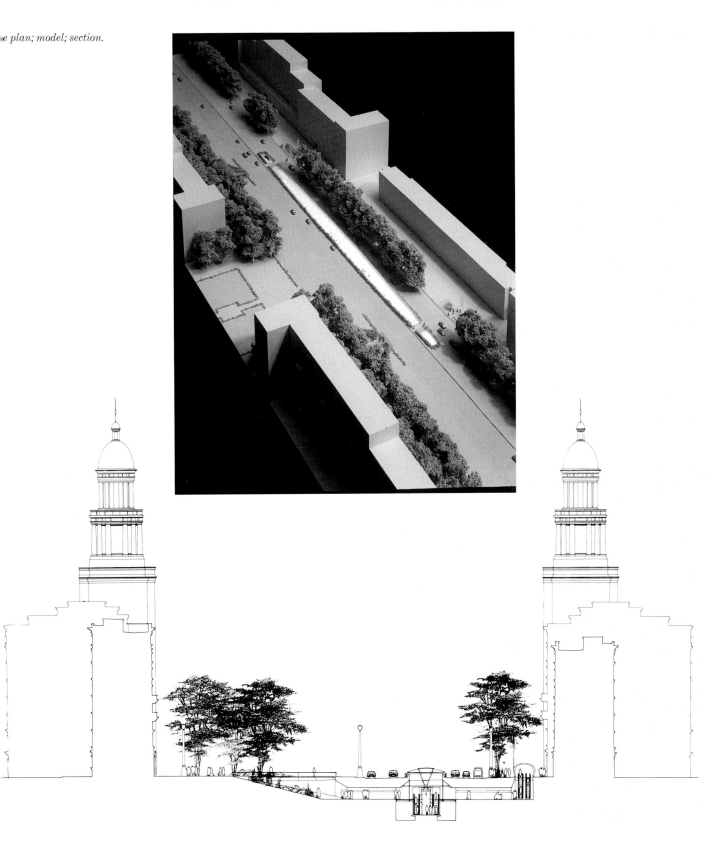

Section; model section showing platform.

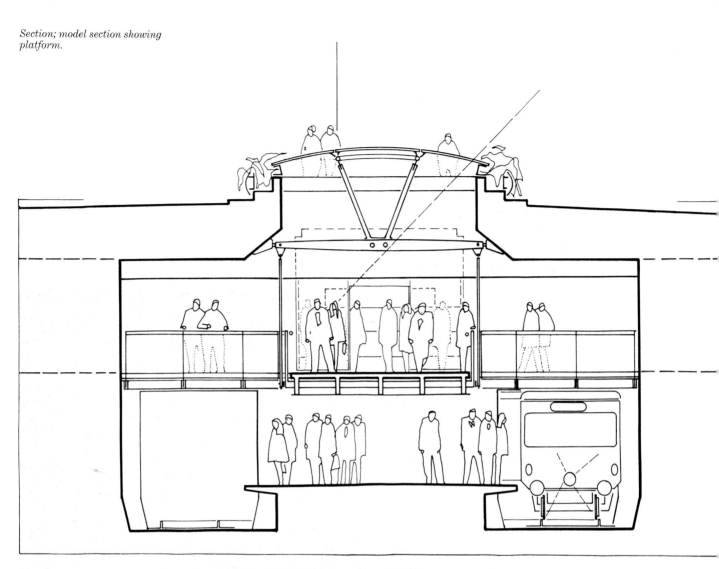

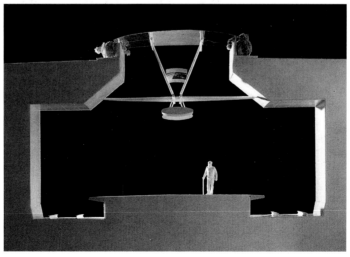

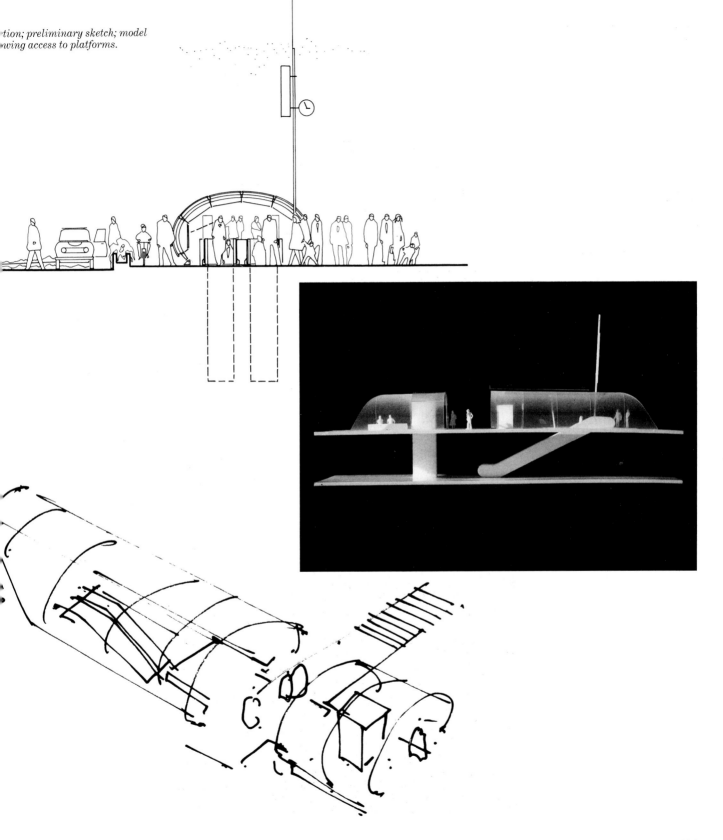

221

Towns and Cities

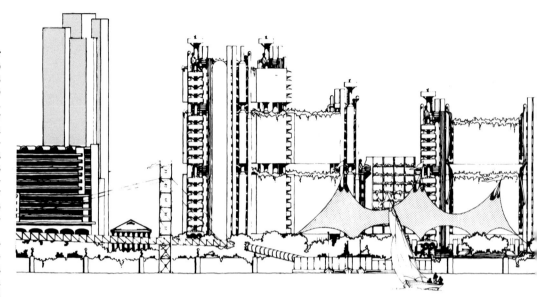

Coin Street is a relatively minor road that runs perpendicular to the Thames on its less glamorous south bank. Across the river to the north is London's West End. This fragmented area at the very heart of London, caught between twentieth-century large-scale institutions and the remains of a dense eighteenth-century street pattern, fails to exploit its metropolitan location and lacks any sense of urban vitality. Despite its proximity to the river, public access to the water is limited

Rogers' design for a mixed-use development—including housing, offices, and retail—provides a new spinal cord for the area. A glazed pedestrian arcade flanked by new buildings threads its way through the existing structures. A series of public spaces punctuates the linear route providing views and access from the landside area to the river. As the arcade reaches the river the route bends northward, extending into an encased glass pedestrian bridge that connects the two banks of the Thames. At the metropolitan level the scheme shifts the epicenter of central London southward, giving greater emphasis to the Thames River as an urban phenomenon. At the local level it provides a series of new public spaces, shops, and houses that integrate the existing community with the new development and the river.

The scheme is designed around a clear section with a sixteen-story glazed arcade, vertical circulation towers, and flexible floor plates that coincide with the spatial organization and expression of the Lloyd's Building. The tower clusters are stepped, increasing in height as they reach the river frontage, creating an appropriately scaled panorama when viewed from the south. At ground level the glass-topped arcade is lined by shops and cafés while a service road runs parallel to the river. A series of south-facing low-level semicircular housing units acts as a landscaped buffer between the arcade and the neighboring residential communities.

The sketchy physiognomy of the Coin Street buildings (only a sketch design) has had a significant impact on the architectural vocabulary of the practice. The interplay of planar metallic surfaces, vertical skewers topped by circular dishes, and linking glazed pavilions has become a Rogers trademark in a number of more recent buildings, including Brau und Brunnen in Berlin and the recent projects in Japan.

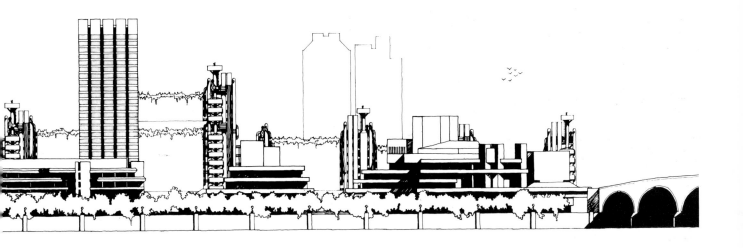

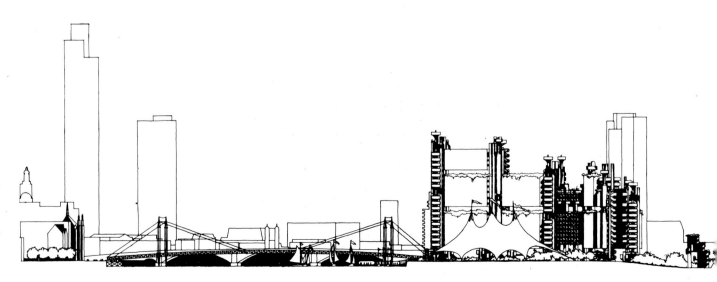

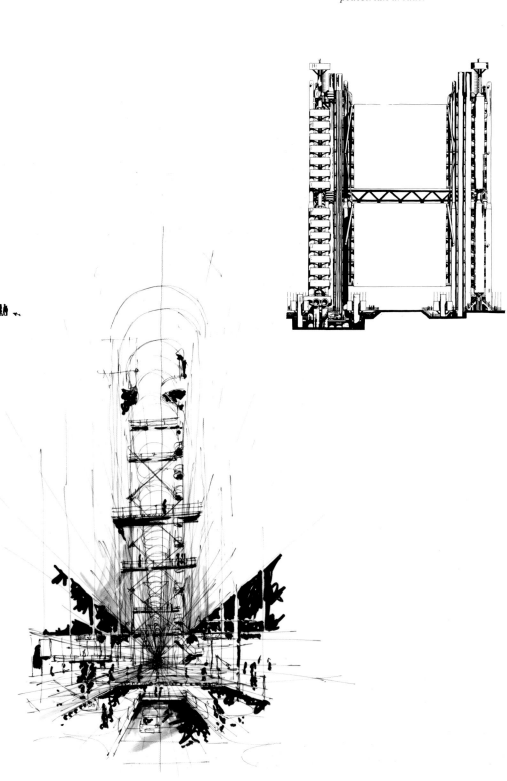

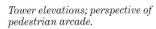

227

National Gallery Extension, London, 1982

The project for a major extension of the National Gallery in Trafalgar Square, in the heart of London, takes advantage of the extremely important location of the building to resolve urban problems.

The scheme envisages a pedestrian walkway underneath Pall Mall East, forming a direct public route from Leicester Square to Trafalgar Square. The idea is elaborated with a proposal to stop traffic on the northern edge of Trafalgar Square and to pedestrianize the entire area between the National Gallery and the church of St. Martin-in-the-Fields, forming a vast, south-facing public plateau that steps down toward Nelson's Column with axial views of Big Ben and the Houses of Parliament. Like the Place Beaubourg in Paris, the new piazza becomes London's major public space in front of the National Gallery.

A tower structure functions as an unchanging urban point of reference and balances St. Martin-in-the-Fields at the opposite corner of the public plateau.

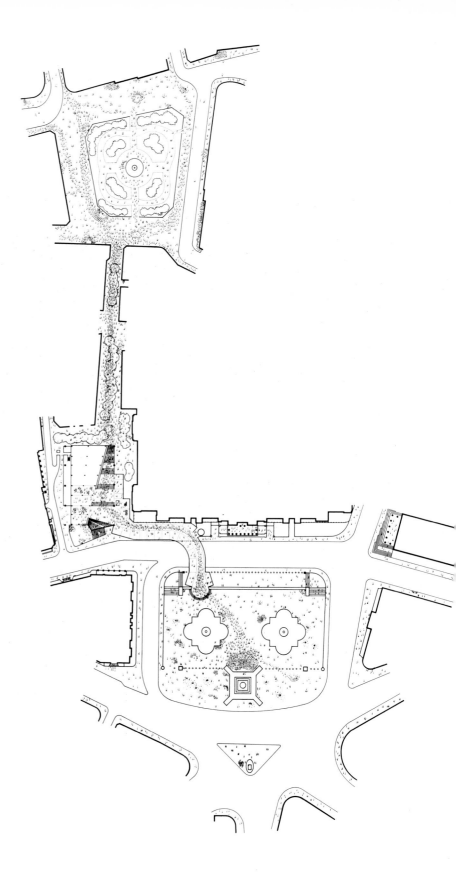

Elevation; model.

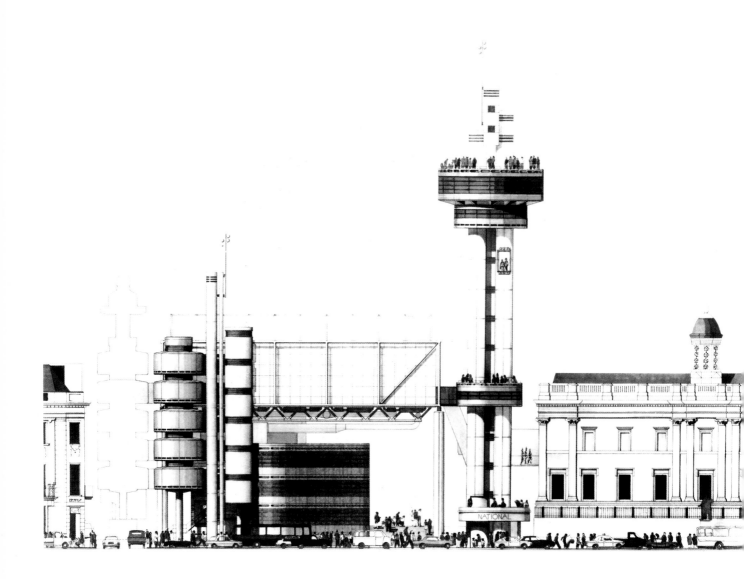

231

The competition anticipated the reconstruction of an area of great historical and urban significance: that around St. Paul's Cathedral in the center of the City of London. The site is occupied by a complex of neo-Corbusian office buildings with access ramps and raised public spaces.

The Rogers project extends the urban fabric of the surrounding neighborhood, integrating the isolated site with the old and varied structure of the City. The scheme reflects the interest of the Rogers studio in critic Colin Rowe's figure-ground urban theories. A hierarchy of public spaces defines volumes for a series of buildings that maintains street-level continuity with stores, bars, cafés, and other commercial activities.

A diagonal axis connects the Underground station to St. Paul's. It forms a grand public space in the heart of the area, integrating the old and the new.

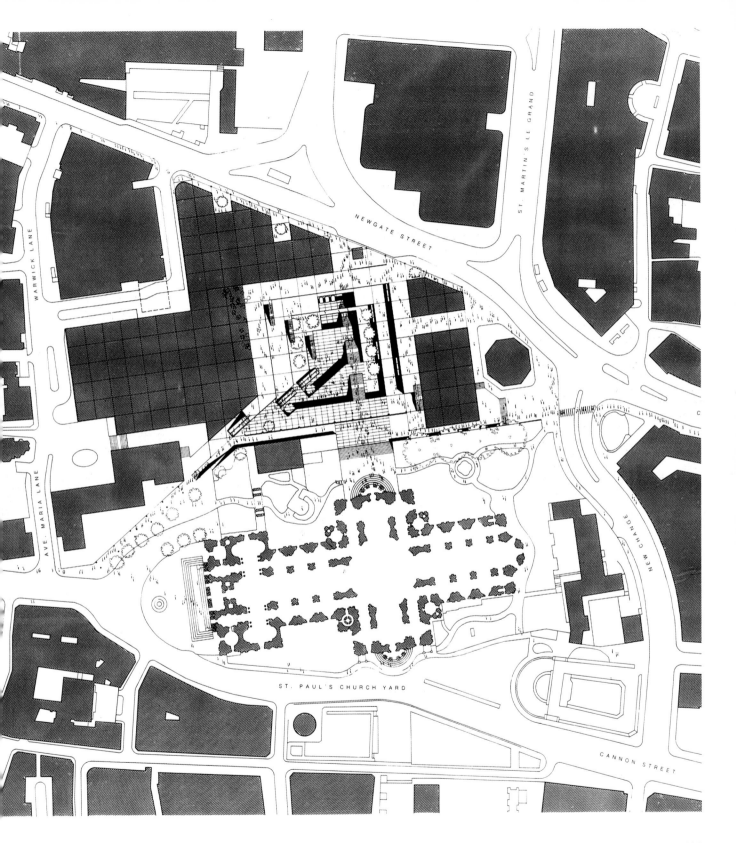

ST. PAUL'S CHURCH YARD

WARWICK LANE

AVE. MARIA LANE

NEWGATE STREET

ST. MARTIN'S LE GRAND

NEW CHANGE

CANNON STREET

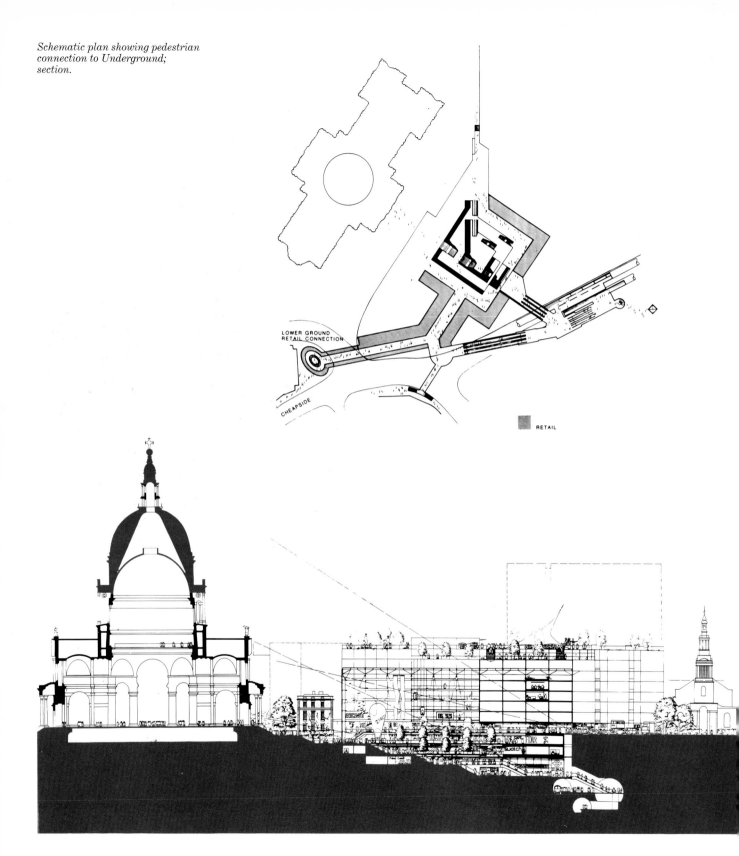

Schematic plan showing pedestrian connection to Underground; section.

LOWER GROUND
RETAIL CONNECTION

CHEAPSIDE

RETAIL

The string of projects for London were triggered by a major public exhibition held at the Royal Academy in 1986 to celebrate the work of Norman Foster, James Stirling, and Richard Rogers. While Foster and Stirling focused on their completed buildings and current projects, the Rogers practice used the opportunity to explore new ideas for London. Their contribution to the exhibition centered on a large-scale reconstruction of the central section of the Thames River, complete with water, detailed models of new bridges, viewing platforms, pontoons, and floating islands. It is amusing to note that at the formal opening ceremony the much-missed "Big Jim" Stirling, who had briefly taught Richard Rogers at architecture school, surreptitiously placed two goldfish in the vast black pond to "animate the river"!

The project proposed a framework of urban design initiatives for key public spaces in central London. The overriding principle is the improvement of the "public realm" in London, which, to Rogers' mind, has deteriorated substantially in the last decades of the twentieth century. Rogers' interventions, which recall the grand Regency plans and Victorian street improvements in London, establish a clear sequence of public routes across central London, from Leicester Square through Trafalgar Square, linking the north and south banks of the Thames.

Despite their grandeur and sense of history, Trafalgar Square and Parliament Square—the hearts of London and the British Empire, containing the National Gallery and the Houses of Parliament—are, in effect, traffic round-abouts where the pedestrian is stranded. By closing off strategic routes to car traffic, the Rogers plan transforms these round-abouts into "people places," where pedestrians can enjoy the sense of urban scale and appreciate the presence of major public monuments.

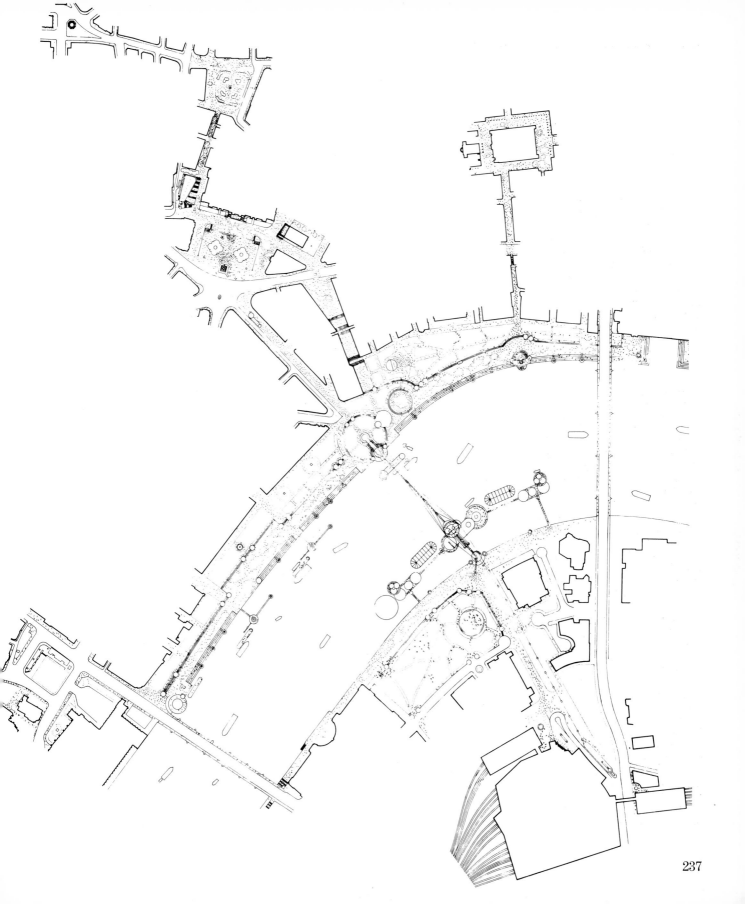

237

*Perspective showing Underground
and below-grade highway;
preliminary sketch; model.*

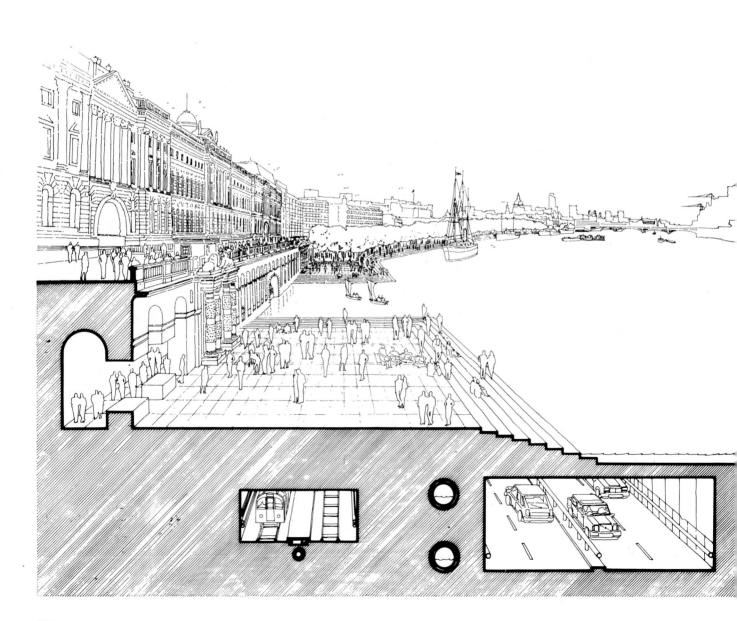

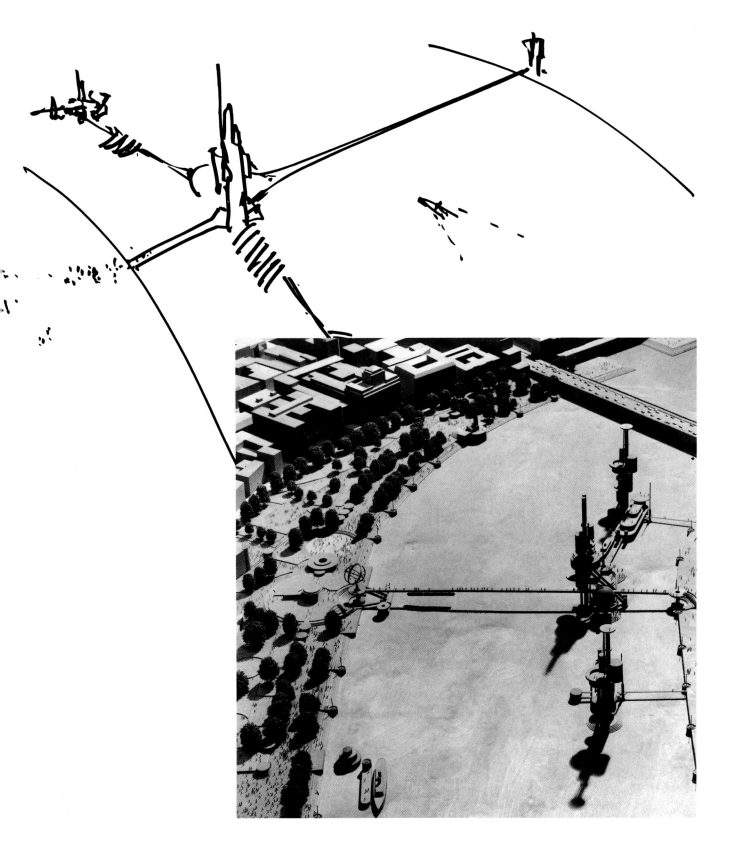

Model of pedestrian bridge over the Thames; elevation.

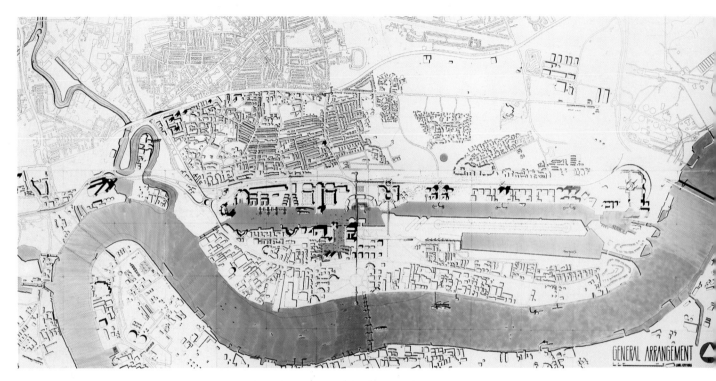

GENERAL ARRANGEMENT

The first of Rogers' large-scale urban master plans, the Royal Docks Strategic Plan is an appropriately robust framework for the vast, derelict urban wasteland on the fringes of central London which until the 1960s was the thriving mercantile heart of the city's river-based industry. Docklands is one of the greatest casualties of the laissez-faire policies of the Thatcher government of the 1980s, which left the redevelopment of inner-city sites to market forces. The Royal Docks, composed of three interconnected water basins with fifteen kilometers of quayside, covers nearly one thousand acres currently occupied by empty warehouse buildings and surrounded by a fragmented array of low-quality housing. Promoted by a consortium of private developers, Rogers sought to provide a physical infrastructure for an area that has no development plan promoted by central or local government.

The strategic plan envisages an overlapping grid of roads, railway, water, services, and landscape systems integrated by a continuous structure of public spaces and visual axes. A series of linear developments along the quayside are punctuated by strong geometric shapes—circular or radial forms marked by vertical elements—that act as visual reference points to the main axes of communication. The master plan provides the rudimentary skeleton for the flexible development of mixed-use neighborhoods that relate to the scale of the docks and the presence of the water.

A more detailed proposal for the Royal Albert Dock, the longest of the three basins, envisages a two- and three-level crescent-shaped shopping complex at the eastern end of the basin. A toplit radial route acts as an internal street for the retail area, culminating in a grand pavilion overlooking the full length of the basin. Along the northern edge of the dock is a number of regular development plots for a business park, while a series of leisure and recreational buildings support the water-based activities.

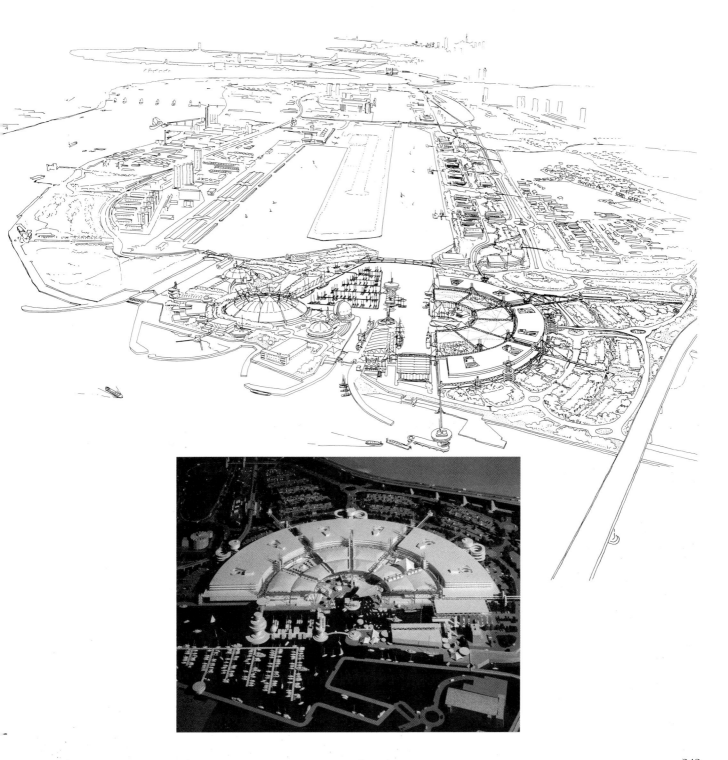

South Bank Centre Crystal Palace, London, 1994

Since the late 1970s, the South Bank has preoccupied Rogers as a missed opportunity for London. With spectacular views of central London and the Thames, and access to the new Channel Tunnel Terminal at Waterloo Station, the South Bank is at the geographical heart of the metropolis, although it is currently perceived as a marginal location. Building on the Royal Academy plans for London, Rogers has tackled the regeneration of the South Bank Centre, a complex of postwar Brutalist arts buildings adjacent to the elegant modernist Royal Festival Hall, designed by Leslie Martin and Peter Moro in 1951. The site is bounded by Waterloo and Hungerford Bridges and is close to Denys Lasdun's National Theatre and IBM Building. The tired but heroic arts center, with its overhead concrete walkways and empty terraces, is well known for the caliber of its performances and exhibitions but is notorious for the poor quality of its public spaces. The principal design objective of the competition-winning scheme is to transform the South Bank Centre from an unwelcoming arts complex into a vibrant, mixed-use area that is open and accessible for most hours of the day.

The practice's approach is characteristically bold. The Crystal Palace, which refers directly to Joseph Paxton's pioneering glass-and-iron construction for the Great Exhibition of 1851, is an all-embracing curved glass roof that encloses a large open public foyer for the individual arts buildings within the South Bank Centre. The sailing roof encloses the Hayward Gallery, the Queen Elizabeth Hall, and the Purcell Room, the three main institutions that clus-

ter around Waterloo Bridge, but stops short of the Royal Festival Hall. The glass-and-steel structure is a social and environmental canopy that recaptures the under-utilized and windswept terraces, giving a unified architectural expression to the disparate buildings. A sequence of protected public spaces relates directly to the arts buildings and their entrances. The overall form of the grand curved roof, composed of modular steel components, assists patterns of air movement through the canopy skin with natural air forces driving ventilation in the non-air-conditioned volume.

Pedestrian movement is mainly at ground level, reinforcing connections between the arts complex and the surrounding street pattern. A central spine between the Royal Festival Hall and the expanded Hayward Gallery forms a direct route to the river's edge, leading to a new underground auditorium and open-air arena along the embankment in front of the Royal Festival Hall. A new pedestrian *passarelle* with travelators creates a direct link between the north and south banks, increasing accessibility to the South Bank Centre and the rest of London. Two float-

ing islands under Waterloo and Hungerford bridges are conceived as floating villages, with shops and public activities along the river's edge.

By casting a protective net over the existing public space and riverside walkway, the master plan for the South Bank extends Rogers' notion of the totally flexible framework to its natural limits. If built, the proposals may have a regenerative impact on the wider South Bank neighborhood, as did the Centre Pompidou and Place Beaubourg on the surrounding Marais district in Paris.

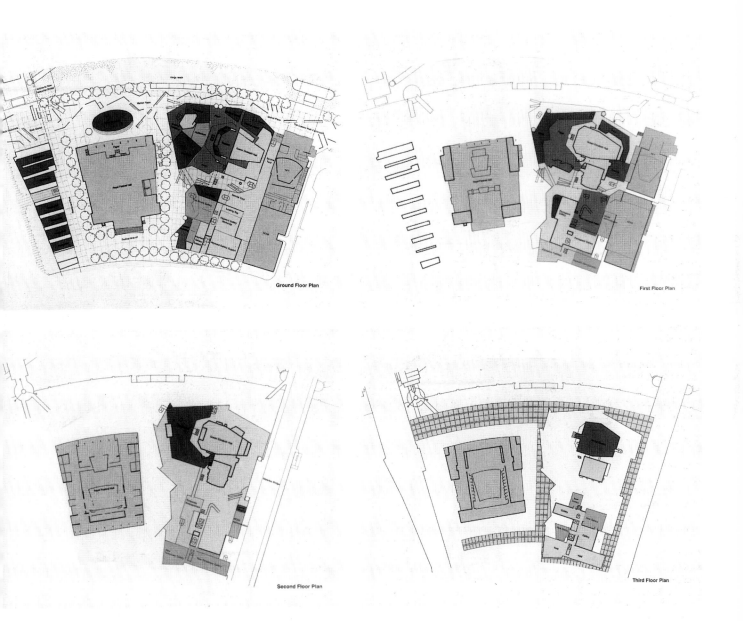

Ground Floor Plan

First Floor Plan

Second Floor Plan

Third Floor Plan

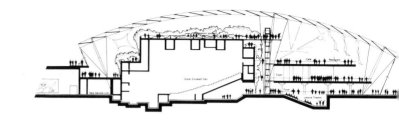

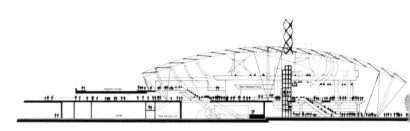

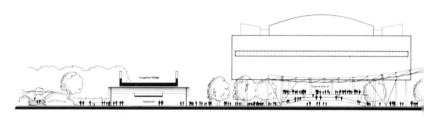

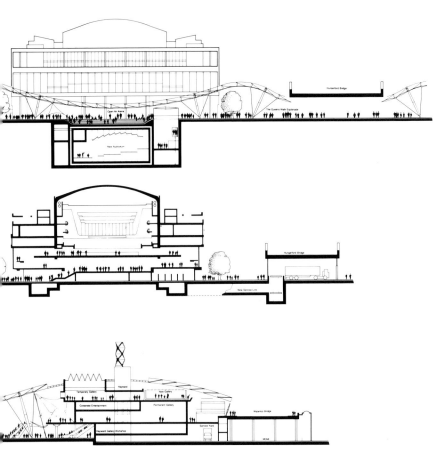

Redevelopment of the Banks of the Arno River, Florence, 1983

A detailed scientific and historical analysis of the city's relationship with its river generates a comprehensive master plan for the entire length of the Arno's urban trajectory. The scheme recognizes the river's role as a double-edged sword in the life of the city: it is both a resource and a threat. Until recently the Arno, lined by streets and riverside facilities, was an active element in the city's social and commercial fabric. Increased vehicular traffic and the erection of antiflood balustrades (following the serious flood of 1969) have cut off pedestrians from the river. As a result, the Arno has been used more as a rubbish heap and collector of silt and rubble than as an extension of the public realm.

Rogers' strategy is a linear park that complements and enhances the public space of the city, bringing visitors and residents into direct contact with the water. A new serviced route runs for eight kilometers between the suburbs of Varlungo and Indiano, consolidating and extending ancient paths in the city center adjacent to Florence's historic monuments and the Ponte Vecchio. Temporary structures, tents, stalls, and booths cutting into the banks or floating on rafts re-create a pleasant waterside environment for the exclusive use of the pedestrian. Lightweight steps and ramps provide access for pedestrians and service vehicles, supplementing existing routes.

The linear park acknowledges the changing nature of the river's water levels. Rather than designing a cumbersome structure that would be immune to flooding, the design simply accepts the fact that at certain times of year the pedestrian embankment will be flooded and become inaccessible. As the water lev-

els rise, the activities recede. Happily, the "danger period" does not coincide with the intense tourist season, when Florence suffers most from overcrowding and needs relief from human congestion. By developing an alternative strategy that does not slavishly respond to "peak demands" (this would have required impermeable concrete walls permanently cutting off the city from the river), the proposal turns a potential liability into an asset, a characteristic of Rogers' design approach to traffic flows, energy demand, and environmental performance of buildings and cities. The concept of the linear park that consolidates and extends the public realm of a city has become a prototypical urban device employed by Rogers in the practice's plans for London, Berlin, and Shanghai .

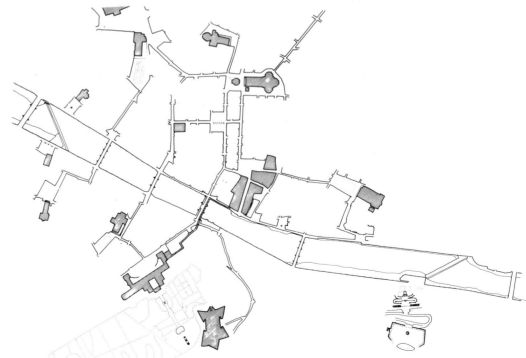

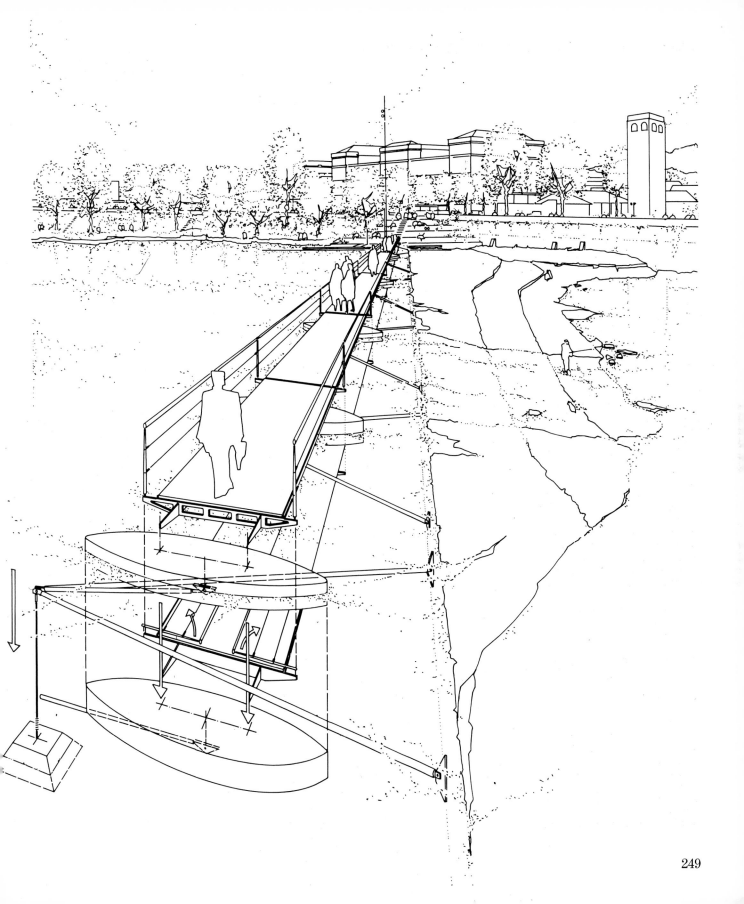

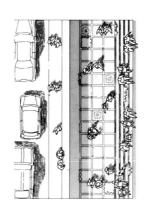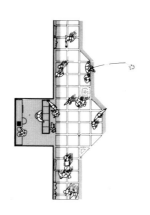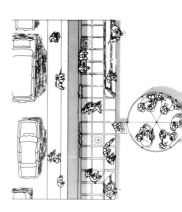

*Overall perspective of proposal;
details showing specific elements.*

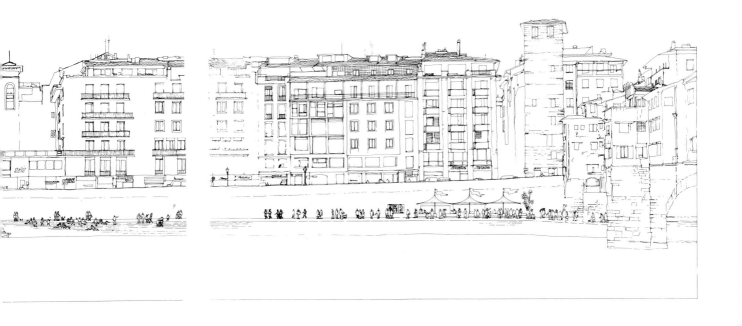

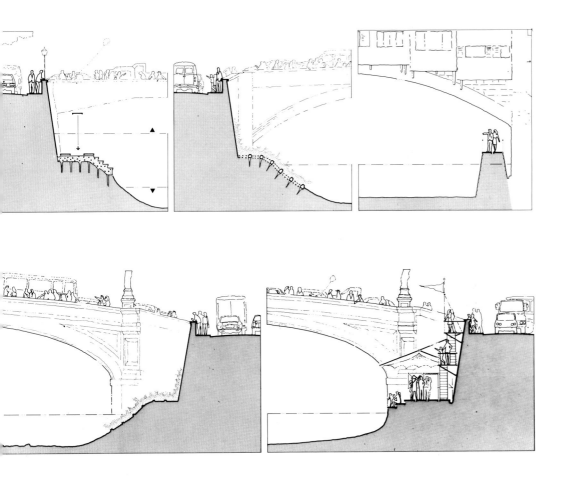

With the sudden reemergence of Berlin's Potsdamerplatz as a symbol of Germany's reunification, the site has become a polemical battleground for the contemporary architectural and urban debate. Rogers' master plan is a statement of faith in the dense, twenty-four-hour-a-day city: a contemporary reinterpretation of the Baroque city plan creating an environmentally balanced continuum of public spaces, streets, and squares.

Until 1945 Potsdamerplatz was the liveliest place in Berlin, the city's main transport hub, full of vitality and architectural variety. Originally a market, it became a circus with roads leading to Potsdam and Charlottenburg, which was subsequently separated by city gates from the octagonal Leipzigerplatz and the seventeenth-century Baroque quarter of Friedrichstadt. After 1945, the area was leveled into a no-man's-land between East and West Berlin. Adjacent to the Kulturforum (with Mies van der Rohe's National Art Gallery and Hans Scharoun's Philharmonic) and the Friedrichstadt, the redevelopment of the Potsdamerplatz represents a "collision between potentially conflicting forces: between the search for private profit and the making of a public monument, and between the creation of a confident contemporary architecture and the re-creation of traditional forms" (Dan Cruickshank, "Potsdamer Platz Designs Strive to Reunite Berlin," *Architectural Review*, Jan. 1992, 20).

The master plan developed by Rogers for a consortium of private companies, including Daimler Benz and Sony, reestablishes Potsdamerplatz as a major civic space. A fan-shaped, radiating grid of streets emanates from the square, emphasizing and defining its role as a central urban node. A dense pattern of buildings and open spaces occupies the resulting triangular urban segments, establishing a hierarchy of public and semipublic spaces. A north-south landscaped wedge acts as a "green lung" for the new development and as a major new civic amenity for the neighborhood. The generous open space is the centerpoint of the ecological strategy that will contribute to energy conservation by maximizing daylight and natural ventilation for adjoining buildings.

Acknowledging and reinforcing the public transport potential of the area, the master plan envisages a car-free environment that would transform the nature and quality of the spaces between the buildings, knitting together the fragmented no-man's-land with a new infrastructure of landscaped urban routes in central Berlin. By increasing the height and density of development as one moves away from the square, the retail and commercial potential of the area is maximized. While daytime activity animates the wider district, evening and nighttime activities are focused around Potsdamerplatz and Leipzigerplatz, with cinemas, theaters, streetside cafés, and bars complementing the urban density and variety of Berlin city life.

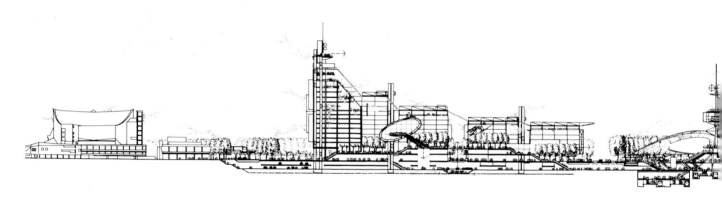

254

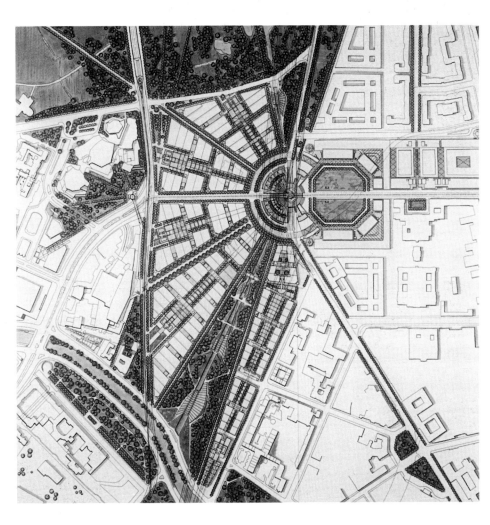

The new financial and business district for Shanghai is the practice's most comprehensive design for a sustainable, compact twenty-four-hour city. The population in Shanghai is expected to grow from thirteen million to seventeen million in five years, consolidating its role as the commercial hub of China and a major force in world finance. Shanghai is a dense, vibrant city with the tree-lined riverside promenade of the Bund facing the one-kilometer-wide Huangpo River. Across the river lies the Pudong, a vast development area that contains the teardrop-shaped site for a new financial district. The city authorities intended to turn the new district into a Western-style inward-looking ghetto planned around the car.

Rogers' environmentally driven approach creates a mixed-use commercial and residential area that relies on an extensive public transport network. The circular diagram is organized around a central park with radiating landscaped boulevards linked by three concentric avenues. The first carries pedestrians and cyclists; the second, trams and buses; and the third, the main car routes. In this way, the needs of the local community are located within walking distance, away from through-traffic.

New neighborhood units, each with its own distinct character and massing, are focused on the six main transport interchanges. Offices and shops are concentrated around the underground stations, while residential buildings, together with the hospitals, schools, and community facilities for the district, are near the central park and the river. By varying the height of buildings along the streets and squares,

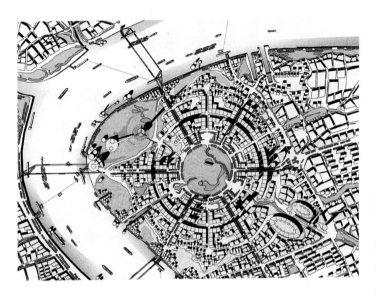

daylight penetration is ma[x]imized, presenting a strong skyl[ine] to the river and old Shanghai.

With roads, traffic, cong[es]tion, and pollution kept to a mi[ni]mum and with the design of en[er]gy-conscious buildings, the n[ew] district would reduce overall en[er]gy consumption by 70 perce[nt] compared to a conventional co[m]mercial development of a simi[lar] size. In effect, the Lu Jia Zui m[as]ter plan constitutes a blueprint [for] sustainable urban developme[nt] that offers a radically different [al]ternative to most commerc[ial] projects of this scale. While [its] approach suggests an innovati[ve] ecological and physical framew[ork] for the city of the future, it [re]flects the influence of late-ni[ne]teenth- and early-twentieth-c[en]tury concepts of urban grow[th,] community, and containment [by] Patrick Geddes, Ebene[zer] Howard, and in particular, Patr[ick] Abercrombie's ideas enshrined [in] the 1943 Plan for London.

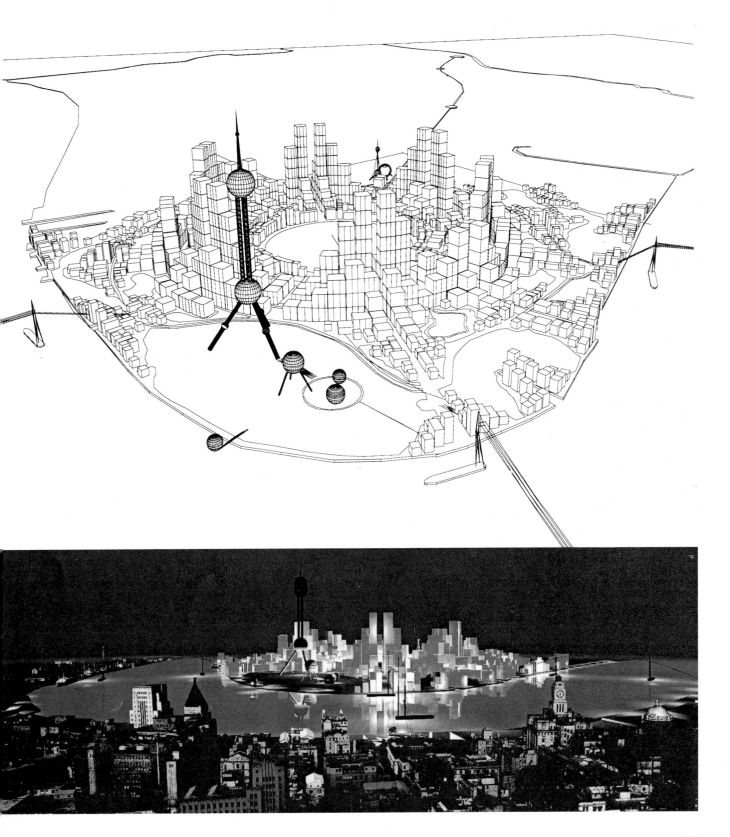

Computer-generated model; study of volumes for environmental impact; model.

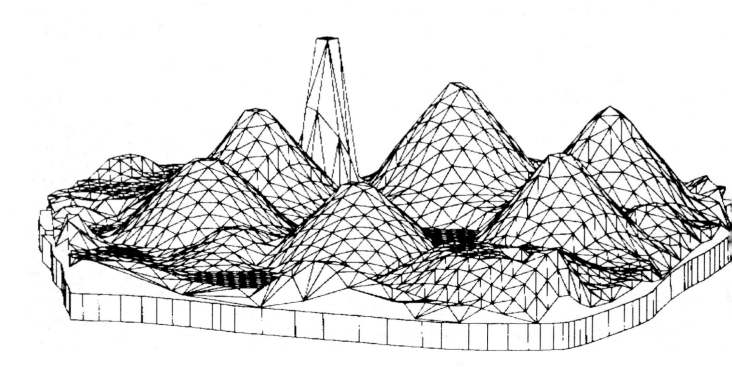

Appendices

Richard Rogers was born of Italian parents in Florence in 1933. He studied at the Architectural Association in London and with Norman Foster at Yale University. In 1963 Rogers and Foster returned to England, where they founded Team 4, a small, avant-garde studio responsible for the famous project for the Reliance Controls factory. He worked with Su Rogers from 1967 to 1971 and, starting in 1970, with Renzo Piano. Rogers and Piano collaborated on the winning competition entry for a cultural center in Paris; that project, the Centre Georges Pompidou, was completed in 1977.

The same year, Rogers, along with John Young, Marco Goldschmied, and Mike Davies, founded the Richard Rogers Partnership in London. In 1978 the firm won the competition for the Lloyd's Building, and since then they have had numerous commissions, both public and private, in the United Kingdom, Germany, France, the United States, and Japan, many of which have won awards for their innovative character and quality. Most recently, the firm built the Channel 4 Television Headquarters in London and the European Court of Human Rights in Strasbourg. In addition to its headquarters in London, the firm has offices in Berlin and Tokyo. The firm's work has been widely published; it has also been exhibited at the Museum of Modern Art in New York, the Venice Biennale, the Centre Pompidou, and London's Royal Academy of Arts (in a 1986 show "New Architecture: Foster, Rogers, Stirling").

Rogers has taught and lectured throughout England and the United States. He was knighted in recognition of his contributions to architecture. He has received the Royal Gold Medal for Architecture from the Royal Institute of British Architects in 1985. He became a Chevalier de l'Ordre Nationale de la Legion d'Honneur in 1986 and was elected to the Ordre des Artes et des Lettres in 1985. He is president of the Architecture Foundation and of the National Tenants Association; he was chairman of the board of directors of the Tate Gallery from 1981 to 1989. Other cultural activities include the promotion and explanation of contemporary architecture on radio and television. Rogers has been a juror for many international competitions. He has participated in conferences and written essays and articles on his work, including *Architecture: A Modern View* and *A New London*. He was vice president of the Arts Council of England in 1994, and in 1995 he delivered the Reith Lectures for the BBC.

Project Credits

Projects are listed in chronological order.

reek Vean House
*eock, Cornwall, United Kingdom,
'66–68*

lient: Marcus and Rene Brumwell
esign Team: Team 4
aurie Abbott, Norman Foster,
'endy Foster, Frank Peacock,
ichard Rogers, Su Rogers
 structural Engineer: Anthony Hunt
ssociates
ervices Engineer: Hanscombe
artnership
andscape Architect: Landscape
esign Partnership
wards: RIBA Award for Work of
utstanding Quality 1969 (first
IBA award for a private house)

ogers House
*imbledon, United Kingdom,
'68–69*

lient: Dr. and Mrs. Rogers
esign Team: Richard + Su Rogers
ierre Botschi, John Doggart,
agrid Morris, Richard Rogers, Su
ogers, Richard Russell, John
oung
structural Engineer: Anthony Hunt
ssociates
uantity Surveyor: Hanscombe
artnership
andscape Architect: Landscape
esign Partnership
wards: Representative of British
rchitecture at the 1967 Paris Bien-
ale

ip-Up House
968–71

lient: Various
esign Team: Richard + Su Rogers
ally Appleby, John Doggart, Marco
oldschmied, Richard Rogers, Su
ogers, John Young
structural Engineer: Anthony Hunt
ssociates
ervices Engineer: Max Fordham
uantity Surveyor: Hanscombe
artnership
wards: First "House for Today,"
968, sponsored by Dupont; RIBA
esearch Award, 1970

Centre Georges Pompidou
Paris, 1971–77

Client: Ministère des Affaires Cul-
turelles/Ministère de l'Education
Nationale
Design Team: Piano + Rogers
Laurie Abbott, Cuno Brullmann,
Hans-Peter Bysaeth, Michael Davies,
Mike Dowd, Philippe Dupont, Gian-
franco Franchini, Claude Gallot,
Marco Goldschmied, Françoise
Gouinguenet, Eric Holt, Shunji
Ishida, Arika Komiyama, William
Logan, Johanna Lohse, Peter Merz,
Hiroshi Naruse, Nori Okabe, Renzo
Piano, Bernard Plattner, Judith Ray-
mond, Richard Rogers, Ken Rupard,
Jan Sircus, Claudette Spielmann,
Alan Stanton, Hiroyuki Takahashi,
Colette Valensi, Reiner Verbizh,
John Young, Walter Zbinden
Structural Engineer: Ove Arup &
Partners
Services Engineer: Ove Arup &
Partners
Quantity Surveyor: Ove Arup &
Partners
Awards: International Union of
Architects August Perret Prize,
1975–78

Patscentre Research Laboratory
*Melbourn, Hertfordshire, United
Kingdom, 1976–83*

Client: PA International Manage-
ment Consultants, Inc.
Design Team: Piano + Rogers
Sally Appleby, Pierre Botschi,
Michael Burkhart, Michael Davies,
Sally Eaton, Peter Flack, Marco
Goldschmied, Don Gray, John
McAslan, Natalie Moore, Alphons
Oberhofer, Brendan O'Brien, Renzo
Piano, Mark Roche, Richard Rogers,
Richard Soundy, David Thom, Peter
Ullathorne, Neil Winder, John Young
Structural Engineer: Felix J.
Samuely & Partners
Services Engineer: Hancock Design
Co-ordinates/David WG Bedwell &
Partners/YRM Engineers/Cressey
Wilder Associates
Quantity Surveyor: Gleeds
Landscape Architect: Landscape
Design Partnership

Awards: Financial Times Award for
Most Outstanding Work of Indus-
trial Architecture, 1976; RIBA
Regional Award, 1977

Lloyd's of London
London, 1978–86

Client: Corporation of Lloyd's of
London
Design Team: Richard Rogers Part-
nership
Laurie Abbott, Graham Anthony,
Robert Barnes, Susan Blythe, Kieran
Breen, Julieann Coleman, Ian David-
son, Michael Davies, Maureen Diffley,
Janet Dunsford, Michael Fairley,
Marco Goldschmied, Mark Guard,
Philip Gumuchdjian, Ivan Harbour,
Roger Huntley, Eva Jiricna, Andrew
Jones, Wendy Judd, Amarjit Kalsi,
Kathy Kerr, Stig Larsen, Malcolm
Last, John McAslan, Michael
McGarry, Colin MacKenzie, Sue
McMillan, Peter McMunn, David
Mark, Richard Marzec, Andrew Mor-
ris, Niki van Oosten, Frank Peacock,
Robert Peebles, Gennaro Picardi,
Elizabeth Post, Richard Rogers,
Peter St. John, Henrietta Salveson,
Georgina Savva, Kiyo Sawoaka,
Richard Soundy, Stephen Stang, Alan
Stanton, Graham Stirk, Clare
Strasser, Jude Taylor, Peter Thomas,
Jamie Troughton, Andrew Weston,
Chris Wilkinson, Joseph Wilson, Yasu
Yada, John Young
Structural Engineer: Ove Arup &
Partners
Services Engineer: Ove Arup &
Partners
Quantity Surveyor: Monk Dunstone
Mahon & Sears
Lighting: Friederich Wagner of
Lichttehnische Planung
Acoustics: Sandy Brown Associates
Awards: Civic Trust Award, 1987;
Financial Times Architecture at
Work Award, 1987; Eternit Eighth
International Prize for Architec-
ture, Special Mention, 1988; RIBA
National Award, 1988

Fleetguard Manufacturing Plant
Quimper, Brittany, France, 1979–81

Client: Cummins Engine Company/

Ville de Quimper
Design Team: Richard Rogers Part-
nership
Ram Ahronov, Sally Eaton, Ian
Davidson, Marco Goldschmied,
Kunimi Hayashi, Amarjit Kalsi, Sue
McMillan, Richard Rogers, Richard
Soundy, John Young
Structural Engineer: Ove Arup &
Partners
Services Engineer: Ove Arup &
Partners
Quantity Surveyor: Northcroft
Neighbour & Nicholson
Awards: Premier Award for Excep-
tional Steel Structure, France, 1982;
Constructa-Preis, 1986

Coin Street Redevelopment
London, 1979–83

Client: Greycoats Commercial
Estates Limited
Design Team: Richard Rogers Part-
nership
Laurie Abbott, Michael Davies, Jan
Dunsford, Marco Goldschmied,
Philip Gumuchdjian, Amarjit Kalsi,
Sue McMillan, Andrew Morris, Tim
Oakshott, Richard Rogers, John
Sorcinelli, Peter Thomas, Chris
Wilkinson, John Young
Structural Engineer: Ove Arup &
Partners
Services Engineer: Ove Arup &
Partners
Quantity Surveyor: Gardiner &
Theobald

Inmos Microchip Factory
Newport, Gwent, Wales, 1982

Client: Inmos Limited
Design Team: Richard Rogers Part-
nership
Julia Barfield, David Bartlett,
Pierre Botschi, Michael Davies,
Sally Eaton, Michael Elkan, Marco
Goldschmied, Kunimi Hayashi, Tim
Inskip, Amarjit Kalsi, Peter
McMunn, Richard Rogers, John
Young
Structural Engineer: Anthony Hunt
Associates
Services Engineer: YRM Engineers
Quantity Surveyor: Hanscombe
Partnership

Awards: Eurostructpress Award, 1983; Financial Times Architecture at Work Award, Commendation, 1983; The Structural Steel Design Award, 1982; Constructa-Preis, 1986

PA Technology Centre
Princeton, New Jersey, 1982–85

Client: PA International Management Consultant Inc.
Design Team: Richard Rogers Partnership with Kelburgh & Lee Architects (USA)
Ram Ahronov, Pierre Botschi, Michael Davies, Marco Goldschmied, John McAslan, Gennaro Picardi, Richard Rogers, John Young
Structural Engineer: Ove Arup & Partners/Robert Silman (USA)
Services Engineer: Ove Arup & Partners/Syska & Hennesy Inc. (USA)
Quantity Surveyor: Hanscombe Partnership
Associate Architect: Kelburgh & Lee Architects (USA)

National Gallery Extension
London, 1982

Client: Speyhawk plc/Secretary of State for the Environment
Design Team: Richard Rogers Partnership
Laurie Abbott, Julia Barfield, Michael Davies, Marco Goldschmied, Philip Gumuchdjian, Di Hope, Sue McMillan, Andrew Morris, Gennaro Picardi, Richard Rogers, Peter St. John, John Sorcinelli, Richard Soundy, Peter Thomas, John Young
Structural Engineer: Ove Arup & Partners
Services Engineer: YRM Engineers
Quantity Surveyor: Axtell Yates Hallet

Redevelopment of the banks of the Arno River
Florence, 1983

Client: Comune di Firenze
Design Team: Richard Rogers Partnership with Claudio Cantella

Claudio Cantella, Michael Davies, Marco Goldschmied, Philip Gumuchdjian, Andrew Morris, Gennaro Picardi, Richard Rogers, Alan Stanton, John Young
Hydraulic Engineer: Enrico Bougleux

Royal Docks Strategic Plan
Docklands, London, 1984–86

Client: London Docklands Development Corporation
Design Team: Richard Rogers Partnership
Laurie Abbott, Kieran Breen, Michael Davies, Marco Goldschmied, Mark Roche, Richard Rogers, John Young
Services Engineer: Ove Arup & Partners
Transport Planning: Ove Arup & Partners
Commercial Advice: Debenham Tewson & Chinnocks
Landscape Architect: William Gillispie & Partners
Townscape Advice: Gorden Cullen, Kenneth Brown

Thames Reach Housing
London, 1984–87

Client: Croudace Construction Ltd.
Design Team: Richard Rogers Partnership
Peter Angrave, Paul Cook, Ian Gibson, Marco Goldschmied, Sarah Granville, Ian Hopton, Tim Inskip, Janette Mackie, Mark Roche, Richard Rogers, John Young
Structural Engineer: Hay Barry & Partners
Services Engineer: The Sinnett Partnership
Quantity Surveyor: Melvyn Newell
Landscape Architect: Rendel & Branch
Awards: Royal Institute of British Architects Housing Design Award, 1989

Billingsgate Securities Market
London, 1985–88

Client: Citicorp/Citibank
Design Team: Richard Rogers Partnership

Peter Angrave, David Bartlett, Pierre Botschi, John Cannon, Philip Chalmers, Tim Colquhoun, Michael Davies, Patrick Davies, Sally Draper, Marco Goldschmied, Ian Hopton, Shahab Kasmai-Tehran, Lester Korzilius, Clodagh Latimer, Mary Le Jeune, Amanda Levete, Kevin Lewenden, Avtar Lotay, John Lowe, Ernest Lowinger, Luke Lowings, Janette Mackie, Richard Marzec, Malcolm McGowan, Arif Mehmood, Natalie Moore, Frank Peacock, Mark Roche, Richard Rogers, Seth Stein, Peter Thomas, John Young
Structural Engineer: Ove Arup & Partners
Services Engineer: Ove Arup & Partners
Quantity Surveyor: Hanscombe Partnership
Lighting: Lighting Design Partnership
Awards: Royal Institute of British Architects Regional Awards, 1988; Royal Institute of British Architects Awards, 1989; Civic Trust Award, 1989; BBC Design Awards Finalist, 1990

London As It Could Be
Royal Academy, 1986

Client: Royal Academy
Design Team: Richard Rogers Partnership
Laurie Abbott, Philip Gumuchdjian, Stephen Pimbley, Richard Rogers
Structural Engineer: Ove Arup & Partners

Pump House
Docklands, London, 1987–88

Client: LDDC/Williams Halcrow & Partners
Design Team: Richard Rogers Partnership
Brian Bell, Paul Cook, Michael Davies, William Firebrace, Marco Goldschmied, Tim Inskip, Amarjit Kalsi, Maralyn Lai, Werner Lang, Richard Rogers, John Sorcinelli, John Young
Structural Engineer: William Halcrow & Partners
Awards: Constructa-Preis, 1992

Paternoster Square
London, 1987

Client: Paternoster Consortium Limited
Design Team: Richard Rogers Partnership
Laurie Abbott, Tim Colquhoun, Michael Davies, Ruth Elias, Marco Goldschmied, Ivan Harbour, Tina Himsley, Andrew Jones, Shahab Kasmai-Tehran, John Lowe, Richard Rogers, Graham Stirk, Josh Wilson, John Young
Structural Engineer: Ove Arup & Partners
Quantity Surveyor: Davis Bellfield & Everest
Collaborator: Lifschutz Davison
Design: Doris Saatchi, Jim Allan Design

Autocity
Massy, France, 1987

Client: Groupement Rhodanien de Construction, Lyon
Design Team: Richard Rogers Partnership
Laurie Abbott, Kieran Breen, Michael Davies, Florian Fischötter, Marco Goldschmied, Lennart Grut, Stig Larsen, John McFarland, Richard Rogers, Stephen Spence, John Young
Structural Engineer: Ove Arup & Partners/OtH Paris/RFR, Paris
Services Engineer: OtH, Paris
Quantity Surveyor: Thorne Wheatley Associates

Reuters Data Centre
London, 1987–92

Client: Reuters Ltd.
Design Team: Richard Rogers Partnership
Laurie Abbott, Keith Allison, Peter Angrave, Michael Davies, Fiona Galbraith, Marco Goldschmied, Lindsay Gwillam, Ivan Harbour, Sze-King Kan, Swantje Kühn, John Lowe, Ernest Lowinger, Robert Peebles, Cynthia Poole, Richard Rogers, John Young
Structural Engineer: Ove Arup & Partners
Services Engineer: YRM Engi-

ers/Matthew Hall
antity Surveyor: Webb & Tapley
ards: Royal Institute of British
chitects Nation Award, 1993

buki-cho Tower
kyo, 1987–93

ent: K-One Corporation
sign Team: Richard Rogers Part-
rship
urie Abbott, Maxine Campbell,
chael Davies, Florian Eames,
chael Elkan, Stuart Forbes-
ller, Marco Goldschmied, Horishi
bio, Eric Holt, Miyuli Kurihara,
g Larsen, John Lowe, Richard
gers, Atsushi Sasa, Kyoko
mioka, Yoshi Uchiyama, Christo-
er Wan, Benjamin Warner, John
ung
ructural Engineer: Umezawa
sign Office
rvices Engineer: ES Associates
-architect: Architect 5

arseille International Airport
arignane, France, 1989–92

ent: Chambre de Commerce et
ndustrie de Marseille
esign Team: Richard Rogers Part-
rship
ter Barber, Pierre Botschi, Tim
lquhoun, Michael Davies, Pascale
bbon, Marco Goldschmied,
nnart Grut, Enrique Hermoso-
era, Oliver Kühn, Swantje Kühn,
chael McNamara, Andrew Par-
dge, Gregoris Patsalosavvis, Kim
aazi, Richard Rogers, John Smith,
hn Young
ructural Engineer: Ove Arup &
rtners
rvices Engineer: OtH Mediter-
née
antity Surveyor: CEC
-architect: Atelier 9/ETA

rminal 5, Heathrow Airport
ndon, 1989–2016

ient: BAA
esign Team: Richard Rogers Part-
rship
urie Abbott, Andy Bryce, Oliver
llignon, Mark Collins, Tim
lquhoun, Michael Davies, Chris

Dawson, James Finestone, Florian
Fischötter, Marco Goldschmied,
Jorge Gomendio, Lennart Grut,
Ivan Harbour, John Höpfner, Jenny
Jones, Sze-King Kan, Shahab Kas-
mai- Tehran, Marcus Lee, Carmel
Lewin, Avtar Lotay, Steve Martin,
Mark Newton, Robert Peebles,
Cynthia Poole, Tim O'Sullivan,
Susan Rice, Richard Rogers, Simon
Smithson, Andrew Strickland, Taka
Tezuka, Yuli Toh, Fai Tsang,
Andrew Tyley, Katherina Walter-
spiel, Christopher Wan, Megan
Williams, Yoshiyuki Uchiyama,
John Young
Structural Engineer: Ove Arup &
Partners
Services Engineer: Ove Arup &
Partners
Quantity Surveyor: Bovis

European Court of Human Rights
Strasbourg, France, 1989–95

Client: Conseil de l'Europe
Design Team: Richard Rogers Part-
nership with Atelier Claude Bucher
Laurie Abbott, Peter Angrave,
Eike Becker, Michael Davies, Karin
Egge, Marco Goldschmied, Lennart
Grut, Ivan Harbour, Amarjit Kalsi,
Sze-King Kan, Carmel Lewin,
Avtar Lotay, John Lowe, Louise
Palomba, Kim Quazi, Richard
Rogers, Pascale Rousseau, Yuli
Toh, Sarah Tweedie, Andrew Tyley,
Yoshiyuki Uchiyama, John Young
Structural Engineer: Ove Arup &
Partners/Ominium Technique
Europeén
Services Engineer: Ove Arup &
Partners/Ominium Technique
Europeén
Quantity Surveyor: Thorne Wheat-
ley Associates
Co-architects: Atelier Claude Bucher
Landscape Architect: David Jarvis
Associates/Dan Kiley
Lighting: Lighting Design Partner-
ship

Tokyo Forum
Tokyo, 1990

Client: Mitsubishi
Design Team: Richard Rogers Part-

nership
Laurie Abbott, Peter Angrave,
Michael Davies, Fiona Galbraith,
Marco Goldschmied, Shahab Kas-
mai-Tehran, Hiroshi Kawana, Avtar
Lotay, Michael McNamara, Mark
Newton, Richard Rogers, Masaaki
Sekiya, Stephen Spence, Graham
Stirk, Benjamin Warner, John
Young
Structural Engineer: Ove Arup &
Partners
Services Engineer: Ove Arup &
Partners
Acoustics: Arup Acoustics

Michael Elias House
Los Angeles, California, 1990–91

Client: Michael Elias
Design Team: Richard Rogers Part-
nership
Laurie Abbott, Michael Davies,
Stuart Forbes-Waller, Marco Gold-
schmied, Cynthia Poole, Richard
Rogers, Atsu Sasa, Christopher
Wan, John Young
Structural Engineer: Ove Arup &
Partners
Services Engineer: MB & A, Bur-
bank
Co-architect: Appleton, Mechor and
Associates

Channel 4 Television Headquarters
London, 1990–94

Client: Channel 4 Television Co.
Design Team: Richard Rogers Part-
nership
Laurie Abbott, Yasmine Al-Ani,
Helen Brunskill, Oliver Collignon,
Mark Collins, Mark Darbon,
Michael Davies, Jane Donnelly, Flo-
rian Fischötter, Marco Gold-
schmied, Philip Gumuchdjian,
Jackie Hands, Bjork Haraldsdottir,
Stig Larsen, Carmel Lewin,
Stephen Light, Avtar Loray, Steve
Martin, Andrew Morris, Louise
Palomba, Elizabeth Parr, Kim
Quazi, Susan Rice, Richard Rogers,
Daniel Sibert, Stephen Spence,
Kinna Stallard, Graham Stirk, Yuli
Toh, Alec Vassiliades, Martin
White, Adrian Williams, Megan
Williams, John Young

Structural Engineer: Ove Arup &
Partners
Services Engineer: YRM Engineers
Quantity Surveyor: Wheeler Group

Daiwa Headquarters
London, 1991–92

Client: Daiwa Europe Properties
plc
Architect: Richard Rogers Partner-
ship
Marco Carlini, Fiona Charlesworth,
Alan Davidson, Michael Davies,
Max Fawcett, Russel Gilcrest,
Marco Goldschmied, Jorge Gomen-
dio, Philip Gumuchdjian, Bjork Har-
aldsdottir, Claudia Hoge, Sze-King
Kan, Oliver Kühn, Stig Larsen,
Carmel Lewin, Avtar Lotay, Ernest
Lowinger, Tim O'Sullivan, Louise
Palomba, Matt Parker, Andrew
Partridge, Gregoris Patsalosavvis,
Cynthia Poole, Richard Rogers,
Ulreika Seifritz, John Smith, Simon
Smithson, Stephen Spence, Kinna
Stallard, Graham Stirk, Amarjit
Tamber, Taka Tezuka, Yuli Toh,
Sarah Tweedie, Andrew Tyley,
Yoshiyuki Uchiyama, Duncan Web-
ster, Martin White, Adrian
Williams, Megan Williams, John
Young
Structural Engineer: Ove Arup &
Partners
Services Engineer: Ove Arup &
Partners
Quantity Surveyor: Gardiner &
Theobald

Zoofenster Building
Berlin, 1991–95

Client: Brau und Brunnen, Dort-
mund
Design Team: Richard Rogers Part-
nership
Laurie Abbott, Peter Barber,
Pierre Botschi, Helen Brunskill,
Sabine Coldrey, Oliver Collignon,
Penny Collins, Tim Colquhoun,
Julian Coward, Mark Darbon,
Michael Davies, Katrin Dzenus,
Karin Egge, Stuart Forbes-Waller,
Peter Gibbons, Marco Goldschmied,
Lennart Grut, Jackie Hands, Bjork
Haraldsdottir, John Höpfner, Oliver

Kühn, Swantje Kühn, Naruhiro Kurishima, Stephen Light, Steve Martin, Andrew Partridge, Gregoris Patsalosavvis, Robert Peebles, Cynthia Poole, Richard Rogers, Atsu Sasa, Birgit Schneppenseifen, Yoshiki Shinohara, Simon Smithson, Kinna Stallard, Graham Stirk, Taka Tezuka, Alec Vassiliades, Atsu Wada, Wolfgang Wagner, Christopher Wan, Megan Williams, Andrew Wright, John Young
Structural Engineer: Ove Arup & Partners
Services Engineer: YRM Engineers/Schmidt Reuter
Quantity Surveyor: ECE/Hanscomb
Model Makers: Michael Faibrass, Jackie Hands

John Young Apartment
Thames Reach Housing, London, 1986–89

Client: John Young
Design Team: John Young
Peter Angrave, Amarjit Kalsi
Structural Engineer: Hay Barry & Partners
Services Engineer: Ove Arup & Partners
Quantity Surveyor: Melvyn Newell
Lighting: Lighting Design Partnership
Audiovisual Consultant: Michael Holden
Awards: RIBA Regional Award, 1992

Potsdamerplatz Master Plan
Berlin, 1991

Client: Daimler Benz AG; Sony AG; Hertie; ABB; Haus Vaterland
Design Team: Richard Rogers Partnership
Laurie Abbott, Peter Barbour, Oliver Collignon, Mark Darbon, Alan Davidson, Michael Davies, Marco Goldschmied, Lennart Grut, Ivan Harbour, Amarjit Kalsi, Oliver Kühn, Swantje Kühn, Avtar Lotay, Andrew Partridge, Richard Paul, Richard Rogers, Stephen Spence, Graham Stirk, Hugh Turner, Adrian Williams, John Young

---

Structural Engineer: Ove Arup & Partners
Services Engineer: Ove Arup & Partners

Industrialized Housing System
Korea, 1992

Client: Hanseem
Design Team: Richard Rogers Partnership
Laurie Abbott, Michael Davies, Stuart Forbes-Waller, Marco Goldschmied, John Lowe, Jackie Moore, Richard Paul, Richard Rogers, Andrew Wright, John Young
Structural Engineer: Ove Arup & Partners
Services Engineer: Ove Arup & Partners

Tomigaya Exhibition Space and Turbine Tower
Tokyo, 1992–93

Client: Internal Research
Design Team: Richard Rogers Partnership
Laurie Abbott, Michael Davies, Marco Goldschmied, Richard Rogers, Harriet Watson, Andrew Wright, John Young
Structural Engineer: Ove Arup & Partners/Battle & MacCarthy
Services Engineer: Ove Arup & Partners/Battle & MacCarthy
Quantity Surveyor: Aeronautics Imperial College; Mike Graham

Inland Revenue Headquarters
Nottingham, United Kingdom, 1991

Client: Inland Revenue
Design Team: Richard Rogers Partnership
Laurie Abbott, Yasmin Al-Ani, Mark Darbon, Michael Davies, James Finestone, Stuart Forbes-Waller, Philip Gumuchdjian, Carmel Lewin, Avtar Lotay, John Lowe, Andrew Morris, Louise Palomba, Kim Quazi, Richard Rogers, Stephen Spence, Andrew Tyley, Chris Wan, Andrew Wright, John Young
Structural Engineer: Ove Arup & Partners

Services Engineer: Ove Arup & Partners
Quantity Surveyor: Turner Townsend

Lu Jia Zui Master Plan
Shanghai, 1992

Client: Shanghai Development Corporation
Design Team: Richard Rogers Partnership
Laurie Abbott, Hal Currey, Michael Davies, Marco Goldschmied, Philip Gumuchdjian, Richard Rogers, Simon Smithson, John Young, Andrew Wright
Structural Engineer: Ove Arup & Partners/Guy Battle
Research: Cambridge Architectural Research

Office and Residential Buildings for Daimler Benz
Berlin, 1993–98

Client: Debis Immobilienmanagement GmbH
Design Team: Richard Rogers Partnership
Laurie Abbott, Michael Davies, Marco Goldschmied, Lennart Grut, Dennis Ho, Douglas Keys, James Leatham, Dan Macorie, Nick Malby, Richard Paul, Richard Rogers, Neil Southard, Wolfgang Wagner, Andrew Wright, John Young
Structural Engineer: Weiske & Partner GmbH
Services Engineer: RP & K Sozeitäe
Quantity Surveyor: Davis Langdon Everest

Lloyd's Register of Shipping
Liphook, United Kingdom, 1993

Client: Lloyd's Register of Shipping
Design Team: Richard Rogers Partnership
Yasmin Al-Ani, Mark Darbon, Michael Davies, Janes Finestone, Marco Goldschmied, Jackie Hands, Bjork Haraldsdottir, Ivan Harbour, Stig Larsen, James Leatham, Nick Malby, Jackie Moore, Louise Palomba, Kim Quazi, Richard

---

Rogers, Richard Rose-Casemore Simon Smithson, Neil Southard, John Young
Structural Engineer: Anthony Hunt/YRM Engineers
Services Engineer: Ove Arup & Partners
Landscape Architect: Janet Jack

Law Courts
Bordeaux, France, 1993–96

Client: Ministère de la Justice
Design Team: Richard Rogers Partnership
Stephen Barrett, Elliot Boyd, Michael Davies, Pascale Gibbon, Marco Goldschmied, Lennart Grut, Philip Gumuchdjian, Jackie Hands, Ivan Harbour, Avery Howe, Amarjit Kalsi, Stig Larsen, Carmel Lewin, Avtar Lotay, Louise Palomba, Kim Quazi, Richard Rogers, Simon Smithson, John Young
Structural Engineer: OtH SudOuest/Ove Arup & Partners International Ltd.
Services Engineer: OtH SudOuest
Quantity Surveyor: Interfaces Pa
Acoustics: Sound Research Laboratories
Lighting: Lighting Design Partnership

Bahnhof (Underground Station Prototype)
Berlin, 1993

Client: BVG
Design Team: Richard Rogers Partnership
Sabine Coldrey, Michael Davies, Marco Goldschmied, Jackie Hands, John Höpfner, Avery Howe, Neil Merryweather, Cynthia Poole, Kim Quazi, Richard Rogers, Neil Southard, Stephen Spence, Wolfgang Wagener, John Young
Structural Engineer: David Glover, Gerhard Prodöhl, Ove Arup
Services Engineer: Schmidt Reuter & Partner
Lighting: Lighting Design Partnership
Acoustics: Akustik Labor Berlin

th Bank Centre Crystal Palace
don, 1994

nt: South Bank Centre
ign Team: Richard Rogers Part-
ship
dy Atkin, Elliot Boyd, Maurice
nnan, Maxine Campbell, Fiona
rlesworth, Chris Curtis, Mike
ies, Chris Dawson, Mike Fair-
ss, Pascale Gibon, Russel
hrist, Marco Goldschmied,
lip Gumuchdjian, Jackie Hands,
n Harbour, Dennis Ho, Paul
nson, Amo Kalsi, Richard
gers, Simon Smithson, Yuli Toh,
riet Watson, John Young
ctural Engineer: Ove Arup &
tners
vices Engineer: Ove Arup &
tners
antity Surveyor: Davis Langdon
erest
lestrian Movement: Alan Penn
dscape Architect: Edward
tchinson

tersea Flour Mills Housing
don, 1994–95

nt: British Land
sign Team: Richard Rogers Part-
ship
urice Brennan, Mark Darbon,
ke Davies, Jane Donnely, Mike
rbrass, Marco Goldschmied,
lip Gumuchdjian, Jackie Hands,
ery Howe, Richard Rogers,
ven Spence, Graham Stirk, John
ing
uctural Engineer: Buro Happold
vices Engineer: Buro Happold
antity Surveyor: Hanscomb
tnership

General Bibliography

Entries are listed in chronological order.

General Works on Richard Rogers and on the Richard Rogers Partnership
By Their Own Design. Granada: St. Albans, 1980.
Richard Rogers + Architects. London and New York: Academy Editions, 1985 (hereafter *Rogers + Architects*).
Appleyard, Bryan. *Richard Rogers: A Biography.* London: Faber & Faber, 1986.
Sudjic, Deyan. *New Directions in British Architecture: Foster, Rogers, Stirling.* London: Thames & Hudson, 1986.
"Richard Rogers 1978–1988." *Architecture + Urbanism* 12, 1988 (hereafter "Rogers 1978–1988").
Richard Rogers Partnership: Flexible Framework, London, Tokyo, Berlin, 1991. Berlin: Aedes Gallery, 1991.
Powell, Kenneth. *Richard Rogers.* London/Zurich: Artemis, 1994.
Sudjic, Deyan. *The Architecture of Richard Rogers.* London: Fourth Estate, 1994.

Books and Essays by Richard Rogers
"Patronage." *Architects' Journal,* July 9, 1980, 68–83.
"Observations on Architecture." *Rogers + Architects.*
"Order, Harmony and Modernity." "Rogers 1978–1988."
"Belief in the Future is Rooted in Memory of the Past." *RSA Journal* 136 (Nov. 1988): 873–84.
"Public Responsibility and Private Buildings." *Architecture: Shaping the Future.* La Jolla, Calif: University of California, San Diego, 1989.
"A Case for Modern Architecture." The Smallpiece Lecture, 1989.
"In Praise of the Modern." *Marxism Today,* Mar. 1989, 26–31.
"Pulling Down the Prince." *Times* (London), July 3, 1989, 10–11; reprinted in *Architectural Design* Profile 79, vol. 59, no. 5–6, 70.
Architecture: A Modern View. New York: Thames & Hudson, 1990.

"Streets for People." *Arch +,* Oct. 1990, 85–87.
"The Future is Just Beginning." *Independent,* Feb. 13, 1991, 19.
A New London. With Mark Fisher. London: Penguin, 1992; extracts in *Sunday Times Magazine* (London), Mar. 1, 1992, 16–24.
Architektur: Ein Plädoyer für die Moderne. Campus Verlag, 1993.
"Civic Duties." *Sunday Times: Culture* (London), Oct. 24, 1993, 7–9.
"Cities for a Small Planet." The Reith Lectures 1995, BBC Radio 4; reprinted in *Independent,* Feb. 13–Mar. 13, 1995 (on Mondays).

Interviews with Richard Rogers
Sharp, Dennis. "Rogers inside out." *Building,* Apr. 6, 1979, 86–73.
Bragg, Melvyn. "Melvyn Bragg Interviews Richard Rogers." *Art & Design,* Nov. 1985, 34–41.
"Richard Rogers: Architect and Influence." *Vogue,* Oct. 1986, 302–3, 362.
"Vision for London." *Controspazio,* "Richard Rogers," Feb. 1992, 8–24.
Pawley, Martin. "Sir Richard Rogers." *World Architecture,* July 1992, 32–33.
"Das Tor zum Osten." *Lettre Internationale,* June 1993, 76–79.

Profiles of Richard Rogers
"Rogers Goes Gold." *Building,* Feb. 8, 1985, 33–35.
Silver, Nathan. "Royal Gold Medal for Architecture 1985." *Architect & Builder,* Mar. 1985, 14–19.
Glancey, Jonathan. "High Tech Midas." *RIBA Journal,* June 1985, 18–21.
"Rogers: School, Survival and Success." *Architects' Journal,* Mar. 12, 1986, 36–53.
Banham, Reyner. "A proper old-fashioned biography." Review of *Richard Rogers: A Biography,* by Bryan Appleyard. *Architecture,* Mar. 1987.
"An Architecture of Possibilities." *New Yorker,* Nov. 14, 1988, 47–96.
"Men at Work." *Arena,* Jan.–Feb. 1989, 42–50.
Davies, Colin. "On being big in France." *World Architecture,* July 1992, 34–55.

"Una scolta per sognare." *Costruire,* Mar. 1993, 170–74.
"Richard Rogers ou l'écologie urbaine." *Urbanisme,* Dec. 1993, 21–24.

Works on or by John Young
Young, John. *Designing with GRC: A brief guide for architects.* London: Architectural Press, 1978.
"Apartment: London Architect John Young." *Blueprint,* extra edition 1, 1990.
"Gets ideas then stands them up." Interview. *Times* (London), Apr. 14, 1993.

Works on or by Marco Goldschmied
"Self-Development for Architects." *Building,* Feb. 1986, 44–46.
"Against all odds." Interview. *Building,* Feb. 1991, 36–37.

Works on or by Michael Davies
"A Wall for All Seasons." *RIBA Journal,* Feb. 1981, 55–57.
"Design for New Technology." Chapter 5 in *Intelligent Buildings.* New York: Halsted Press, 1988.
"Richard Rogers Partnership: due progetti di riuso a Londra." *Parametro,* Sept.–Oct. 1990, 38–45, 92.
"Das Ende des mechanischen Zeitalters." *Arch +,* "Wohltemperierte Architektur," Sept. 1992, 49–56; reprinted in *Architectural Design,* "Visions," July–Aug. 1993, 48–51.

General Articles
"Piano + Rogers." *Architectural Design,* May 1975, 275–311.
"Piano + Rogers, Architectural Method." *Architecture and Urbanism,* June 1976, 63–121.
"Richard Rogers, un decouvreur passionné." *Techniques & Architecture,* Nov. 1983, 79–100.
"Low Profile, High Tech." *Blueprint,* Dec. 1984–Jan. 1985, 10–12.
"Sir Richard Rogers: Twenty years in France." *World Architecture,* July 1988, 32–55.
"Le Rêve d'une Londres moderne." *L'Architecture d'Aujourd'hui,* Sept. 1988, 1–32.

Radio and Television Programs
"Richard Rogers: 'Building Change.'" *Arena,* BBC 2, Jan.
"Don't shoot the architect." *Di Reports,* Channel 4, 1985.
"Showing the Works: Profil Richard Rogers, one of Brit most successful architects." *K doscope,* BBC, June 1985.
"Architecture at the Crossroa BBC 2, Jan. 1986.
Industry Year Debate, Chann Apr. 1986.
Tchalenko, John. "Wall of Lig Channel 4, July 1986.
Saturday Review, BBC 2, Mar. Oct. 1986.
Visions of Britain, BBC 2, 1988.
On the Record, BBC 1, May 19, Craig-Martin, Michael. "Lloyd London." *Building Sites,* BB 1992.
London's South Bank, BBC 2, 30, 1992.
"The New London." *Open Sp* BBC 2, Feb. 29, 1992.
"The New Alchemists." *Hori* BBC 2, Apr. 14, 1993.

estic Environments

k Vean House
side House in Cornwall." *Ar-
ectural Review*, Aug. 1968,
6.
i Häuser in England." *Deutsche
eitung*, Mar. 1969, 153–59.
camente francescana." *Interni*,
1970, 26–28.
e Burg." *Architektur &
nen*, 1971, 10–13.
hard + Su Rogers." *Architects'
nal*, Jan. 20, 1971, 151–53.
ology for your own backyard."
se & Garden*, June 1971, 56–102.
ard-Winning House in Corn-
" *Homes & Gardens*, July 1971,
3.
) Private Houses." *Architects'
nal*, Oct. 1971, 753–66.
hnhaus mit Dachgarten an der
ste von Cornwall." *Die Kunst*,
1979.
'ortino Belvedere." *Abitare*,
1982, 32–41.
igning with plants." *Architects'
nal*, Apr. 25, 1984, 61.
ek Vean house, Cornwall." *Ar-
ecture and Urbanism*, May
, 28–33.

ers House
totypen aus Stahl." *Bauen +
nen*, Dec. 1968, 406.
hlhaus-Prototyp in Wimbledon,
land." *Bauen + Wohnen*, Dec.
.
hilterra: per una edilizia indus-
lizzata." *Domus*, Mar. 1971,
4.
e Maison Signée Richard
ers." *Plaisir de France*, Oct.
, 42–45.
o Private Houses." *Architects'
nal*, Oct. 6, 1971, 753–66.
New System in Wimbledon."
gressive Architecture*, May
, 116–19.
Mysterious Parkside House."
s*, Jan. 21, 1977.
h-Tech a Wimbledon." *Interni*,
–Aug. 1984, 16–17.
cks Went Out of the Window."
day Times Magazine*, "Good
ng," fall 1991, 30–33.

Zip-Up House
Rogers, Richard and Su. "A place to
find out what happens if." *Ark*, win-
ter 1969, 45–49.
"Judges play safe." *Architects'
Journal*, Feb. 12, 1969, 424.
"Choosing a Home Off the Peg." *Ob-
server Magazine*, Mar. 9, 1969, 34–35.
"Du Pont Competition." *Architec-
tural Design*, Mar. 1969, 118.
"Housing." *Architectural Review*,
Sept. 1970, 195–96.
"Richard + Su Rogers." *Casabella*,
Sept. 1970, 32–36.
"Zip Code." *Building Design*, Nov.
30, 1990.

Thames Reach Housing
Blackwell, Lewis. "Richard Rogers
returns to Housing." *Building De-
sign*, Aug. 9, 1985, 6.
"Rogers on the River." *Architects'
Journal*, Jan. 4 and Jan. 11, 1989,
36–39.
Giordano, Paolo. "Thames Reach
Housing, Hammersmith/Londra."
Domus, June 1989, 33–41.
"Das Hammersmith-Project."
Bauwelt, July 28, 1989, 1332–37.
"Wohnblock am Themseufer." *Mö-
bel Interior Design*, Sept. 1989,
68–73.
Buchanan, Peter. "Thames Reach à
Hammersmith, Richard Rogers."
L'Architecture d'Aujourd'hui, Dec.
1989, 109–11.
"Thames Reach Wohnungsbau in
London, Großbritannien." *Architek-
tur + Wettgewerbe*, June 1990, 10–11.

John Young Apartment
"Apartment: London Architect
John Young." *Blueprint*, extra edi-
tion 1, 1990.
"Die Neuerfindung des Wohnens."
Ambiente, May 1991, 31–40.
"Wo die Liebe zum Detail zur Lei-
denschaft Wird." *Häuser*, June
1991, 112–21.
"Ingeniería doméstica." *Arquitec-
tura Viva*, July–Aug. 1991.
"A Londra come se fosse New
York." *Abitare*, Sept. 1991, 186–94.
"A Celebration of Intricacies." *Pro-
gressive Architecture*, Sept. 1991,
130–35.

"Steeling the Show." *House & Gar-
den*, Nov. 1991, 34–37.
"Apartment John Young in Lon-
don." *Deutsche Bauzeitung*, Sunday
edition, "Bad Keramik Sanitar,"
1992, 26–31.
"Architektenwohnung in London."
Baumeister, Jan. 1992, 34–37.
"Captain of the Industrial." *House
& Garden*, Jan. 1992, 62–69.
"The Deckhouse." *RIBA Journal*,
Jan. 1992, 26–27.
"RIBA award winners." *Building
Design*, Jan. 10, 1992, 5, 9.
"Space Age Man Clears the Deck."
Sunday Telegraph, Feb. 5, 1992, 28.
"Breaking the Mould." *Individual
Homes*, Mar.–Apr. 1992, 10–12.
"John Young, Interview." *Tostem
View*, Apr. 1992, 8–15.
"Apartment London." *Detail*,
Apr.–May 1992, 132–34.
Navi, Sept. 1992, 168–69.

The Workplace

Ackermann, Kurt. *Industriebau*.
Stuttgart: Deutsche Verlags-
Anstalt, 1984.
Schultz, Helmut. *Industrie-
architektur in Europa*. Constructa-
Pries. Berlin: Quadrato Verlag,
1986.
Berlinmodell Industriekultur.
Basel: Birkhäuser Verlag, 1989.
Schultz, Helmut. *Indus-
triearchitektur in Europa*. Con-
structa-Pries. Berlin: Ernst & Sohn,
1992.
Phillips, Alan. *The Best in Industri-
al Architecture*. London: B. T. Bats-
ford, 1993.

Patscentre Research Laboratory
"Patscentre." *RIBA Journal*, Feb.
2, 1977, 57–60.
"Centro Ricerche fuori Cambridge."
Domus, May 1977, 18–21.
"Linking advanced techniques and
architecture." *Building Design*,
May 5, 1978.
"Building Study, Patscentre, Mel-
bourn, Hertfordshire." *Architects'
Journal*, June 28, 1978, 1247–60.

Fleetguard Manufacturing Plant
"Playing the Field." *Building Mag-
azine*, Nov. 1980, 34–39.
"Richard Rogers & Partners à
Quimper." *Architecture Intérieure
Créé*, Mar. 2, 1981, 77–81.
"Fleetguard, Quimper." *Arup Jour-
nal*, Sept. 1981, 11–15.
Knobel, Lance. "Rogers, Quimper."
Architectural Review, Feb. 1982,
23–30.
"Centre de Production et de Distri-
bution." *L'Architecture d'Aujour-
d'hui*, "Industrie," June 1982, 18–29.
"Shed, Supershed, un Nouvel
Archétype dans la Tradition Britan-
nique." *Techniques et Architecture*,
June 1982, 112–23.
"Fleetguard." *L'Architecture d'Au-
jourd'hui*, Sept. 1982, 90–91.
"Fabrik und Lager in Quimper."
Baumeister, Jan. 1984, 44–48.
"Produktions und Lagerhalle in Quim-
per." *Detail*, July–Aug. 1985, 365–70.

Inmos Microchip Factory
Murray, Peter. "Architecture for
the Microchip Era." *RIBA Journal*,
Sept. 1980, 45–48.
Stansfield, Kathy. "Inmos Arche-
type." *Architects' Journal*, Sept. 10,
1980, 476–77.
"Rogers Wins Site Unseen." *Build-
ing Design*, Feb. 20, 1981, 15–17.
Sudjic, Deyan. "Richard Rogers
Ltd: Fast Tracking in Wales." *RIBA
Journal*, Jan. 1982, 31–37.
"Usine Inmos Ltd." *L'Architecture
d'Aujourd'hui*, June 1982, 26–29.
"Shed, Supershed, un Nouvel
Archétype dans la Tradition Britan-
nique." *Techniques et Architecture*,
June 1982, 112–23.
"High Speed, High Tech." *Building
Services*, Nov. 1982, 24–28.
Banham, Reyner. "Inmos, Gwent."
Architectural Review, Dec. 1982,
26–41.
Hunt, Tony. "Usine de composants
de micro-électronique etc." *Acier
Stahl Steel*, Jan. 1983, 11–15.
"Werk für Mikro-Elektronik in
Newport, Gwent." *Detail*, May
1983, 459–64.
"Elegant New Geometry." *News-
week*, June 27, 1983, 88.

"Products in Practice." *Architects' Journal*, June 29, 1983, 4.
"Gli ingredienti della Nouvelle Usine." *Domus*, July–Aug. 1983, 9–15.
"Actualité." *L'Architecture d'Aujourd'hui*, Apr. 1984, 27.
"Fabbrica di microcircuiti a Newport." *L'Industria delle Costruzioni*, July–Aug. 1984, 58–61.
Glancey, Jonathan. "Factory Bespeaks the Craftsmanship of British High-Tech." *Architecture*, Sept. 1984, 172–75.
"Ben Johnson." *RIBA Journal*, "Interiors," Sept. 1985, 12–14.

PA Technology Centre
"Patscentre Princeton." *Architectural Review*, July 1983, 43–47.
"Peter Rice." *Architects' Journal*, Dec. 21 and 28, 1983, 24–31.
Boles, Daralice D. "Rogers' US Debut." *Progressive Architecture*, Aug. 1985, 67–74.
"Another Low-Tech Spectacular." *Architectural Review*, Sept. 1985, 38–43.
Blackwell, Lewis. "Princeton Palace." *Building Design*, Sept. 13, 1985, 10.
"Laboratoire en Suspension." *Architecture Intérieure Créé*, Oct.–Nov. 1985, 92–93.
Carstairs, Eileen. "PA targets Princeton for high tech." *Corporate Design & Realty*, May 5, 1986, 30–35.
Gardiner, Ian. "Patscentre." *Arup Journal*, summer 1986, 8–16.
"Leicht Überspannt." *Deutsche Bauzeitung*, Aug. 1986, 10–14.
"Forschungsgebäude in Princeton, New Jersey." *Baumeister*, Nov. 1986, 40–43.

Lloyd's of London
Hagan, Susan. "Lloyd's Assured." *Architects' Journal*, June 6, 1979, 1144–46.
"The Frontiers of Patronage." *RIBA Journal*, Sept. 1979, 404–8.
"Projet d'immeuble de bureaux pour le Lloyd's, Londres." *L'Architecture d'Aujourd'hui*, Feb. 1980, 56–58.

"Architecture and the Programme: Lloyd's of London." *International Architect*, Mar. 1980, 25–39.
"Projekt für die Lloyd's Versicher in London." *Werk, Bauen + Wohnen*, Apr. 1980, 14–23.
"Lloyd's." *Architectural Review*, May 1981, 278–82.
"Immeuble de la Lloyd's à Londres." *Techniques et Architecture*, Sept. 1981, 52–55.
Thornton, John, and Martin Hall. "Lloyd's Redevelopment." *Arup Journal*, June 1982, 2–7.
"Lloyd's room to last for a hundred years." *Concrete*, Apr. 1983, 36–41.
"Lloyd's takes shape." *Building Magazine*, May 1983, 32–38.
"Richard Rogers: Un découvreur passionné." *Techniques et Architecture*, Nov. 1983, 79–100.
Grover, Reginald. "Lloyd's lift logic is US pacesetter." *RIBA Journal*, Mar. 1984, 36–38.
"Design for Better Assembly: Case Study, Rogers' and Arup's." *Architects' Journal*, Sept. 5, 1984, 87–94.
Waters, Brian. "A Year at Lloyd's." *Building Magazine*, Sept. 21, 1984, 30–37.
"Lloyd's of London." *Art & Design*, Oct. 1985, 38–41.
Waters, Brian. "The inside story." *Building Magazine*, Dec. 20–27, 1985, 38–41.
Knevitt, Charles. "Lloyd's 21st Century Coffee House." *Times* (London), Dec. 23, 1985, 8.
"Lloyd's of London." *Edizioni Tecno* (Milan), 1986.
"Lloyd's." *Arup Journal*, winter 1986, 22–27.
"The Romance of the Machine." *Blueprint*, Mar. 1986, 34–37.
Fillon, Odile. "Lloyd's Londres." *Architecture Intérieure Créé*, Apr.–May 1986, 94–97.
Cullen, Gordon. "A tale of two cities." *Architectural Review*, June 1986, 47–52.
"Rogers' Lloydskantoor in Londen." *De Architect*, July–Aug. 1986, 27–33.
Scheider, Sabine. "High-Tech-Palast." *Deutsche Bauzeitung*, Aug. 1986, 4.

Fillon, Odile. "Contradictions in the City." *Architecture Intérieure Créé*, Aug.–Sept. 1986, 74–89.
Banham, Reyner. "Glazed 'planthouse' atop a cascade of silvery cylinders." *Architecture*, Sept. 1986, 47–51.
"Beyond the City Limits." *Designers' Journal*, Sept. 1986, 40–53.
Architectural Review, Oct. 1986, 40–93.
"Richard Rogers at Lloyd's." *Progressive Architecture*, Oct. 1986, 33–36.
Pawley, Martin, and Colin Davies. "Lloyd's of London." *L'Architecture d'Aujourd'hui*, Oct. 1986, 2–19.
Rice, Peter. "Rogers Revolution." *Building Design*, Oct. 10, 1986, 32–33.
"Lloyd's and the Bank." *Architects' Journal*, special issue, Oct. 22, 1986.
Cheung, Ny Alan. "A Tale of Two Architects." *Architects' Journal*, Oct. 29, 1986, 28–45.
Dietsch, Deborah. "Lloyd's of London." *Architectural Record*, Nov. 1986, 104–17.
Lischner, Karin. "Technische Kathedrale." *Aktuelles Bauen*, Nov. 1986, 38–40.
"Lloyd's of London." *Baumeister*, Nov. 1986, 14–21.
Irace, Fulvio. "I Lloyd's di Londra." *Abitare*, Dec. 1986, 168–75.
"Lloyd's of London." *Vector*, Jan. 1987, 8–29.
"Lloyd's of London." *Deutsche Bauzeitung*, Jan. 1987, 23–28.
"Edificio Lloyd's, Londra." *Domus*, Feb. 1987, 25–37.
"Richard Rogers Partnership: Lloyd's of London." *A+U*, Mar. 1987.
Castellano, Aldo. "Il moderno non è morto." *L'Arca*, Mar. 1987, 20–31.
"Insight: Glass at Lloyd's." *AJ Focus*, Apr. 1987, 36–39.
Brozen, Kenneth. "A Step into the 21st Century." *Interiors*, June 1987, 190–97.
Jones, Peter Blundell. "Eine eigentumliche Mischung aus Tradition und Innovation." *Architese*, Nov.–Dec. 1987, 18–23.

"Lloyd's of London setzt Zeic[...] *Möbel Interior Design*, Dec. [...] 42–51.
"Nella City di Londra: l'impor[...] di essere Lloyd's." *Costruire*, [...] 1988, 122–25.
"Lloyd's of London." *Deutsche [...] chitektenblatt*, Mar. 1988, 355–[...]
Jones, Peter Blundell. "I Lloy[...] Londra: high-tech e cerimon[...] *Spazio e Società*, Apr.–June [...] 44–49.
Murray, Peter. "Quand grin[...] high tech: le 'affaire' des Lloy[...] *L'Architecture d'Aujourd'hui*, [...] 1988, 31–32.
"Concreto e aco high-tech na [...] dres." *Projecto*, Oct. 1989, 64–7[...]
Blackmore, Courtenay. *The Cl[...] Tale*. RIBA Publications, 1990.
"I 'Lloyd's' di Richard Rogers.[...] chitettura: Croniche e Storia*, [...] 1992, 127–29.
Powell, Kenneth. *The Lloyd's B[...] ing*. London: Phaidon Press, 19[...]

Billingsgate Securities Market [...]
"Billingsgate Market." *Archite[...] al Review*, Apr. 1988, 38–42.
Davies, Colin. "From Fish to [...] crochips." *Building Magazine*, [...] 15, 1988, 4348.
"Conversion of Billingsgate [...] Market to Headquarters for [...] corp." *RIBA Journal*, June 198[...]
Weatherhead, Peter. "Gone Fi[...] Bank Later." *Building Maga[...] June 9, 1989, 53–57.
Morris, Nick. "Londres Rén[...] tion." *Architecture Intérieure [...] June–July 1989, 84–89.
"Billingsgate Fish Market." *[...] Journal*, summer 1989, 2–7.
Powell, Kenneth. "From Fish t[...] nance." *RIBA Journal*, Aug. 1[...] 30–34.
"Heroic Transformations." *A[...] tectural Record*, Sept. 1989, [...] 77.
Moore, Rowan. "From Fish to [...] nance." *Architectural Review*, [...] 1989, 50–59.
Lueder, C. "Billingsgate Mark[...] London." *Deutsche Bauzeitsch[...] May 1991, 647–56.

cher, Alfred. *Umnutzung alter äude und Anlagen (New life in buildings)*. Stuttgart: Karl .mer Verlag, Jan. 1992, 98–101.
Restauro della Luce." *Flare*, . 1992, 44–49.

ters Data Centre
.ersey-Willams, Hugh. "A ers for Reuters." *Blueprint*, /. 1989, 16.
.ternario Award. Milan: Electa, 3, 128–29.
.ackwall Yard Phase One." *RIBA .rnal*, Jan. 1993.
gest." *Architects' Journal*, Jan. 993, 5.

.nnel 4 Television Headquarters .ctory for Rogers in Channel 4 .npetition." *Building Design*, . 11, 1991, 1.
.lsh, John. "Winning Channel .mula." *Building Design*, Feb. 1, 1, 12–14.
.ophets without Honour." *New .tesman*, Mar. 1, 1991, 27–28.
.lue added tack." *New Builder*, .. 12, 1993, 22–23.
.chard Rogers per Londra e per .ttingham." *L'Arca*, Oct. 1993, .63.
.site saga." *Building Magazine*, . 29, 1993, 22–26.
.purpose-built television station." .chitects' Journal*, Apr. 24, 1994, .39.
.ints of Order." *Building Maga- .e*, May 20, 1994, 39–44.
.nvironmental Assessment of .ldings." *Environmental Assess- .nt*, June 1994, 49–51.
.e Fourth Estate." *Facility De- .n & Management*, June 1994, .18.
.ation Identification." *Blueprint*, .e 1994, 34–36.
.ur goes green." *Landscape De- .n*, June 1994, 30–32.
.hannel Hopping." *Guardian*, .e 2, 1994, 1–4.
.ide of Place." *Broadcast*, June 3, .4, 17.
.remier Division." *New Builder*, .e 10, 1994, 30–31.

"Through the round window." *Observer*, June 12, 1994, 7.
"Shrine of the Times." *Sunday Times* (London), June 26, 1994, 10.
"Through a Glass, imaginatively." *Independent*, July 6, 1994, 20.
"Channel 4 brings new meaning to street theatre." *Times* (London), July 8, 1994.
"Channel Vision." *Architectural Review*, Dec. 1994, 35–50.
"Broadcast News." *Architecture*, Jan. 1995, 56–65.
"Channel 4 Television Headquarters." *GA Document*, Jan. 1995.
"Ubung in Transparenz." *Leonardo*, Jan. 1995, 16–21.
"Channel Four Television Headquarters, London." *Bauwelt*, Feb. 3, 1995.
Blueprint, extra edition, Mar. 1995.
Avisa, Mar. 1995.

Zoofenster Building
Building Design, Apr. 3, 1991, 40.
"Londoner Star-Architekt baut neues City-Wahrzeichen." *Berliner Morgenpost*, Apr. 6, 1991.
"Fenster zum Zoo Hochaus in der Berliner City." *Bauwelt*, Apr. 26, 1991.
"Brau und Brunnen Building." *Bauwelt*, May 1, 1991, 950–51.
"Berlin Special Report." *Architects' Journal*, May 8, 1991.
"Fenster zum Zoo." *Architektur*, Aug. 1991, 20–21.
"Berlin 1991." *Bauwelt*, special issue, Dec. 1991.
"Una finestra sulla città." *L'Arca*, Jan. 1992, 50–55.
"Projects Preview: The English Abroad." *Architects' Journal*, vol. 195, nos. 1 & 2, 1992, 54.
"Hochhäuser." *Arch +*, Mar. 1992, 13.
Sack, Manfred. "Brau und Brunnen Building." *Bauwelt*, May 1, 1992, 950–51.
"Berlin." *Building Design*, May 22, 1992, 24–25.
"Brau und Brunnen Building." *Architects' Journal*, June 24, 1992, 44.
"Funkelnder Fingerzeig in der City." *Süddeutsche Zeitung*, Aug. 28, 1992.

Nikkei Architecture, Dec. 20, 1993, 102.
"Berlin im Jahre 2010." *Architektur & Wohnen*, May 1994, 99–110.
"Keep the Customer Satisfied." *Building Design*, June 10, 1994, 18.

Inland Revenue Headquarters
"Design Taxonomy." *Building Design*, Jan. 17, 1992, 18.
"Rogers' Scheme Proves Winner." *Nottingham Evening Post*, Feb. 11, 1992.
"A taxing choice for Nottingham." *Architects' Journal*, Feb. 26, 1992, 26–33.
"Intelligente Planung." *Arch +*, Sept. 1992, 32–41, 49–56.
"Inland Revenue Headquarters." *Architectural Design*, July–Aug. 1993, 48–51.
"Inland Revenue HQ, Nottingham." *L'Arca*, Oct. 1993, 64–67.
"Oficinas de Inland Revenue." *Arquitectura*, Aug. 1994, 24–27.

Daiwa Headquarters
"Three Generations of London Wall." *Building Magazine*, June 19, 1991, 41–43.
"Rogers' Daiwa HQ Design Unveiled." *Architects' Journal*, Oct. 2, 1991, 9.
"Daiwa design unveiled by Rogers." *Estates Times*, Oct. 4, 1991.
"New home for Daiwa." *Building Design*, Oct. 4, 1991.
"Rogers gets city blessing." *Building Design*, Dec. 6, 1991.
City Changes. Architecture Foundation, 1992, 31.
"Stepping round a corner." *Architectural Review*, May 1992, 40–43.
"Rogers, Foster, Farrel: tre architetti per tre progetti lungo 'London Wall.'" *Controspazio*, Feb. 1993, 42–53.

Kabuki-cho Tower
"Nine Projects, Japan." *Blueprint*, extra edition 3, 1991.
British Architecture Today: Six Protagonists. Milan: Electa, 1991, 134–54.
"Biennale de Venise." *L'Architecture d'Aujourd'hui*, Oct. 1991.

"Working Capital." *Architectural Review*, Nov. 1991, 48–57.
"Projects Preview: The English Abroad." *Architects' Journal*, vol. 195, nos. 1 & 2, 1992, 54.
"Baumarkt." *Arch +*, June 1992, 91.
"Richard Rogers." *Techniques et Architecture*, June–July 1992, 124–25.
"Kabuki-cho Tower." *Japan Architect*, summer 1992, 214–15.
"Rogers: una Arquitectura de Permanencia y Transformacion." *La Revista*, Nov. 22, 1992.
Shinkenchiku, Aug. 1993, 215–27.
"Kabuki-cho Project." *Kenchiku Bunka*, Aug. 1993, 69–80.
"Embracing Green." *RIBA Journal*, Sept. 1993, 44–47.
"Büroturm in Tokio." *Baumeister*, Nov. 1993, 23–26.
"Richard Rogers." *Architectural Design Profile* 107, 1994, viii–ix.
"What is behind these names?" *Nordic Building & Construction*, Jan. 1994, 6–7.
"Un sofisticato meccano." *Abitare*, Oct. 1994, 182–85.
"Bürogebäude in Tokio." *Detail*, Feb.–Mar. 1995, 63–68.

Tomigaya Exhibition Space and Turbine Tower
"Dessin de mois." *L'Architecture d'Aujourd'hui*, Feb. 1992, 64.
"Tomigaya Exhibition Space." *Japan Architect*, summer 1992, 220–23.
"Intelligente Planung." *Arch +*, Sept. 1992, 32–41, 49–56.
"Turbine Tower." *Architectural Design*, July–Aug. 1993, 48–51.

Public Buildings and Infrastructure

Centre Georges Pompidou
d"Centre du Plateau Beaubourg: Concours d'Idées." *Techniques et Architecture*, Feb. 1972.
Mollard, Claude. *Le Centre National d'Art et de Culture Georges Pompidou*. Paris: Centre Georges Pompidou, 1975.

"Beaubourg Furniture." *Architectural Design*, July 1976, 442–43.

"Centre Beaubourg." *Global Architect* 44, 1977.

"Nuovo oggetto a Parigi." *Domus*, Jan. 1977, 1–32.

"Piano + Rogers, Approach to Architecture." *RIBA Journal*, Jan. 1977, 11–16.

Burgess, Anthony. "A $200 Million Erector Set." *New York Times Magazine*, Jan. 23, 1977, 14–22.

"Le Centre national d'Art et de Culture Georges Pompidou." *CREE*, Jan.–Feb. 1977, 6–98.

"Centre Pompidou." *Architectural Design Profile* 2, Feb. 1977.

"The Pompidolium." *Architectural Review*, May 1977, 271–94.

"Six Million Visitors Can't Be Wrong." *Horizon*, July 1977, 28–33.

"Exoskeletal art container is the rage, literally, and the delight of Paris." *Smithsonian*, Aug. 1977, 20–29.

"The Beaubourg: A Bouillabaisse." *Newsweek*, Jan. 2, 1978, 55.

"Profiles: A Good Monster, Pontus Hulten." *New Yorker*, Jan. 16, 1978, 37–67.

"Les Lieux du Spectacle." *L'Architecture d'Aujourd'hui*, "Ircam," Oct. 1978, 52–63.

"Musikzentrum unter der Erde." *MD*, Apr. 1979, 25–29.

"Beaubourg prolifera per Pierre Boulez." *Architettura: Cronache e Storia*, July 1979, 424–25.

"Boulez Music Centre in Paris." *Deutsche Bauzeitung*, Dec. 1979, 1849–52.

"Centre National d'Art et de Culture Georges Pompidou." *Stahl und Form/Steel and Form/Acier et Forme*, 1980.

"Pompidou Centre, Rage of Paris." *National Geographic*, Oct. 1980, 468–77.

"Centre National d'Art et de Culture Georges Pompidou." *L'Architecture d'Aujourd'hui*, Feb. 1981, 92–95.

"Institute for research and coordination of acoustic/music, Centre Georges Pompidou." *Architecture & Urbanism*, Sept. 1982, 27–32.

"Evaluation: Beaubourg already shows its years." *Architecture*, Sept. 1983, 62–71.

"Engineers as Pioneers." *Architects' Journal*, Nov. 1984, 48–49.

Maheu, Jean. "Centre Georges Pompidou: Dix ans Déjà!" *Atlas* (Air France), May 1987, 142–59.

Centre Georges Pompidou. Paris: Editions du Centre Pompidou, Oct. 1987.

Piano, Renzo. *Du Plateau Beaubourg au Centre Georges Pompidou.* Paris: Editions du Centre Pompidou, 1987.

Silver, Nathan. *The Making of Beaubourg.* Cambridge: MIT Press, 1994.

Tokyo Forum

Welsh, John. "Opportunity Missed." *Building Design*, Nov. 24, 1989, 24–25.

"Unbuilt Tokyo." *Blueprint*, Dec. 1989, 40–41.

"Land of the Rising Complex." *Daily Telegraph*, Mar. 20, 1990.

"Richard Rogers: New Architecture of the 21st Century." *A+U*, May 1990, 7–22.

European Court of Human Rights

Melhuish, Claire. "Rogers Palace of Justice." *Building Design* 95, Oct. 13, 1989, 12.

"Ancorage à Strasbourg du palais des droits de l'homme." *Architecture Intérieure Créé*, Oct.–Nov. 1989, 22.

"Per i diritti dell'uomo." *L'Arca*, Mar. 1990, 52–59.

"Architektur: Im Zweifel Für die Moderne." *Häuser*, Mar. 1990, 12.

"French woo the British who wow the French." *Independent*, July 25, 1990.

"European Court of Human Rights, Strasbourg." *TAS* (Australian Post Publication), Mar.–Apr. 1991, 35–38.

"L'Urbanisme à Strasbourg." *Urbanisme et Architecture*, Sept. 1991, 103–7.

"Le Renouvellement Strasbourgeois." *Techniques et Architecture*, Feb. 1992, 40–49.

"Practice." *Architecture Today*, July 1992, 68–69.

"Un Béton Brut Parfaitement Lisse." *Le Moniteur*, Sept. 25, 1992, 70–71.

Pump House

"Pumps Primed." *New Civil Engineer*, Apr. 6, 1989, 28–31.

"Docklands Duet." *New Builder*, July 6, 1989, 16–20.

"Station Technique à Londres." *Techniques et Architecture*, special edition, 1991, 96–97.

Industrial Architecture in Europe. Germany: Constructa Preis Catalogue, 1992, 56–63.

Marseille International Airport

"Aéroport de Marseille Provence Parasols pour Europe." *Urbanisme et Architecture*, Feb. 1990, 50.

"Cities in the air." *Blueprint*, Oct. 1992, 34–38.

"Ein Engländer in Marseille." *Baumeister*, Jan. 1993, 40–43.

"Aéroport de Marseille Provence." *Techniques et Architecture*, special edition, Feb. 1993, 28.

"Una Dársena a cubierto." *Arquitectura Viva*, Mar.–Apr. 1993, 46–51.

"Ampliamento dell'aeroporto di Marsiglia." *Domus Dossier*, "Aeroporti," Apr. 1993, 60–69.

"Flying Carpet." *AJ Focus*, Apr. 1993, 11–14.

"Gli ombrelli galleggianti." *L'Arca*, May 1993, 54–61.

"Marseille International Airport." *Nikkei Architecture*, June 1993, 46–47.

"L'Efficacité Comme Emblème." *Techniques et Architecture*, Aug.–Sept. 1993, 32–33.

"French Connection." *Architectural Review*, Sept. 1993, 51–56.

Terminal 5, Heathrow Airport

"Heathrow's Futuristic New Terminal." *Business Life*, Dec. 1992–Jan. 1993, 22–23.

"Flying High." *Building Design*, May 15, 1992, 1.

"Heathrow Airport Terminal 5." *Nikkei Architecture*, June 1993, 40–41.

"Heathrow at the Centre of Chan[ge]." *FX Magazine*, July–Aug. 1993, [.]

"Temples of Flight." *Arena*, J[uly–] Aug. 1994, 70–71.

Law Courts

"Doing Justice to Bordeaux." *Bu[ild-]ing Design*, Jan. 22, 1993, 8.

"Open Court." *Architectural [Re]view*, Mar. 1993, 48–51.

"L'Extension du Tribunal, [Bor-]deaux." *Techniques et Architect[ure],* Aug.–Sept. 1993, 34–37.

"Tribunales de Burdeos, Franc[e]." *Arquitectura*, Aug. 1994, 10–15.

Bahnhof (Underground Stat[ion] Prototype)

"Rogers moves in on Berlin Und[er]ground." *Building Design*, Sep[t.] 1993, 1.

Nikkei Architecture, Dec. 1993, [.]

"Tageslicht im Untergrund." *De[tail],* Aug.–Sept. 1994, 443.

Towns and Cities

London As It Could Be

Sudjic, Deyan. *New Direction[s in] British Architecture: Foster, Rog[ers,] Stirling.* London: Thames & H[ud-]son, 1986.

"The English School." *Bluepr[int],* Oct. 1986, 19–25.

"A bridge for people." *Illustra[ted] London News*, Oct. 1986, 50–57.

"Maestro Buildings." *Cosmop[oli-]tan*, Oct. 1986, 58–65.

"Le Meilleur des mondes." *Conn[ais-]sances des Arts*, Oct. 1986, 29.

Cruickshank, Dan. "Visions [of the] modern city." *Architects' Jour[nal],* Oct. 1, 1986, 28–31.

"Big Three Architects Honoured [at] the Royal Academy." *Build[ing] Magazine*, Oct. 3, 1986, 18–19.

"Model Exhibition." *Archite[cts'] Journal*, Oct. 8, 1986, 22–23.

Blanc, Alan. "Golden Years." *Bu[ild-]ing Design*, Oct. 10, 1986, 26–29.

Saldarriaga Roa, Alberto. "Ar[qui-]tectura inglesa en Londres." *P[roa],* Nov. 1986, 56.

he big three." *Building Design*, ov. 14, 1986, 22.

atton, Brian. "Three architects at e Royal Academy." *Progressive rchitecture*, Dec. 1986, 30.

lte Technologie oder neue Re- aissance?" *Frankfurter Allge- eine Zeitung*, Dec. 5, 1986.

hree Dimensions of Architec- re." *Magazine for the Friends of e Royal Academy*, winter 1986, –31.

tre grandi dell'architettura in- ese alla Royal Academy." *Domus*, n. 1987, 14–16.

ldersey-Williams, Hugh. "New rchitecture: Foster, Rogers, Stir- ng." *Architectural Record*, Mar. 87, 73–77.

avey, Peter. "North Bank Show." *rchitectural Review*, June 1987, –74.

hampenois, Michele. "Richard ogers: le rêve d'une Londres mod- ne." *L'Architecture d'Aujour- hui*, Sept. 1988, 32.

owan, Robert. "Designing Lon- n." *Architects' Journal*, Apr. 17, 91, 26–71.

ast and present of the inhabited idge." *Rassegna*, Dec. 1991, 10–19.

Capital Ideas: Lost Visions for ondon." *Architects' Journal*, Dec. –18, 1991.

onati, Christina. "Londra oggi ensa . . ." *Controspazio*, Feb. 92, 5–24.

ational Gallery Extension Richard Rogers with Speyhawk c." *Architects' Journal*, Aug. 25, 82, 65.

nside Story." *Architects' Journal*, pt. 15, 1982, 60–63.

Britain, Gallery Competition." rogressive Architecture*, Oct. 1982, .

uchanan, Peter. "National Gallery amble." *Architectural Review*, ec. 1982, 19–21.

he English School." *Blueprint*, ct. 1986, 19–25.

laying to the Gallery." *Sunday mes Magazine* (London), June 23, 91, 16–24.

"Capital Ideas: Lost Visions for London." *Architects' Journal*, Dec. 11–18, 1991.

Coin Street Redevelopment Cruickshank, Dan. "Bright Future for the South Bank." *Architects' Journal*, Aug. 8, 1979, 270–71.

"South Bank Vision." *Architects' Journal*, Mar. 26, 1980, 598–600.

"Saviour of the South Bank." *RIBA Journal*, Apr. 1980, 43–46.

Buchanan, Peter, Jonathan Glancey, and Dan Cruickshank. "Foster: Rogers—High-Tech: Classical, Gothic." *Architectural Review*, May 1981, 265–82.

"Capital Ideas: Lost Visions for London." *Architects' Journal*, Dec. 11–18, 1991.

Paternoster Square "Royal worries over St. Paul's de- sign." *Building Design*, Aug. 7, 1987.

"Unbuilt London." *Architectural Review*, Jan. 1988, 36–38.

"Paternoster Square." *Architectur- al Design*, Feb. 1988, vii.

Champenois, Michele. "Rogers, Lon- dres et le prince." *Monuments His- toriques*, Feb.–Mar. 1988, 118–22.

"Paternoster Square." *Arch +*, Aug. 1988, 44–51.

"Shifting Ground." *RA Summer Magazine*, 1990, 54–56.

"Capital Ideas: Lost Visions for London." *Architects' Journal*, Dec. 11–18, 1991.

Royal Docks Strategic Plan "Land of lost opportunities." *Blue- print*, July 1987, 32–40.

"The Royals alternative." *Building Design*, Aug. 7, 1987, 2.

"Die Docklands in London." *Bau- welt*, Dec. 23, 1988, 2070–74.

"London's Docklands." *Landscape Architect*, Apr. 1989, 14.

"Quays to Design." *Architectural Review*, Apr. 1989, 38–44.

"Royals set to go." *New Civil Engi- neer*, May 19, 1989, 28–31.

"Time for building to replace the build-up." *Estates Times*, July 21, 1989, 32–34.

"Bridge fears delay Royal Docks plan." *Building Design*, Oct. 13, 1989, 6–7.

"Stanhope pulls out of the Royals." *Building Design*, May 18, 1990, 3.

South Bank Centre Crystal Palace "Balancing the Bank Statements." *Building Design*, July 15, 1994, 8.

"A Knight to Remember." *London Architect*, Sept. 1994, 9–10.

"Medieval Monster eats Architect." *Blueprint*, Sept. 1994, 24.

"Cinderella Complex." *New States- man & Society*, Sept. 9, 1994, 32.

"South Bank Competition." *Ar- chitects' Journal*, Sept. 15, 1994, 10.

"Richard Rogers Partnership's 'crystal palace' wins South Bank re- design competition." *Building Mag- azine*, Sept. 16, 1994.

"All wrapped up." *Building Design*, Sept. 16, 1994, 2.

"Slipping into clichés." *Building De- sign*, Sept. 23, 1994, 2.

Jencks, Charles. "High-tech slides to organi-tech." *ANY 10*, 1995, 45–49.

Redevelopment of the Banks of the Arno River "The Banks of the Arno." *Building Design*, Mar. 18, 1983, 32–33.

"Réaménagement des Bords de l'Arno, Florence, Italie." *Tech- niques et Architecture*, Nov. 1983, 93–94.

"Proposal for the Banks of the Riv- er Arno, Florence." *Architectural Design*, Jan.–Feb. 1984, 62–68.

"'Cara Firenze più coraggio,' Il fu- turibile di Rogers." *La Repubblica*, Feb. 16, 1989.

Potsdamerplatz Master Plan *Ein Stück Großstadt als Experi- ment Planungen Platz in Berlin*. Verlag Gerd Hatje.

"Berlin Special Report." *Architects' Journal*, May 8, 1991.

"Ein zähes Stück Filet." *Stern*, Oct. 17, 1991, 286–87.

"Rogers' scheme is platz du jour." *Architects' Journal*, Oct. 23, 1991, 9.

Welsh, John. "Potsdamer 'farce.'" *Building Design*, Oct. 25, 1991, 48.

Bauwelt, Potsdamer Platz issue, Nov. 1, 1991.

Baker, Nick. "Mending Spirit." *Building Design*, Nov. 8, 1991, 22.

"United Berlin." *Economist*, Nov. 9–15, 1991, 23–27.

"Rogers' Berlin plan snubbed." *Ar- chitects' Journal*, Nov. 27, 1991, 5.

"Phönix aus der Asche." *Ambiente*, Dec. 1991, 110–13.

"Potsdamer Platz." *Arch +*, Dec. 1991, 94–99.

"Berlin 1991." *Bauwelt*, special edi- tion, Dec. 1991.

"Vecchia nuova Berlino." *Panora- ma*, Dec. 1, 1991, 33.

"Potsdamer Platz Designs Strive to re-unite Berlin." *Architectural Record*, Jan. 1992, 20.

"Menetekel der Moderne Das Scheitern zweier Entwurfe am Potsdamer Platz." *Werk, Bauen + Wohnen*, Jan.–Feb. 1992, 45–60.

Tschanz, Martin. "Nochmals Pots- damer Platz." *Archithese*, Mar.–Apr. 1992, 44–56.

"United Berlin Struggles with Site at its Heart." *Progressive Architec- ture*, Apr. 1992, 25.

"Unifying projects." *Architects' Journal*, June 24, 1992, 30–39.

"Beschränkter Realisierungswett- bewerb Potsdamer Platz, Berlin, Daimler Benz AG." *Wettbewerbe Aktuelle*, Oct. 1992, 54–55.

"Daimler Benz-Wettbewerbe." *Bauwelt*, Oct. 9, 1992.

"Cross Road Berlin." *Architectural Review*, Jan. 1993, 20–28.

Building Design, Sept. 30, 1994.

Lu Jia Zui Master Plan "Birth of a brave new city." *Guard- ian*, Dec. 2, 1992, 2–3.

"Shanghai Expressed." *Building Design*, Dec. 4, 1992, 16–17.

"Alles Rogers." *Deutsche Bauzeit- ung*, Feb. 1993, 8.

"New UK business." *China Britain Trade Review*, Feb. 1993, 5.

"Shanghai's new Bund." *China Now*, spring 1993, 24–25.

"Proposal for New Commercial Centre." *SD*, May 1993, 110.

"Rogers lands Shanghai job." *Estates Times*, Dec. 4, 1993, 1.

"Shanghai of the Future." *Britain-China*, Jan. 1994, 1–3.

Photography Credits

Thanks to the Richard Rogers Partnership for having supplied the graphic material for this book, as well as:

Matthew Antrobus: 196
Otto Baitz: 84–86, 88, 89 bottom
Keith Barron: 10
BBC Hutton Picture Library: 106
Richard Bryant: 30, 48, 49, 51–53, 55, 5, 92, 95, 99 bottom, 101, 102, 104, 09, 110 bottom, 111, 130, 131
Camera Craft: 37
Martin Charles: 97, 169 left, 174, 176, 77
Keith Collie: 47
Jim Colquhoun: 204 right
Peter Cook: 98, 100, 103, 195, 202, 04 left, 205
Hayes Davidson: 144, 172, 208, 209, 11, 213, 216, 217, 244, 246, 247, 257, 58, 261
Richard Davies: 118, 121, 122, 222, 39, 240, 241
Michel Denancé: 169 right
John Donat: 99 top, 225, 228, 229, 231
Barry Dunnage: 89 top
Richard Einzig: 32–35, 39 top and bottom left, 40, 41, 43–45, 167 center and right
Florian Fischötter: 39 bottom right
Dennis Gilbert: 69
Andrew Holmes: 71
Katsuhisa Kida: 147
Ken Kirkwood: 70, 72, 74–77, 79, 81–83
John Lindon: 128, 129, 200, 201, 203
Eamon O'Mahony: 18, 19, 27, 57, 60, 3, 64, 90, 96, 107, 108, 110 top, 124, 25, 127, 133, 134, 136–38, 140, 142, 43, 145, 153, 154 bottom right, 155, 57, 180, 181, 188, 189, 198, 207, 215, 19–21, 243, 253, 254 bottom, 259
Renzo Piano Building Workshop: 120
Marc Riboud: 163
Christian Richter: 192 bottom, 193
Yesaaki Sekiya: 146, 148–51
Larry Sowden: 172
Bernard Vincent: 173
Morley Von Sternberg: 185, 191
Paul Wakefield: 160, 166, 168, 170, 71
Harriet Watson: 215
Matthew Weinrebb: 113–17